'This book by one of the most influential contemporary thinkers on sustainable food systems explains why we should relocalise food, and how schools and other local public bodies can contribute to this, by using a largely underestimated yet crucial tool: the power of the purse. It will inspire policymakers to do better, and it will encourage food activists, including parents, to demand more.'

Olivier De Schutter, former UN Special Rapporteur on the right to food and Co-Chair of the International Panel of Experts on Sustainable Food Systems

'Food in schools, hospitals and prisons is the "canary" in the food system. How often do we hear politicians promise to address tricky matters by sorting out public provision? The private sector, meanwhile, barely receives political attention. This book explains why public food provision is often a mess and doesn't need to be. It's full of learned stories, great people and wobbly structures on the food frontline. A gem.'

Tim Lang, author of *Feeding Britain: Our Food Problems and How to Fix Them*

'Kevin Morgan describes the political, economic and social causes of appallingly unhealthful and disrespectful institutional feeding programmes in schools, hospitals and prisons, and the human and societal consequences. His book provides compelling examples and arguments for why and how we can – and must – do better.'

Marion Nestle, author of *Food Politics: How the Food Industry Influences Nutrition and Health*

'Why do poor people so often eat poor food? To answer that question, Kevin Morgan takes us on a tour through school dinners, hospital meals and prison kitchens, from Malmö to Oldham. His answer is that our diet is as politically constructed as our housing or our schooling, and all the apps in the world will be of little use. Writing of imagination and sympathy.'

Aditya Chakra'

'Good food and great cities go together: cuisine has long helped to certify the status of global cities. But the sad reality is far too many people lack access to safe, healthy food. Kevin Morgan shows how the "good food" revolution can help us create better, more sustainable cities and improve the health and well-being of their residents.'
Richard Florida, author of *The Rise of the Creative Class*

'One in twenty meals served in the UK is paid for by the government. That is why the transformation of catering in our public sector is key to any long-term improvement in our food culture. A catering service that has the competence and confidence to cook from scratch is essential, because it nourishes the most vulnerable people in society and safeguards our planet at the same time. This book highlights both the challenges and the solutions, and I urge politicians to read it.'
Henry Dimbleby, food campaigner and author of the *National Food Strategy*

'A compelling look at the power of public food procurement to transform our food system into one that is fairer, healthier and more sustainable. Morgan deftly weaves together inspiring examples of local innovation with a sober assessment of the administrative and economic obstacles to systemic change. This book is an essential read for policymakers and activists alike.'
Nevin Cohen, Director, CUNY Urban Food Policy Institute

'A tour de force that dissects, critiques and champions the role and importance of Good Public Food. Morgan brings to life a topic often dismissed as dull and unimportant. How we feed our most vulnerable members of society underpins how we value food more generally. This book talks eloquently about embracing the power of public food, improving standards, showcasing what can be achieved with thoughtful leadership and ensuring that key vulnerable groups are well fed in order to support them reaching their potential.'
Mary Brennan, Chair of the Scottish Food Coalition

'The public owes a debt of gratitude to Kevin Morgan for writing this book. Not only is public food procurement perhaps the most frequently enacted food-related strategy to achieve sustainable development goals, making this a timely and important discussion, but Kevin's first-hand witness to these conversations make him uniquely positioned to tell a nuanced story. A must read for government officials, researchers and advocates working on sustainable food policy development.'
Becca Jablonski, Co-Director, Food Systems Institute, Colorado State University

'In examining the role of food in public and civil society contexts, Kevin Morgan has highlighted how good food can improve the wellbeing of the most vulnerable people in society.'
Yvonne Thomas, Chief Executive, The Clink Charity

'Prison, school and hospital food have long been among the most problematic examples of institutional food in the UK and the US, emblematic of systems that prioritise the bottom line and contribute to poor health outcomes, as Kevin Morgan identifies in this insightful, accessible and hopeful book. His elaboration of what constitutes good food and a sustainable food system provides an alternative route for the type of food system we need.'
Robert Gottlieb, author of *Care-Centered Politics: From the Home to the Planet*

'It's been said that one true measure of a civilisation's greatness is how well it treats its prisoners. In this clearly written and deeply researched investigation, Kevin Morgan extends this measure to how well we feed our school children and hospital patients as well. By Morgan's account, civilisation is clearly in decline, yet its ascent may once again be assured by the spirited and determined guardians showcased in this inspiring book.'
Mark Winne, author of *Stand Together or Starve Alone: Unity and Chaos in the U.S. Food Movement*

'If budgets are a reflection of a society's values, then public food procurement is our ultimate test. Kevin Morgan's step-by-step account shines a much-needed light on how communities in the UK and beyond have transformed the complex and opaque public food procurement process into one that from farm to fork demonstrates how our public dollars can and must serve the public good.'

Alexa Delwiche, Co-Founder and Executive Director, Center for Good Food Purchasing

'Our current food system is not sustainable. Long-term trends are heading in the wrong direction, including rates of obesity, diabetes and hunger. Intensive farming practices are causing significant harm to our environment. *Serving the public* shows that it does not have to be that way, that we can ensure the food system becomes one we would be happy for future generations to inherit. Goodness knows they'll have enough on their plate. Let's not land them with a food system that is broken too.'

Derek Walker, Future Generations Commissioner for Wales

'Morgan takes a fascinating and erudite deep dive into the history of school meal provision. He tells the story of an essential and cost-effective intervention that has been sacrificed on the altar of consumer choice and individual responsibility, despite the well-evidenced reports, campaigns and initiatives (such as our own Food For Life scheme) that have shown the way forwards. There are green shoots of hope though – may Morgan's book inspire policy makers to build on them.'

Helen Browning, Chief Executive, The Soil Association

Serving the public

Manchester University Press

The Manchester Capitalism book series

Manchester Capitalism is a series of short books that follow the trail of money and power across the systems of financialised capitalism. The books make powerful interventions about who gets what and why, with rigorous arguments that are accessible for the concerned citizen. They go beyond simple critiques of neoliberalism and its satellite knowledges to re-frame our problems and offer solutions about what is to be done.

Manchester was the city of both Engels and Free Trade where the twin philosophies of collectivism and free market liberalism were elaborated. It is now the home of this venture in radical thinking that primarily aims to challenge self-serving elites. We see the provincial radicalism rooted here as the ideal place from which to cast a cold light on the big issues of economic renewal, financial reform and political mobilisation.

Books in the series so far have covered diverse but related issues. How technocratic economic thinking narrows the field of the visible while popular myths about the economy spread confusion. How private finance is part of the extractive problem not the solution for development in the Global South and infrastructural needs in the UK. How politics disempowers social housing tenants and empowers reckless elites. How foundational thinking about economy and society reasserts the importance of the infrastructure of everyday life and the priority of renewal.

General editors: Julie Froud and Karel Williams

To buy or to find out more about the books currently available in this series, please go to: https://manchesteruniversitypress.co.uk/series/manchester-capitalism/

Serving the public

The good food revolution in schools, hospitals and prisons

Kevin Morgan

Manchester University Press

Copyright © Kevin Morgan 2025

The right of Kevin Morgan to be identified as the author of this work has been asserted in accordance with the Copyright, Designs and Patents Act 1988.

Published by Manchester University Press
Oxford Road, Manchester, M13 9PL
www.manchesteruniversitypress.co.uk

British Library Cataloguing-in-Publication Data
A catalogue record for this book is available from the British Library

ISBN 978 1 5261 8283 8 hardback
ISBN 978 1 5261 8046 9 paperback

First published 2025

The publisher has no responsibility for the persistence or accuracy of URLs for any external or third-party internet websites referred to in this book, and does not guarantee that any content on such websites is, or will remain, accurate or appropriate.

Typeset
by Cheshire Typesetting Ltd, Cuddington, Cheshire
Printed in Great Britain
by Bell & Bain Ltd, Glasgow

To the memory of Wayne Roberts,
whose warmth, wit and wisdom leavened the Good Food
movement in and beyond his native Canada.

Contents

Introduction	1
Part I: Food in the public sphere	
1 Reclaiming the public plate	25
Part II: Schools, hospitals and prisons	
2 Food for life: the whole school approach	67
3 Catering for health: the quest for good food	105
4 Doing time: food behind bars	141
Part III: Foodscapes of hope	
5 The Good Food movement	177
6 Prospects for change	221
Acknowledgements	251
List of exhibits	253
Notes	254
Index	274

Introduction

Good food means different things to different people. In certain circles, it is synonymous with fine dining, exclusive restaurants and celebrity chefs, but in the following pages it is understood to mean food that is appetising, nutritious, culturally appropriate and sustainably produced. Seldom is good food associated with public canteens in schools, hospitals and prisons. While pupils, patients and prisoners are clearly very different groups, operating in radically different institutional settings, they nevertheless have one thing in common: they are all made up of highly vulnerable people whose well-being depends on a nutritious diet. Because of its unique role in sustaining life, and shaping our physical and cognitive development, food is the universally accepted index of our capacity to care for ourselves and for others, be they our 'nearest and dearest' or 'distant strangers'.

In this book we'll encounter public bodies that are endeavouring to serve good food against the odds and in places that defy shallow stereotypes. Take Oldham in Greater Manchester for example, a post-industrial town that features in Chapter 2. Oldham was one of the first municipalities in the UK to win a Food for Life Served Here (FFLSH) Gold Award for the quality of its school meals service, despite its Cinderella status as the 'poorest town in England'. What this accolade meant in practice was that every meal served in its schools met the most exacting quality standards in the country and every child had a nutritious hot meal, no mean feat for a highly deprived locality.

As the local newspaper proudly declared: 'All of Oldham's menus are freshly prepared daily on site by the catering teams, using a range of organic products, high animal welfare produce, and free range ingredients.'[1] National newspapers have also been impressed with Oldham's school meals service: 'Any council would be proud of serving meals that prompt children to present teachers their cleaned-out plates as if they were sports day trophies.'[2]

How had such a poor municipality managed to scoop the top award for quality school meals when it was spending no more than the average for its region? As we'll discover later, Oldham's success was attributed to a combination of internal and external factors: the calibre and commitment of the catering team, the sustained support of local politicians and long-term relationships with tried and tested suppliers, most of whom were based in the region. Over the years I got to know the head of catering, Anne Burns, and she was clearly a force of nature for whom the service was a vocation rather than just a job. Although the catering service won a clutch of awards under her leadership, including the Gold Award for five consecutive years between 2014 and 2019, she was fond of saying 'there's no I in our team'.

The experience of Oldham is instructive on two counts: (1) because it gives the lie to the notion that poor places are congenitally incapable of designing and delivering high-quality public services, and (2) because it provides a compelling illustration of

Introduction

the *power of purchase* and the *calibre of catering* when these functions are managed by a competent and confident municipal workforce. Sadly, Oldham is also instructive for the fact that it was unable to retain its Gold Award, highlighting the fragility of progressive localism in a highly centralised national environment that has denuded municipalities of capacity and resources.

The plight of Oldham stands in stark contrast to the situation in Malmö in Sweden, which also features in Chapter 2. Malmö has acquired an international reputation for the quality of its school meals service, the result of a *thirty-year* sustainable food strategy that was aided and abetted by a supportive national environment in the form of a universal free school meals system funded through general taxation. But local innovation was just as important. As there were no national guidelines for sustainable food in Sweden in the early years of the new millennium, Malmö had to build the road as it travelled by working from projects to policy, not the other way around. Through a learning-by-doing process, involving constant experimenting and testing, the school meals service rapidly learned about how to design and deliver new recipes that were appreciated by young people; how decentralised food preparation and production reduced food waste; and how the reduction of food waste offset the additional cost of organic products.

In 2010 the city council adopted the Policy for Sustainable Development and Food, a strategy that had just two goals: to improve the quality of public food by procuring organic produce and to reduce the environmental impact of the public food system. As we will see, Malmö has gone a long way to achieving both goals. Apart from clear goals, the city attributes its success to continuous educational training for care providers, educators and kitchen staff along with the recruitment of competent chefs. The policy was allocated a budget of one million krona for its development, most of it devoted to staff training.[3] Having greater fiscal autonomy than its English counterpart, Malmö was able to sustain its strategy.

Oldham and Malmö are microcosms of their national political systems, illustrating the radically different possibilities for local innovation in public services in the UK and Sweden. Their contrasting fortunes are part of a global struggle to improve the quality of food served in public sector settings – what I and others call the *public plate*. This book aims to establish the importance of the public plate as a focus for action and politics.[4] Although the focus is largely on the UK, I draw on examples from the US and Sweden for comparative purposes at certain points. But everywhere, it seems, governments are increasingly turning to the public plate to help them resolve the problems spawned by an unsustainable agrifood system, particularly the problems of diet-related diseases, environmental harms and climate change.

While national governments could be doing so much more to promote a fairer, healthier and more sustainable agrifood system, they remain deeply torn. This is because, while the scientific evidence suggests the need for more robust regulatory action on public health and climate change, governments seem unable or unwilling to consider stronger regulations for fear of alienating the food industry and incurring the wrath of right-wing media accusing them of intrusive 'nanny state' policies. As we'll see in Chapter 1, this has been the experience in the UK, where successive governments have not only recoiled from regulating the production and consumption of ultra-processed foods but also rolled back on measures to combat obesity and

Introduction

delayed plans to strengthen public sector food procurement standards, all because of an unwarranted belief in 'light touch' regulation.

Fortunately, the good food cause does not depend on such national governments. On the contrary, when the history of the good food revolution comes to be written, a prominent role will be found for locally based civil society groups along with the health trusts and local governments that are serious about their duty of care. A combination of civic energy and public sector innovation in these localities demonstrates that the food system can be rendered healthier and more sustainable in the here and now, confirming the adage that 'the future is already here – it's just not very evenly distributed'.[5]

But the core message of this book is that optimism must be tempered with realism. There is indeed a good food revolution underway in and beyond the UK but it is a work in progress. In the following chapters I try to do justice to these twin sentiments by documenting how the good food cause is being advanced at the local level in the UK and the US and why it is still the exception not the norm.

A cautionary tale

A public duty of care is a concept that is rightly revered because it contributes so much to social well-being. But the significance of the concept is perhaps more powerfully conveyed when a duty of care is absent. It may take a tragedy to remind us of this grim reality, but that's precisely what happened following an E.coli outbreak in Wales in 2005. The report of the public inquiry succinctly summarised what happened: 'Most cases were children in 44 schools across four local authority

Serving the public

areas. Thirty-one people were admitted to hospital. Tragically, Mason Jones aged five, died.[6]

The ensuing public inquiry is etched in my mind because I sat through the sessions in which local authority officers were subjected to the forensic skills of a seasoned barrister, who exposed a sorry saga of unremitting incompetence. The outbreak occurred because of food hygiene failures at the premises of John Tudor and Son, a local meat supplier. The responsibility for the outbreak was attributed to William Tudor, the proprietor, who pleaded guilty to seven food hygiene offences. He was sentenced to twelve months' imprisonment and banned from participating in the management of any food business.

John Tudor and Son had been supplying meat to the four local authorities since 1996 and, despite dozens of complaints from school caterers about the quality of the meat and the standards of hygiene, the company had managed to retain the contract because it was cheap, because of its status as a local supplier, and because of the failure of the lead authority to exercise a public duty of care. An aspect of the crisis that was never addressed was the official endorsement that the company received from the Welsh government. Prior to the crisis, John Tudor and Son had featured as a local supplier in the government's 'Lamb for Lunch' school meals pilot project, a scheme designed to promote the use of local food in public procurement contracts. Being extolled as a local supplier helped the company secure a privileged status in the school catering sector, a status that was totally unwarranted given its woeful performance.

It beggars belief that the company could be extolled in an official publication promoting quality local food when the hygiene standards in the company's abattoir were even worse

Introduction

than the factory. An inspection conducted some years earlier resulted in a hygiene assessment score of 11 out of 100, the lowest hygiene score ever recorded in Britain. The official report failed to establish a reason as to why the abattoir's licence was not revoked when the problems were well known. But in a chilling paragraph of the report, the chairman wrote: 'I conclude that although the safety rules were being broken, those who had the power to act must have accepted that the breaches could be lived with. There was, in effect, a "normalization of deviance".'[7]

For Mason's parents, the agony of losing a child was compounded by the light sentence imposed on William Tudor, reflecting the fact that he was charged with food hygiene offences rather than corporate manslaughter. Although he was given a twelve-month prison sentence, he only served twelve weeks in jail, presumably because food hygiene offences were not deemed a serious crime. Recognising the errors of its ways, the Crown Prosecution Service later admitted it should have pressed corporate manslaughter charges.[8]

The E.coli tragedy may seem a purely localised event, but it highlights the problems that litter the history of public food provisioning in the UK, such as the high cost of a 'cheap food' culture; the shortcomings of 'light touch' regulation; the dangers of being seduced by the 'local food' label; and the fatal conceit that 'food standards' are effectively monitored and implemented.

The power of purchase

Two decades on from the tragedy, public food procurement is becoming de rigueur in political circles. Having moved from the margins to the mainstream in food policy debates, analysts

Serving the public

and policymakers have come to realise that the power of purchase can help to fashion a fairer, healthier and more sustainable food system *if* it is deployed with professional skill and political purpose. In international food policy forums, public food procurement is now perceived to have 'the potential to profoundly influence both food consumption and food production patterns and to deliver multiple social, economic and/or environmental benefits to a multiplicity of beneficiaries, including the producers and consumers of publicly procured food and the wider community'.[9]

The power of purchase is sometimes gauged by its monetary value. Worldwide, the value of the public procurement market is estimated to be more than $13 trillion, while in the UK alone it amounts to over £300 billion a year, roughly equivalent to a third of all public sector spending. As vast as these sums appear on paper, the real impact is much diminished by the fact that they are spread across countless public bodies, each of which operates in its own organisational silo, which further dilutes the effect. And as we'll see later, the promise of public procurement is also stymied by a whole series of other barriers, including inadequate public sector skill sets and the lack of political leadership.

Although food is far from being the largest procurement category in financial terms, its *social* significance is so much greater than its monetary value would suggest. This is due to the unique status of food. Since we ingest it, food is vital to human health and well-being in a way that other commodities are not, and this constitutes its unique status.

If food has a universal significance for us as human beings, it also has a particular significance for us as *individual* beings. Beyond the banal sense of each of us having different individual

Introduction

tastes, preferences and needs, medical scientists are beginning to appreciate the biological significance of the gut microbiome, where a diverse population of microbes aids digestion and conveys information to the immune system and the brain. These insights have fuelled the rapidly growing field of personalised nutrition, which aims to link our unique microbiomes with our individual responses to particular foods.

Tim Spector, a genetic epidemiologist at Kings College London, has shown that even identical twins, who share the same genes, can have radically different responses to the same meals largely because of their unique microbiomes. In other words, there is no such thing as a one-size-fits-all diet, according to Spector, because 'our guts and brains are so individual, and the ways we react to food so different and yet flexible'.[10]

Whatever its benefits, personalised nutrition has the potential to exacerbate health inequalities if current trends are any guide. Spector has already developed a personal nutrition app called ZOE, which has over 100,000 subscribers paying up to £600 in their first year for a personalised nutrition plan and a glucose blood monitor usually used by diabetics. Apart from the fact that only the wealthy among the worried well can afford it, critics argue that ZOE's scientific foundations are not as robust as its creators have claimed.[11]

But perhaps the main danger of personalised nutrition apps such as ZOE is that they fuel the neoliberal belief that access to a healthy diet is a personal and private matter at a time when it is more imperative than ever to affirm the *public duty of care* that governments owe their citizens, especially poor and vulnerable citizens. Why is it more imperative than ever to affirm this public duty? Because the multiple crises of food insecurity, hunger and a host of diet-related diseases, to say nothing of the existential threats from climate change, are becoming more pronounced in the low-income countries of the Global South as well as in the high-income countries of the Global North.

The spectres of poverty and hunger

Throughout the Global South the initial optimism that greeted the launch of the UN's seventeen Sustainable Development Goals (SDGs) is rapidly receding. Cast as a 'promise in peril', the latest progress report on the SDGs is truly alarming. They are rapidly disappearing in the rear-view mirror, it said, along with the hope and rights of current and future generations: 'It is time to sound the alarm. At the midpoint on our way to 2030, the Sustainable Development Goals are in deep trouble.' The parlous condition of SDGs 1 and 2, the foundational goals, is particularly concerning:

- *SDG 1 – No Poverty*: if current trends continue, 575 million people will still be living in extreme poverty and only one-third of countries will have halved their national poverty levels by 2030.
- *SDG 2 – Zero Hunger*: the number of people facing hunger and food insecurity has been rising since 2015, with the pandemic, conflict, climate change and growing inequalities exacerbating the situation. In 2022, about 9.2 per cent of the world population was facing chronic hunger, equivalent to about 735 million people – 122 million more than in 2019. An estimated 29.6 per cent of the global population – 2.4 billion people – were moderately or severely food insecure, meaning they did not have access to adequate food. This figure reflects an alarming 391 million more people than in 2019.[12]

Introduction

Poverty and hunger are no longer strangers in the countries of the Global North, if they ever were. That's why it's important to remember that the SDGs are *global* goals, applicable to all countries, and not confined to the countries of the Global South. One of the common challenges facing all countries is what the public health community refers to as the double burden of malnutrition, the coexistence of undernutrition and hunger with overweight, obesity and associated diet-related non-communicable diseases.[13]

This means it's time to abandon the antiquated stereotype in which countries are characterised either as low income and undernourished or as high income and overweight because the double burden is a global phenomenon. In high-income countries, where overweight and obesity affect more than half of the population, food insecurity among people with low incomes is associated with low-quality diets dominated by high consumption of ultra-processed foods, snacks and beverages high in energy, sugar and fat.

To address this new nutritional reality, public health campaigners are calling for a new *double-duty* strategy to deal with both sides of the double burden because different forms of malnutrition have hitherto been addressed in separate policy silos. The international evidence shows that common actions are needed to address the double burden, and the most efficacious actions are widely agreed to be: (1) actions that promote healthy growth in early life, (2) nutritious diets throughout the life course, (3) healthy food environments, (4) adequate income and education and (5) the knowledge and skills to support these goals.[14]

Far from making progress on these wider determinants of health and well-being, some countries in the Global North are seriously backsliding. The UK, for example, is witnessing deeply alarming societal trends, especially with respect to the poverty, health and well-being of its children:

Poverty

Children have consistently had the highest poverty rates throughout the past twenty-five years according to the Joseph Rowntree Foundation.[15] Twenty-five years ago a third of children lived in poverty, falling to 28 per cent in 2004–2005 before climbing to 31 per cent in 2019–2020. Recent analysis from UNICEF shows that this increase over the last decade was not mirrored in the majority of the other thirty-eight countries of the EU and Organisation for Economic Co-operation and Development (OECD). British children who grew up during the years of austerity have also fallen behind their European peers in terms of height according to an international group of health scientists tracking risk factors for non-communicable diseases.[16]

Early childhood

Early years, defined as the first five years of childhood, forms the basis for physical and mental health and well-being throughout the life course. A study by the Academy of Medical Sciences summarised its sombre findings:

> The messages of our report are urgent, because, despite its importance, health in the early years is under serious threat. The infant survival rate in the UK has stalled in recent years, and is worse than in 60 per cent of other Organization for Economic Cooperation and Development (OECD) nations. Other metrics

Introduction

of child health and wellbeing point in a similar direction. The prevalence of obesity is increasing, demands on all childhood mental health services are growing, breastfeeding rates are amongst the lowest of comparable high-income countries, ranking 15th out of 19 countries, the majority of childhood vaccination rates have fallen below the World Health Organization (WHO) recommended levels, and dental extractions due to preventable tooth decay remain a top reason for hospital admission of children.[17]

We'll encounter these problems again in later chapters because, while there is no single cause of such a complex array of health problems, the noxious interplay of prolonged poverty and poor diets is clearly implicated in many of these conditions, especially obesity, dental extractions and mental health.

But this brings us to a political paradox. There may be an international consensus around the nature and causes of diet-related health conditions, and widespread agreement as to many of the solutions, but governments around the world have been unable or unwilling to act on the consensus. Some of the reasons for this disconnect between scientific consensus and political action – such as the formidable lobbying power of the industrial food industry and the free market disposition of governments in thrall to neoliberal ideology – are explored in Chapter 1.

Sustainable diets

The mainstreaming of 'sustainable diets' is a key part of this international consensus and one of the most widely canvassed solutions to the challenges of malnutrition and climate change. 'Sustainable diets', says the UN's food and agriculture agency,

Serving the public

'are those diets with low environmental impacts which contribute to food and nutrition security and to healthy life for present and future generations. Sustainable diets are protective and respectful of biodiversity and ecosystems, culturally acceptable, accessible, economically fair and affordable; nutritionally adequate, safe and healthy; while optimizing natural and human resources.'[18]

This may be a perfectly sound definition in principle, but in practice it's difficult to translate into actual meals on a plate, especially when different diets vary so much in terms of their impacts on health and the environment. Tara Garnett has explored this issue at great length, and she contrasts 'win-win' diets that are both healthy and have a low environmental impact with 'lose-lose' diets that have high environmental impacts and damage health (see Exhibit 0.1).

She is surely right to argue that 'lose-lose' diets such as the Western diet are the point of departure when considering alternatives. One of the great merits of her work is that she makes explicit what is implicitly assumed in many studies of sustainable diets – that synergies are possible but not guaranteed. 'Healthy diets', she argues, 'may have high environmental impacts if rich in dairy, lean meats, and fresh produce grown under protected conditions or transported by air, while less environmentally damaging diets are not necessarily nutritionally adequate.'[19]

Trade-offs are inevitable, she argues. While livestock intensification may reduce greenhouse gases per kilogram of meat or milk output, it will raise animal welfare concerns. Nutritious food should certainly be affordable but should it be cheap? Garnett's work calls for more ambitious policies from governments and for more humility in recognising the limits of our knowledge: 'We know little about how to move eating patterns

Health and environmental impacts of different diets

This figure compares 'win-win' diets that are both healthy and have a low environmental impact with other dietary patterns seen around the world today. The typical Western diet, which is both unsustainable and unhealthy, is growing in prevalence around the world.

	Dietary diversity	Food energy intake/ expenditure	Animal products	Fish & related	Vegetables & fruits	Whole grains tubers & legumes	Processed foods	Food losses & waste	Cooking fuels
Healthier & more sustainable diets	High	Balanced	Low (all parts eaten)	Low to moderate (sustainable)	High (minimally processed)	High	Avoided	Low	Efficient
Diets of the healthy wealthy	High	Balanced	Moderate to high (lean meats)	High	High	Low to high	Avoided	High (consumer)	Heavy use
Western-type diets (global)	Low	Excessive	High	Low to high (unsustainable)	Low	Low	High	High	Inefficient
Diets of the poor in poor countries	Low	Insufficient	Low	Low	Low	High (legumes often low)	Low (but growing)	High (spoilage) Low (consumer)	Inefficient

Source: Garnett (2016)

Exhibit 0.1 Health and environmental impacts of different diets

Serving the public

in healthier, let alone more sustainable, directions, except that education and awareness-raising alone achieve little ... Policymakers must also be willing to test promising approaches where evidence is scarce; experimentation builds evidence.'[20]

Another implication of this work is that context is king. Generic definitions of sustainable diets can only take us so far because actual diets are so profoundly context-dependent, reflecting the cultural economy of a country and the values of its communities. But since governments have a *public duty of care*, they ought to draw on the best available knowledge when issuing dietary guidelines (e.g. the *Eatwell Guide* in the UK) on what constitutes 'good food' and 'healthy diets'. As we'll see in later chapters, there are many interpretations of good food, but they are all consistent with the conception proposed earlier – food that is appetising, nutritious, culturally appropriate and sustainably produced.

Cities, regions and nations have been striving to put good food on the political agenda for many years and for many different reasons. While the relief of hunger has the greatest claim on our moral sensibilities, the good food agenda can't be reduced to a single issue because, by its very nature, food has a multifunctional character. Therefore, we need to resist the temptation to reduce the meaning of 'good food' to a narrow nutritional agenda because a purely needs-based perspective cannot possibly do justice to the kaleidoscopic character of our food and the multiple prisms – social, economic, political, ecological, cultural, physiological, psychological – through which food is viewed, valued and used in society. But whatever the prism, there is now a worldwide consensus that radical action is needed to reform the food system for the sake of people and planet alike.

Introduction

Themes and arguments

Turning to the main themes and arguments of the book, let me begin by clarifying the subtitle. The *good food revolution* refers to the struggle – locally, nationally and globally – to create a fairer, healthier and more sustainable food system. Because this is clearly a work in progress rather than an accomplished reality, some critics might be tempted to say that a sustainable food system is merely an ideal. But the well-worn dichotomy between the ideal and the real is misleading according to Martha Nussbaum, the moral philosopher, because '[i]deals are real: they direct our striving, our plans, our legal processes'.[21]

The quest for a sustainable food system is a perfect example of Nussbaum's argument because it represents a compelling ideal for many people around the world, young and old alike, and it begins with an unequivocal refusal to accept that certain types of food – food that is harmful to human health and damaging to the environment – are socially acceptable in societies that aspire to be sustainable in any meaningful sense of the term. In the chapters that follow, I focus on one small part of this quest: the struggle to improve the quality of food served in public places.

Chapter 1 sets the scene by examining the evolving international debate about the food system and its role in the multiple crises of health, environment and climate change. Although global summits are belatedly trying to craft a reform agenda for the food system, the *nation*al level remains the key arena where food policy reforms are fostered or frustrated. Taking the UK as an example, I argue that more than forty years of neoliberalism – the political ideology that demonises the public sector and lionises the private sector – have bequeathed a noxious legacy in the form of a food system that is dysfunctional for producers and consumers and a public sector that has been denuded of capacity and resources.

Despite this inauspicious political context, Chapter 1 also highlights progressive efforts to reclaim the public plate, tapping the potential of the power of purchase through regulatory reform from above and grassroots innovations from below. Here I draw on the innovative Food for Life (FFL) programme to illustrate the scope for reform as well as the limits to reform. While public food procurement is now fashionable in political circles, I argue that it is being set up to fail unless it is part of a food system approach that integrates the interdependent domains of purchasing, production and consumption. A food system approach presupposes a food strategy, but successive Conservative governments have been ideologically averse to embracing such ideas because they smack of too much state intervention.

The chapters in Part II of the book present deep dives into public food provisioning systems in their respective institutional settings: schools, hospitals and prisons. Each of these chapters aims to frame the challenge of public food provisioning in its institutional context before exploring the quest to improve the quality of food.

Chapter 2 outlines three models of school food provisioning from the welfare model of collective provision, through the neoliberal model of consumer choice under Thatcherism, to what I call the ecological model of sustainable provision, a model that is emergent rather than fully realised. Having outlined the historical context of school food policy, I focus on two key themes: first, the *whole school approach* that aims to align the

Introduction

pedagogy of the classroom with the food served in the dining room; and second, the campaign for *universal free school meals*. The whole school approach is analysed through the prism of the FFL programme, what I consider to be the gold standard in the world of public sector food provisioning. The campaign for universal free school meals is the most exciting development in school food policy in the UK since the creation of the welfare state in the 1940s. In the UK it has been pioneered in Scotland, Wales and some London boroughs, all of whom have much to learn from leading municipalities in Sweden, such as Malmö, whose experience I also include because it is an internationally acclaimed exemplar of good food provisioning.

Chapter 3 shifts the spotlight to the National Health Service (NHS) in the UK. Here, the poor quality of hospital food has been a perennial problem and there are many reasons for this sorry state of affairs. The main argument is that hospitals are essentially clinical treatment sites rather than health promotion sites. In this overly medicalised culture, a low status has been attached to food and nutrition by both hospital management and the clinical profession. Yet the real costs of malnourished patients – which involve longer stays in hospital and poor recovery rates – are rarely factored into the financial equations of the medical-industrial complex. The chapter highlights the paradox of the hospital, which consists of the Sisyphean task of trying to provide a *clinical* solution to a *societal* problem – the problem of diet-related diseases associated with the rapid growth of cheap, ultra-processed food. Notwithstanding these problems, the chapter focuses on the agents of change within and without the health service who have collaborated to try to embed a good food culture in the NHS through local experiments.

Serving the public

The final deep dive in Chapter 4 focuses on the prison, a unique public sector setting because the consumers are incarcerated. I include a vignette of the US along with the UK because these are the liberal democracies where the carceral state is most pronounced. The chapter begins with a scene-setting section about prisons and prisoners in the UK and the US, focusing on their conditions of life, their poor state of health and the hugely important role that food plays in their daily lives. Thereafter the chapter explores two key themes: the carceral diet and the prospects for rehabilitation.

Regarding the carceral diet and its discontents, I focus on two extraordinary aspects of prison life: the *Aylesbury mystery* in the UK (where successive governments refused to act on evidence that showed a clear link between nutritional supplements and antisocial behaviour) and the *nutraloaf controversy* in the US (where a gross food concoction that allegedly meets nutritional guidelines is used to discipline and punish prisoners in a manner that evokes the carceral analysis of Michel Foucault).

To assess the prospects for rehabilitation, I examine the food training programme of the Clink charity in the UK, which runs a network of gardens, kitchens and restaurants through which prisoners are trained within the prison and mentored afterwards in the community to find gainful employment, which reduces the incentive to reoffend.

Chapter 5 shifts the focus from the *sectoral* world of public food systems to the *spatial* world of place-based food movements. This chapter charts the rise of what I call the Good Food movement, one of the aims of which is to mobilise the progressive forces of cities and other localities to utilise municipal and civic power to fashion more sustainable foodscapes by

Introduction

harnessing the public plate as part of an integrated suite of local food policies. The chapter focuses on the dynamics of the movement in the UK and the US. In the UK, the Sustainable Food Places network is the most significant example of the emergent food movement, a network that aims to overcome the limits of purely local action. Forming a national network yields a double political dividend: it raises the profile of cities and regions as agents of change, and it enhances the voice of localities as advocates for sustainable food systems. Although local food movements have done remarkably well to survive the age of austerity in the UK, many of them are struggling to sustain themselves financially despite the vital contributions they make to food security.

In the US the Good Food movement has a much longer lineage, where it emerged to fight the scourge of hunger in a country with a notoriously weak welfare state. Although it is impossible to do justice to such a diverse food movement here, I focus on three significant expressions of the movement: the Food Policy Councils that exist throughout the whole country; federal-level networks and alliances such as the Good Food Purchasing Program; and the inspiring case of New York City, a pioneer of good food policies.

One of the challenges for the movement in both the UK and the US is how to build durable alliances for change to enable localities to learn from each other and to become more engaged in national and international food policy forums. In the absence of a progressive political agenda, which strives to promote the public plate and fashion sustainable foodscapes, local food movements can easily degenerate into an exclusive form of green gentrification, which amounts to sustainability for the few and not the many.

Serving the public

Chapter 6, the final chapter, explores the prospects for change. This chapter examines the prospects for reforming the food system by focusing on three dimensions of change: (1) the clash between the power of new ideas and the power of vested interests; (2) the role of civil society organisations and public sector bodies as key agents of change; and (3) the need for more powers and resources to be devolved to cities and regions in the name of subsidiarity, because these subnational agents are pioneering climate-friendly food policies and fashioning new spaces of deliberation in which local citizens can be actively engaged in shaping the process of change.

Part I

Food in the public sphere

1
Reclaiming the public plate

Introduction

We cannot hope to understand the challenges facing public catering if we confine our attention to the institutions themselves: the schools, hospitals and prisons in which the food is served and consumed. In other words, we need to step back to appreciate the wider context in which the food system operates. It may seem a stretch to suggest that what happens in places such as Rio or Paris can affect the food on a public plate in the UK, but that is precisely what has happened. The Earth Summit in Rio in 1992 put sustainability on the public agenda and the Paris Agreement in 2015 agreed new targets for the control of greenhouse gas emissions. Slowly but surely, this sustainability perspective is beginning to change the way we view and value food, raising new and searching questions about how and where our food is produced. From farm to fork, however, the modern agrifood system has reached a crisis point, not least because the pace of reform is dwarfed by the scale of the challenges.

The crisis can be understood at two different levels. At the international level we are facing a polycrisis in which multiple crises intersect, making the whole greater than the sum of its parts. Food is so deeply implicated in this process that I suggest it embodies its very own polycrisis because the problems of health, diet and environment are so closely interwoven. Although there is a growing international consensus around the solutions to what I call the *agrifood polycrisis*, we shall see in the following section the formidable forces arrayed against reform, which helps to explain why progress has been so sluggish.

While globalists claim that nation-states have been rendered redundant by globalisation, the national level remains an important arena for political change. If anything, the national arena is arguably *the* most important level for reforming the food system because it's the level where reforms are fostered or frustrated. As one of the pioneers of neoliberalism, the UK provides a distinctive context to study the scope and limits of the public plate as a vehicle for progressive food politics. Successive Conservative governments in the UK developed a deep ideological aversion to the public sector and this proved especially corrosive to the integrity of the public plate when it was subjected to compulsory competitive tendering (CCT) under Thatcherism, bequeathing a low-cost catering legacy that lingered on.

Despite this inhospitable neoliberal environment, the UK has managed to generate alternative visions in which the public plate was a catalyst for a fairer, healthier and more sustainable food system. These alternative visions appeared in 2003, when the Department of Food and Rural Affairs (DEFRA) launched its vision of a sustainable public food procurement system, and again in 2021, when Henry Dimbleby issued his transformational *National Food Strategy* (NFS). These high points deserve

Reclaiming the public plate

to be acknowledged and acclaimed because they demonstrate that, while the UK had a vision of how to serve good food on the public plate, the vision was never embedded in public sector practice for one very simple reason: the government of the day had no interest in doing so.

As we will see, when alternative visions for good food on the public plate have taken root in practice, they invariably came from small-scale experiments sponsored not by national governments but by civil society groups working in concert with local public bodies.[1]

Confronting the polycrisis

We have entered 'the world of the polycrisis' according to Adam Tooze, the influential historian. This refers to the interplay of multiple crises that are linked in such a way that the overall impact becomes so much greater than the sum of each part.[2] The idea has been fuelled by a confluence of environmental crises (crop failures, water stress, biodiversity loss), human health crises (the double burden of malnutrition in the form of hunger and obesity), socio-economic crises (growing inequalities and widespread precarity) and geopolitical crises (escalating global tensions between the US and China and the full-scale Russian invasion of Ukraine, which triggered huge spikes in energy and food prices). These crises are being amplified by 'comparatively new developments in the global risks landscape, including unsustainable levels of debt, a new era of low growth, low global investment and de-globalization, a decline in human development after decades of progress ... Together, these are converging to shape a unique, uncertain and turbulent decade to come.'[3]

Serving the public

Although the notion of a polycrisis has its critics, it helps us to appreciate two important aspects of our current global predicament. First and foremost, it underlines the deep interdependencies between economy, society and the biosphere, a simple but fundamental point that was obscured in the heyday of neoliberalism, when these complex connections received little attention from market fundamentalists. Second, the polycrisis idea serves as a powerful reminder that conventional policymaking, based as it is on discrete, hierarchically ordered departmental silos, is profoundly ill-equipped to deal effectively with the interdependencies of complex societal challenges such as climate change, food security, energy transitions and the like, all of which require whole-of-government action along with the active involvement of civil society. As we'll see later, these complex challenges demand behavioural change at societal as well as the individual and household levels because citizens and consumers need to be actively involved in the transformation if low-carbon lifestyles are to be normalised.

The agrifood system would seem to embody its very own polycrisis when we consider the interlinked crises of health, climate change and nature/biodiversity. On the *health* front, as we have seen, most countries around the world are grappling with the double burden of malnutrition. Although there is no single cause, it is largely driven by the worldwide access to processed and unhealthy foods that are higher in saturated fats, salt and sugar, and lower in vitamins and minerals, than the traditional or local diets they often replace. Dramatic changes in the agrifood system, towards more and more ultra-processed foods, interact with megatrends such as globalisation and urbanisation to create more homogenised diets.[4] These diets – high in sodium and low in whole grains and fruit etc. – are now responsible for more deaths worldwide than any other risks globally, including tobacco smoking.[5]

The dynamic interconnections at the heart of the agrifood polycrisis are perhaps most apparent with respect to *climate change*. Agrifood trends contribute to climate change while the latter has negative impacts on agrifood systems. Global agrifood systems are the single greatest cause of terrestrial biodiversity loss, one-third of all greenhouse gas (GhG) emissions, 80 per cent of deforestation and 70 per cent of freshwater use. Although the majority of GhG emissions still comes from primary production, the increase in recent years has come mainly from pre- and post-production processes, such as fertiliser production, food packaging, processing, transport, retail and household consumption and waste disposal.[6]

As regards *biodiversity*, the Dasgupta Review showed quite conclusively that, far from neglecting to value nature, we actively devalue it by damaging it through a panoply of perverse incentives. The review noted that governments around the world spend some $500 billion every year subsidising practices that destroy nature, such as fossil fuel subsidies and intensive agriculture subsidies. Even allowing for the subsidies that aim to conserve or enhance nature, 'subsidies that are harmful to the environment vastly outweigh those which are beneficial'.[7]

According to the TEEB study, which adopted a holistic food system approach rather than a narrow production-centric view, the key challenge is how to find a solution to the 'diet-environment-health trilemma'. The best solution, it argued, would be to reduce excessive consumption of animal products in high-income countries, a move that would furnish healthier diets, lower emissions and more sustainable land use patterns because less meat production would require less land for feed grains.[8] But this raises what many reformers consider to be the most controversial issue in the entire agrifood policy debate, namely what is to be done about livestock farming?

The best illustration of the controversial nature of this issue was the political reaction to *Livestock's Long Shadow*, a seminal report which the UN's Food and Agriculture Organisation (FAO) released in 2006. To understand the scale and intensity of the reaction, we need to appreciate the novelty of the study. Whereas previous FAO studies analysed livestock–environment interactions from the perspective of the livestock industry, the new study team inverted this approach and analysed the livestock sector from a broad *environmental* perspective in which social, economic and public health concerns were the primary focus. What emerged was a remarkably frank exposé of what it called 'the truly enormous impact' of the livestock sector on land, land use, climate change, water and biodiversity. It found that livestock production was responsible for 18 per cent of global GhG emissions, mostly due to deforestation for pasture and feed crops. It also exposed the public health problems of excessive animal protein in high-income countries: at the time of the study, meat consumption ranged from 123 kg per person per year in the US compared to just 5 kg in India.

From a policy standpoint the main dilemma was clearly defined: how do you reduce the environmental and health impacts of a livestock sector that provides livelihoods for 987 million poor people in the world and supplies a third of the world's dietary protein? Reform was hindered, according to the report, by the lack of awareness regarding the true impact of livestock and by a policy framework that was actually exacerbating the problem by supporting damaging livestock practices. The most remarkable aspect of the report was that the FAO, famous for its diplomatic language, attributed the lack of a sound policy response to the political power of the livestock lobby: 'livestock lobbies have been able to exert an over-proportional influence on public policies, to protect their interests. An indication of this lobbying power is the persistence of agricultural subsidies, amounting to an average of 32 percent of total farm income in OECD countries, with livestock products (dairy and beef, in particular) regularly figuring among the most heavily subsidized products.'[9]

The political reaction was fast and furious. The livestock lobby in many countries, particularly the beef barons from Argentina, Brazil and the US, was vociferous in its condemnation and threatened to defund the FAO, which depends on external funding like all UN agencies. The authors of the report, from the FAO's livestock policy branch, later revealed that they were not prepared for the storm that erupted following publication nor for the way that they were censored, undermined and victimised within the organisation. The head of the livestock policy branch, Henning Steinfeld, was told by a senior FAO official: 'Even if livestock contributes 18 per cent to climate change, the FAO shall not say that. It's not in the interest of the FAO to highlight environmental impacts.'[10]

This crisis was clearly a traumatic experience for the FAO, and its subsequent reports were more cautious and more diplomatic, even to the point of playing down the role of livestock in climate change according to critics. But the reason why the livestock controversy remains so important is because it's a sobering reminder of the lobbying power of the meat industry in international food policy forums. The FAO seems to have learned from the crisis because, more recently, it has approached the delicate task of reforming the agrifood system in more generic terms rather than targeting the livestock sector as the most egregious climate villain. For example, at the annual climate summit in Dubai in 2023, the COP28 summit, it presented its new agrifood strategy by highlighting policy goals for which there was already a strong global consensus, stressing it was 'not only for climate goals but also to boost food security and counter malnutrition, a fundamental aspect of the right to food'.[11] Optimists were greatly encouraged by this new strategy, and especially by the fact that the agrifood system was being given some prominence at COP28, having been ignored in every previous COP despite accounting for nearly a third of global emissions.

Agrifood may have finally arrived at the annual COP summits but it received very little attention in the final text of the summit, the key document of the proceedings, confirming that it was still not being treated as a top priority. Equally disturbing is the fact that two of the greatest barriers to sustainable development – climate change and the double burden of malnutrition – are still treated at the national level in totally separate policy silos. As the FAO conceded in a report that was not tabled in Dubai, national programmes to address both climate change and nutritional security in an integrated fashion 'are still limited, and thus there is currently little direct evidence of the impact of such work'.[12]

One way to overcome the lack of integration in national plans of climate and nutrition is to harness the energies of subnational actors – local and regional governments along with their civil society partners – all of whom are on the front line of climate change and the double burden of malnutrition. These subnational actors became more visible and more vocal at COP28, and they won a small victory by securing direct access

Reclaiming the public plate

to the Loss and Damage Fund that was launched at the Dubai summit. Although the fund is far short of what is required, the fact that multilevel governance is finally being recognised is a welcome change from the days when national and international actors were deemed to be the only legitimate actors in international policy forums. For all its manifest shortcomings, such as its failure to commit to the phase out fossil fuels, COP28 finally began to correct two problems that had stymied all previous summits: the failure to recognise the potential of food system change and the failure to harness the energies of subnational actors.

In UN climate summits, national governments have been given the leading role in managing the Nationally Determined Contributions (NDCs), which represent each country's individual targets and mechanisms for action on climate change. Although NDCs are the central benchmarking device to track and assess progress towards global climate goals, there is currently no formal process to document the contribution of local actions to meeting national climate targets.[13] Subnational actors are on the front line of climate change and the double burden of malnutrition and their key role in citizen engagement and policy implementation needs to be fully recognised by a governance system that has hitherto neglected the role of cities and regions. The political challenge here is to recognise the limits of unilateral action at any single spatial scale and acknowledge the need for a concerted form of multilevel action in which international, national and subnational governments, along with their civic partners, are empowered to collaborate to confront the burgeoning agrifood polycrisis.

The neoliberal *kulturkampf*

In view of the awesome complexity of the crises that make up the agrifood polycrisis, it now seems ludicrous to suggest that the 'free market' is a credible solution to these collective action challenges. Yet for the past forty years this is precisely what was proposed by the neoliberal paradigm that dominated the thinking and policies of both national governments and international organisations such as the World Bank, International Monetary Fund and World Trade Organization (WTO). To understand the nature and legacy of neoliberalism, it is useful to distinguish its philosophical arguments (some of which remain relevant) from its policy prescriptions (which are anachronistic).

Demonising the state: neoliberal critics

Among the philosophical architects of the neoliberal paradigm, Hayek and Buchanan deserve special mention because they played a big role in developing the paradigm and their ideas remain relevant to the debate about the state today. Hayek is rightly considered to be one of the philosophical founders of neoliberalism for two reasons: he made the most compelling intellectual case for a market-based order, and he offered the most perceptive critique of state planning. According to Hayek, the key problem of a 'rational economic order' was the fact that 'the knowledge of the circumstances of which we must make use never exists in concentrated or integrated form but solely as the dispersed bits of incomplete and frequently contradictory knowledge which all the separate individuals possess'. Here he underlined the significance of what we now call *tacit knowledge* by drawing attention to that 'body of very important but

Reclaiming the public plate

unorganised knowledge which cannot possibly be called scientific in the sense of knowledge of general rules: the knowledge of the particular circumstances of time and place'.[14] The fact that knowledge is not given to any single agent in its totality, and because tacit knowledge can never be fully codified let alone centralised, were the insights on which he built his critique of central state planning and his defence of the market as a decentralised system of economic discovery based on trial and error.

Although this knowledge-based critique of central planning is both powerful and pertinent, Hayek's argument has three major limitations: it crudely juxtaposes central planning (the state) with decentralised planning (the market), as though these were the only mechanisms for coordinating economic activity; it views the market as the only discovery mechanism, ignoring the potential of learning through networks; and, by reducing knowledge to an attribute of atomised individuals, it neglects the much more important form of organisational knowledge, which is created and diffused through social interaction.[15]

While Hayek's contribution to neoliberalism is universally acknowledged, Buchanan's role has garnered less attention. This is surprising and paradoxical because no one in the late twentieth century has done more to undermine confidence in the state, and the political sphere in general, than Buchanan's *public choice* theory. Shorn of its academic trappings, public choice theory sought to apply to the political sphere the narrow self-interested values and motivations of the economic sphere. Buchanan famously defined the public choice perspective as 'politics without romance', because it saw the public sphere as a prosaic sphere where the participants – voters, bureaucrats and politicians – sought to advance their own private interests rather than some presumed public interest.[16]

Serving the public

The earliest expression of this perspective, *The Calculus of Consent*, was closer to political philosophy than it was to either conventional economics or political science. Widely hailed as a classic statement of public choice theory, this book sought to integrate two themes that were central to Buchanan's conservative outlook: first, the overriding importance of *rules*, as opposed to policies, parties or personnel, as the primary object of political choice; and second, the egotistical vision of human behaviour based on *Homo economicus*, the so-called economic man who is presumed to be a fully rational and purely self-interested actor in both the private sphere of the market as well as the public sphere of politics.[17]

Buchanan's stress on the 'rules of the game' may seem abstract and abstruse but such rules played a profoundly important political role because they were deemed to be the main means of controlling what he called 'the threat of Leviathan', that is the state, the public sector and public welfare programmes. Democratic political life contained a systemic flaw according to Buchanan – which was that politicians enjoy spending but not taxing, resulting in ever-growing budget deficits – a flaw that could only be corrected by imposing constitutional constraints, such as rules to ensure balanced budgets and the like. Because the democratic process has an inherent tendency to generate budgetary excesses, Buchanan concluded that: 'Democracy may become its own Leviathan unless constitutional limits are imposed and enforced.'[18]

This conclusion carried two implications that Buchanan rarely spelled out explicitly in his formal works: (1) that the public choice perspective was anti-state by its very nature, designed as it was to substitute political failure for market failure; and (2) that it was even antithetical to democracy

Reclaiming the public plate

itself, given its opposition to the principle of majority rule as the ideal for collective decision processes. Once again, if these seem arcane academic issues, we should remember that public choice principles were actually enacted in a real world context because Buchanan was hired as an economic advisor to General Pinochet and his government, with the result that: 'Chile emerged with a set of rules closer to his ideal than any in existence, built to repel future popular pressure for change ... Buchanan had long called for binding rules to protect economic liberty and constrain majority power, and Chile's 1980 Constitution of Liberty guaranteed these as never before.'[19]

During the long postwar boom, the ideas of Hayek and Buchanan were confined to the margins of mainstream politics because they were deemed to be too esoteric. But with the economic crises of the 1970s, neoliberal ideas suddenly found a receptive audience among political elites searching for new solutions to new problems. The political credentials of neoliberalism were eventually forged and mainstreamed in the US and the UK, the heartlands of the neoliberal policy repertoire, where the Reagan and Thatcher governments became evangelical ambassadors for a policy repertoire that involved shrinking the state and elevating the market. Although each country navigated the new era in its own way, the neoliberal policy repertoire was associated with a suite of pro-market policies that involved some or all of the following: the deregulation of product, labour and capital markets, privatisation of public sector assets, lower taxes and as small a state as was necessary to maintain law and order. In Wendy Brown's famous phrase, neoliberalism aims at the 'economization of everything'.[20]

Serving the public

The UK heartland: neoliberal politics

Under the Thatcher governments the UK became the pioneer of the neoliberal policy repertoire in Europe. For Prime Minister Thatcher, the repertoire was always so much more than a mere economic strategy. It was a moral crusade to change hearts and minds in a bid to restore what she considered to be the lost virtues of thrift, self-reliance and individual responsibility, all of which had been eroded by state-sponsored collectivism. It was a political strategy to recalibrate the balance of power between capital and labour to favour the former and discipline the latter. And it was also a form of economic shock therapy to stimulate a sclerotic economy by reducing the grip of the bureaucratic state sector and enhance the space for private enterprise. Taken together, this amounted to a veritable *kulturkampf* against the public sector and the values of the public domain because it signalled an 'astonishingly radical programme of cultural reconstruction, more far-reaching than anything attempted by any British government since the days of Oliver Cromwell, and more reminiscent of Gramscian Marxism than of anything in the British conservative tradition'.[21]

Public sector industries such as water and telecoms were privatised. Where this was not possible, as in the NHS for example, proxy markets were created between purchaser and provider to mimic commercial pressures. Bitter industrial disputes ensued, most notably a near twelve-month miners' strike which resulted in large-scale closures in areas where coalmining was the mainstay of local employment, precipitating further economic deprivation in regions that were already the poorest in the country. Apart from public sector industries and public services, another

Reclaiming the public plate

key target of the neoliberal *kulturkampf* was local government, an institution that was progressively stripped of its functions and subjected to an ever tighter cage of financial control. In the eyes of central government, the role of local authorities was to deliver centrally designed services to centrally mandated standards, a stance that rendered them 'puppets dancing on the centre's strings, not vehicles for civic engagement in the localities for which they are supposed to speak'.[22]

In the historical accounts of Thatcherism, the battle with the miners is understandably given a prominent place, along with the political conflicts with radical local politicians such as 'Red' Ken Livingstone, a conflict that led to the abolition of Greater London Council and the other metropolitan authorities in 1986. But what rarely gets any attention in these standard histories is what the *kulturkampf* meant for public food provisioning, widely regarded as the Cinderella public service. As we'll see in the following chapters, the effect was little short of dramatic because the impact of CCT triggered a cultural revolution in the spheres of public procurement and public sector catering, bequeathing a long-term legacy that outlived the Thatcher governments.

Despite the technical nomenclature, CCT was a profoundly political tool designed to spearhead public sector reform by subjecting public services in local government and the NHS to a competitive challenge from the private sector. First introduced in 1980 into public sector contracts for construction, the CCT regime was expanded in the 1988 Local Government Act to cover a wide array of additional services, including education and welfare catering, refuse collection, building cleaning and vehicle maintenance. Although it was designed to reduce the role of direct service organisations (DSOs), the in-house

Serving the public

local authority delivery teams, the evidence suggests that DSOs managed to retain a majority of the contracts.[23]

Beneath the surface, however, CCT was having the desired effect due to the new rules to which local authorities were subjected – confirming Buchanan's point about the power of rules to promote or prevent certain forms of public sector behaviour. In the case of CCT, local authorities were prohibited from engaging in 'anti-competitive behaviour' and so they were not allowed to reject lower bids from private contractors without 'good reason'. This rule proved to be hugely consequential because 91 per cent of all contracts were awarded to the lowest bidder in the first round of CCT and 85 per cent in the second round.[24]

In the case of public sector catering, a detailed study of services that were outsourced to the private sector found that unskilled workers suffered the most in the liberalised market as they received lower pay and inferior terms and conditions.[25] This reflected the experience in many other sectors, where the cost reductions associated with contracting out were largely secured by cutting wages. As we'll see in Chapter 2, the most egregious examples of neoliberal policy in school food catering included the abolition of all nutritional standards, the decline of kitchen infrastructure, the proliferation of cheap, processed food and poorer terms and conditions for catering staff. More than anything else, then, CCT helped to embed a low-cost culture into the routines of public procurement and public sector catering.

Although the New Labour government clearly tempered the worst excesses of the CCT regime when it entered office in 1997, its own Best Value regime retained the neoliberal rule that was designed to subject local authority provision to competitive pressures. In his polemical essay on the decline of the public sphere, David Marquand captured both the continuities as well as the novelties of the New Labour approach: 'Behind the mantra of public-service "reform", lie the assumptions that the public services should be run, as far as possible, as though they were private firms ... Their goals differ from their predecessors', but the mechanisms through which they pursue them are the same. In a word, market mimicry and central control still rule.'[26]

The New Labour interregnum was precisely that: a period of soft neoliberalism between two periods of hard neoliberalism. The Conservative-led coalition government that assumed office in 2010 may not have displayed the same evangelical fervour as its Thatcherite forebears but its impact on the economy and society was no less dramatic because its austerity programme was without precedent in the postwar period. Austerity flowed from two fiscal rules that the government set itself: first, to eliminate the structural budget deficit by the end of the Parliament; and second, to have the national debt falling by the next election. These self-imposed fiscal rules were used to justify a level of public expenditure cuts that had no parallel in living memory, with the burden falling largely on the poorest and most vulnerable sections of society. Eminent economic scholars criticised the austerity programme for being a political choice rather than an economic necessity and for resurrecting a pre-Keynesian view of the economy that had damaging consequences for economic growth and social cohesion.[27]

The full costs of the austerity programmes between 2010 and 2023 may never be known because they involve tangible and intangible costs as well as short-term and long-term costs to health, wealth and well-being. During these years of

Serving the public

austerity, the poignant image of the food bank became the most compelling and ubiquitous means through which the media tried to convey the depth and scale of the social crisis. As the largest food bank network in the country, the Trussell Trust became the lightning rod for the debate about the pros and cons of food banking. Founded in 1997, the Trussell Trust grew rapidly after 2010, delivering 1.1 million emergency food parcels in 2014–2015 and as many as three million parcels in 2022–2023.[28]

To stem the growth of demand, the trust sought to discuss the problem of food poverty with the government, but Iain Duncan Smith, the Secretary of State for Work and Pensions, not only refused to meet them but warned them to stop the 'political messaging of your organisation' when they claimed that the government's reform of welfare benefits was fuelling the demand for food banks. In his official reply, Duncan Smith said: 'I strongly refute this claim and would politely ask you to stop scaremongering in this way. I understand that a feature of your business model must require you to continuously achieve publicity, but I am concerned that you are now seeking to do this by making your political opposition to welfare reform overtly clear.'[29]

This encounter was arguably the clearest example of the government refusing to acknowledge the role its austerity programme was having in fuelling the demand for hunger relief among the working poor as well as the unemployed and other welfare recipients. The core problem, as the Trussell Trust rightly said, was the rollout of Universal Credit, the largest and most ambitious welfare reform in a generation. Although the principle of the reform was sound enough – consolidating multiple benefits into one universal payment – the five-week wait for the first payment was having disastrous effects as it locked recipients into hardship. A definitive analysis of the problem some years later concluded: 'The minimum five week wait for Universal Credit – either without income or with a Department for Work and Pensions Advance Payment – has led to acute financial hardship, and damaged households' longer-term financial resilience. This includes destitution, housing insecurity and debt.'[30] The rationale for the five-week payment delay eventually became clear when the minister in charge of welfare reform, David Freud, publicly admitted that the UK Treasury was totally 'unyielding' on the principle of the delayed payment because Universal Credit recipients would be forced to find work, thereby reducing the number of claimants as well as the cost of the scheme.[31] For the Treasury, then, the five-week wait was justified as part of its overriding commitment to reduce the budget deficit, the totemic issue that trumped everything and caused such destitution.

Welfare reform was clearly subordinated to the fiscal strategy of deficit reduction and both were driven by central government. But it fell to *local* governments to announce the bulk of the cuts because they were the ones responsible for delivering local services, allowing central government to distance itself from its own austerity policies. As we will see later, local authorities became locked into a highly precarious financial predicament as a result of austerity, not least because central the government grant was reduced by 40 per cent between 2010–2011 and 2019–2020. Perversely, these cuts fell heaviest on the most deprived authorities because, even though grant funding was cut by a uniform percentage, it had a disproportionate impact on the poorest authorities as they were more dependent on central government support.[32]

Serving the public

Although the costs of austerity are still being debated, it is already clear that its impact on the economy and society was systemic and traumatic. As the following chapters show, the effects manifested themselves in different ways: teachers reported children arriving hungry in school even though they were not eligible for free school meals; patients arriving malnourished in hospitals, making their treatment more time-consuming, less effective and more costly; and all these problems were exacerbated by the twin pressures of the COVID-19 pandemic and the cost-of-living crisis. But the greatest inequalities in any society are the inequalities of mortality and morbidity. Perhaps for this reason, one of the most controversial debates since 2010 was prompted by a study from a team at the Glasgow Centre for Population Health. They argued that mortality rates across the UK had stopped improving in the early 2010s, a trend that was largely attributable to the UK government's austerity policies. Changes in trends were observed for both men and women, especially for those living in the 20 per cent most deprived areas, and their analysis concluded by saying: 'Approximately 335 000 more deaths occurred between 2012 and 2019 than was expected based on previous trends, with the excess greater among men.'[33] The finding caused a political furore when Ruth Dundas, one of the co-authors, put the findings in a wider perspective and said: 'This study shows that in the UK a great many more deaths are likely to have been caused by UK government economic policy than by the Covid-19 pandemic.'[34]

As in other crises, the pandemic saw the state play a new and more proactive role than it had been assigned by neoliberal ideology. But the pandemic was only one factor among many others that helped to rehabilitate the state, by which

Reclaiming the public plate

I mean that a new cognitive landscape is beginning to emerge in and beyond the UK in which the state is perceived not in the negative and desiccated terms in which neoliberals have framed it but rather as a more benign institution that alone has the power and authority to catalyse collective action in economy and society on the scale required to address societal challenges.

Rehabilitating the state: neoliberal twilight?

In recent years neoliberal nostrums have encountered a growing backlash, especially the crude mantra that lionised the market and demonised the state. At the global scale the UN signalled a new era when it convened an international agreement in 2015 to support seventeen new SDGs, goals that were deemed applicable to *all* countries. Even a brief acquaintance with these goals – such as ending poverty and hunger and promoting good health and well-being for all – demonstrates that they cannot be addressed effectively without effective state action. In the same year the Paris Agreement, a legally binding treaty on climate change was signed at COP21, when 196 parties agreed to 'hold the increase in the global average temperature to well below 2C above pre-industrial levels', another goal that requires a proactive state working in concert with its partners in the private and civil sectors to drive the necessary social and economic transformation. In addition to these exacting global agreements, the leading OECD countries have overcome their neoliberal inhibitions and rediscovered the merits of an active industrial policy to help their national economies decarbonise as part of wider green transition. For its part the EU is framing a new generation of innovation policies around five 'missions', all of which presuppose a more proactive and entrepreneurial state.

Cities and regions are also part of this rehabilitation process, for example by remunicipalising some of the services that were either privatised or outsourced during the neoliberal heyday.[35]

These trends are part of a major reassessment of the neoliberal experiment, a process that some critics argue, after forty years, has finally exhausted itself.[36] The neoliberal experiment – lower taxes on the rich, deregulation of labour and product markets, financialisation and globalisation – has clearly failed according to Joseph Stiglitz and 'must be pronounced dead and buried'.[37] But this might be wishful thinking on the part of such economic critics. A far more judicious assessment comes from the political theorist Wendy Brown, who reminds us that 'nothing is untouched by a neoliberal mode of reason and valuation'.[38] A forty-year legacy does not disappear overnight because the reasoning and the valuations associated with neoliberalism are embedded in the rules and regulations that govern the economy and society. There is perhaps no better illustration of this point than the world of public food procurement, where a low-cost purchasing culture is one of the most enduring hallmarks of neoliberalism in the UK.

Values for money: reimagining the power of purchase

Low cost was allowed to masquerade as best value in civilian procurement circles for many years following the Thatcherite revolution in the 1980s – in contrast to the high-cost culture that was (and is) tolerated in military procurement circles, where the overspends run into billions and where contracts are many years behind schedule.[39] But a low-cost operating culture was not the only distinguishing feature of civilian procurement policy. The first systematic review of civilian procurement in the UK exposed a truly shocking picture:

- No one really knew how much the government was spending on a whole range of products and services.
- The government was not utilising effectively its power of purchase in the marketplace.
- The fragmented approach to procurement resulted in enormous variations in price and performance.
- Public procurement was not regarded as a core competence, so its professional and political status within government suffered as a result.
- There was plenty of scope for government to become a more intelligent customer, but this potential was not being tapped for the above reasons.[40]

Shocked by the Gershon Review, successive British governments have sought to modernise public procurement to render it more 'efficient' and more 'sustainable', two goals that are not easily aligned. But modernisation had to be executed in a regulatory landscape defined by international rules of the game as the UK was a member of the WTO and the EU.

Procurement matters: the evolving regulatory landscape

WTO regulations are embodied in the Agreement on Government Procurement (GPA), a classic neoliberal regulation that aims to promote free trade by exposing national public procurement markets to as much international competition as possible. The GPA tries to ensure that national laws

Serving the public

and regulations are fair and transparent, from a free market standpoint, and do not protect domestic products or suppliers or discriminate against foreign products and suppliers. Over time the GPA has extended its coverage to a growing array of services as well as to the procurement activities of sub-central governmental levels, such as states and provinces. To render the process as competitive as possible, the GPA tries to ensure that neither the location of production nor the nationality of the supplier are considered to be relevant factors in the award of public contracts. These free trade regulations have proved to be highly controversial all over the world, not least because they expanded the 'reach' of trade policy to a wide spectrum of sensitive areas – such as agrifood, services and the environment – areas that were hitherto regarded as domestic policy issues.[41]

For these reasons, even the WTO – that most neoliberal of all international trade organisations – has been obliged to accommodate itself to the sustainable development agenda. The most recent version of the GPA accepts the need to integrate sustainable procurement into the agreement but in such a way that it is compatible with the principle of 'best value for money'.[42] It is also significant that some countries – the EU and the US among them – have expressly excluded the procurement of agricultural goods for human feeding programmes from the coverage of the agreement. This exception allows the US to include 'a specific geographical preference in tenders for the purchasing of locally grown or locally raised agricultural products for child nutrition programmes funded by the government'.[43]

The regulatory landscape has also been shaped by the EU, where the regulations governing public procurement have changed dramatically over the past twenty years. To ensure that procurement practices are compatible with the pro-competitive goals of the Single Market, EU regulations stipulate that public contracts must comply with the principles of transparency, non-discrimination and equal treatment. As a result, only two award criteria were deemed to be appropriate: either 'the lowest price' or 'the most economically advantageous tender' (MEAT). Because these criteria were very economistic in nature, there was always a great deal of legal ambiguity surrounding the status of non-economic criteria. But the ambiguity was gradually clarified by a combination of case law and regulatory reform.

One of the decisive judgements on the case law front was the *Concordia Bus* case. The question here was whether a contracting authority awarding a contract on the basis of MEAT could include criteria promoting environmental policy objectives, even if these criteria did not contribute to the direct economic advantage of the contracting authority. The European Court of Justice clarified that it was not correct that 'each of the award criteria used by the contracting authority to identify the economically most advantageous tender must necessarily be of a purely economic nature' and that 'it cannot be excluded that factors which are not purely economic may influence the value of a tender from the point of view of the contracting authority'. In *Concordia Bus*, the level of nitrogen oxide emissions and the noise level of the buses that were to be procured were criteria that the contracting authority wished to use. This case set a new legal precedent for the development of green and sustainable procurement in the EU.[44]

Regulatory reform also played a major role in allowing public procurement contracts to utilise non-economic criteria following the Gothenburg European Council in 2001, when the EU formally committed itself to sustainable development. Then, in 2014, a new general directive on public procurement was issued to enable the power of purchase to support the Europe 2020 agenda of 'smart, sustainable and inclusive growth'. Crucially, public procurement was recognised as a development tool to promote 'common societal goals such as protection of the environment, higher resource and energy efficiency, combating climate change, promoting innovation, employment and social inclusion and ensuring the best possible conditions for the provision of high-quality social services'.[45]

Although EU procurement regulations clearly allow public bodies to use non-economic criteria alongside economic criteria such as price, contracting authorities are still fearful of acting illegally if they venture too far from a narrow interpretation of the regulations. This is especially the case in the UK, where the procurement profession has been hopelessly torn between two conflicting messages: the 'efficiency message', which implies cutting costs; and the 'sustainability message', which implies using more non-economic criteria to secure *values* for money. The evidence suggests that the former has trumped the latter because a major study found that 'the efficiency message was being interpreted throughout the public sector in ways which drowned out sustainability considerations'.[46]

The sustainability cause was not helped by the fact that its standard-bearer, DEFRA, happened to be one of the weakest departments in central government. This was a great shame because DEFRA produced one of the most innovative procurement initiatives in the world when it launched the Public Sector Food Procurement Initiative (PSFPI) in 2003. Launched in response to the foot and mouth crisis of 2002, the PSFPI offered the most compelling vision of sustainable food procurement that had ever appeared in the UK:

> If we are what we eat, then public sector food purchasers help shape the lives of millions of people. In hospitals, schools, prisons and canteens around the country, good food helps maintain good health, promote healing rates and improve concentration and behaviour. But sustainable food procurement isn't just about better nutrition. It's about where the food comes from, how it's produced and transported, and where it ends up. It's about food quality, safety and choice. Most of all, it's about defining best value in its broadest sense.[47]

While the vision was sound, the practice was poor. The initiative failed to attract support from other central government departments and from the wider public sector for many reasons, not least low awareness of the initiative, the lack of sustainable procurement skills in the public sector, a perceived cost premium and the absence of high-level political support. The official evaluation found that procurement practitioners believed it would be too costly to implement the PSFPI and they found it difficult to reconcile the goals of efficiency and sustainability, quoting one official who said that 'PSFPI is trying to swim against the tide of rationalisation and cost cutting'.[48] These sentiments were echoed in a survey by the National Audit Office, which outlined the main perceived barriers to sustainable procurement in central government departments:

- *Cost*: perception of increased costs associated with sustainable procurement. Value for money is perceived to be inconsistent with paying a premium to achieve sustainability objectives.

- *Knowledge:* lack of awareness of the need for conducting procurement more sustainably and the processes required for this.
- *Awareness and information*: lack of information about the most sustainable options. Lack of awareness of products; lack of monitoring of suppliers.
- *Risk:* risk-averse buyers prefer to purchase from suppliers with a good track record. Organisations fear criticism from the media and are therefore less keen to innovate.
- *Legal issues*: uncertainty as to what can and cannot be done under existing rules on public procurement.
- *Leadership:* a lack of leadership, both organisational and political, leading to a lack of ownership and accountability at all levels.
- *Inertia*: lack of appetite for change. Lack of personal or organisational incentives to drive change.[49]

The tension between 'efficiency' and 'sustainability' has persisted ever since, not so much at the high level of official rhetoric, where the tension is elided and conjured away, but at the operational level where procurement officers are obliged to deal with the relentless pressure to cut costs in the context of austerity. Two things have helped their cause: the rise of the Social Value agenda and post-Brexit procurement reform. In 2012 the Public Services (Social Value) Act required all public sector bodies and their suppliers to look beyond the financial costs of a contract to consider how the goods and services they procure can improve the economic, social and environmental well-being of an area. This legislation was a response to concerns that competitive tendering was focusing exclusively on cost in the narrowest sense, a frank admission that non-economic forms of value were being excluded in the commissioning process.

Although the benefits of Brexit are proving to be elusive, quitting the EU allowed the UK to introduce some modest reforms to its procurement regulations (though its freedom of manoeuvre was still constrained by its international trade obligations under the GPA). One of the most important reforms in the post-Brexit period is the shift away from a narrow value-for-money metric and towards a *values-for-money* approach. As the government said:

> Rather than referring to Most Economically Advantageous Tender, contracts will be awarded on the basis of Most Advantageous Tender. This change in terminology will provide further clarity for contracting authorities that when determining evaluation criteria, they are able to take a broader view of what can be included. It will support levelling up by encouraging contracting authorities to give more consideration to social value when procuring public contracts in their areas.[50]

Dropping the reference to 'economically' may seem a trivial revision to the lay person, but in the arcane world of public procurement regulation it signals a very important shift to a broader, more capacious set of values.

Harnessing the power of purchase: values-driven food procurement

Even though the regulatory landscape has become more favourable over the past twenty years, harnessing the power of purchase for social and environmental ends is still no easy matter. This is especially the case for sustainable *food* procurement, where progress in the UK has been stymied by the barriers identified above and by the chilling cost-cutting mentality spawned by the age of austerity. However, one of the goals of the sustainable food movement is to increase the share of local food that is procured by the public sector, which is a challenging goal because it is illegal to specify local produce under EU regulations as it runs counter to the EU principle of non-discrimination. While this was often believed to be an insurmountable barrier in the UK, other countries realised that they could practice local sourcing in all but name if they utilised quality labels – such as fresh, seasonal, organic and certified – as proxies for local food. A senior official from the European Commission confirmed the legitimacy of such values-driven procurement when he said: 'If it is set out in a non-discriminatory way … it is legitimate to say "we want foodstuff that is no older than". If that means in practice that it will have to be locally grown, so be it!'[51]

Although local food is not necessarily synonymous with sustainable food, as the E.coli outbreak in Wales tragically demonstrated, the Good Food movement invariably includes localisation as one of its goals because shorter food chains can potentially generate multiple benefits, including: the health benefits of fresher, more nutritious produce; the ecological benefits of lower food miles; the economic benefits of local supply chains; and the social and cultural benefits of closer linkages between producers and consumers that enable the latter to become better informed about the provenance of their food. It was to try to realise these multiple benefits that FFL was launched in 2003, the most ambitious values-driven food procurement programme ever designed in the UK. Its nearest equivalent is the equally ambitious Good Food Purchasing Program in the US, which uses a set of five values (animal welfare, environmental sustainability, nutrition, valued workforce and local economies) alongside price to select successful bids.

FFL was a practical response to the frustration felt by parents, health and education professionals and food campaigners about the poor quality of primary school meals. Orchestrated by the Soil Association in conjunction with key players in the sustainable food movement, FFL was established to run a pilot project in a small group of primary schools keen to upgrade their menus, source new supplies and cultivate a discerning, healthy food culture through better classroom food education and farm visits. Pilot schools were invited to work towards a series of targets designed to raise awareness and appreciation of good food, reform menus and localise sourcing. In its pilot stage, the schools had five targets:

- *Good nutrition*: primary school lunches will provide food that meets the quantitative nutritional targets first published in 1992 by the public health charity, the Caroline Walker Trust.
- *Organic food*: at least 30 per cent by weight of the foods served should be from certified organic sources. This target aims to steer schools towards food supplies of high quality that incur minimum 'food miles' and enjoy known provenance.
- *Sustainable supply chains*: at least 50 per cent of meal ingredients should be sourced from the local region. The term 'local' refers to food derived from a system of producing, processing and trading, primarily of organic and sustainable forms of food production, where the physical and economic activity is largely contained and controlled within the locality or region where it was produced, which delivers health, economic, environmental and social benefits to the

communities in those areas. FFL schools were encouraged to avoid 'local food' produced in highly intensive production systems employing pesticides, the routine use of antibiotics and growth promoters.
- *Less processed foods*: to meet the other FFL nutritional targets, at least 75 per cent of all foods eaten should be prepared from unprocessed ingredients. Processed ingredients offer poor value for money because their nutritional values are often low, providing fewer nutrients for the money spent compared to less processed ingredients.
- *Better food education*: curriculum time was to be made available for classroom and school trips to cover the subjects of why eating well matters, where good food comes from, how to cook and animal welfare. In particular, FFL schools were encouraged to develop a long-term relationship with a working organic farm to nurture children's knowledge of food and farming. This holistic approach to school food reform became known as the whole school approach.[52]

From this modest pilot, the Food for Life Partnership (FFL) was created in 2003 by the Soil Association together with Focus on Food, Garden Organic, the Royal Society for Public Health and the Health Education Trust. Its principal aim was to respond to increasing concerns over the health of English children, particularly in relation to rising obesity rates. In 2015 it evolved into the FFL programme, led solely by the Soil Association, and it has subsequently expanded from schools to cover both public and private sector catering facilities.

I examine the pros and cons of the programme in the context of school meals provision, where it is most successful, but the important point to register here is that FFL, the gold standard

Reclaiming the public plate

for sustainable food procurement in the UK, has struggled to embed itself as the norm throughout the public sector despite the fact that its merits have been widely acknowledged by government departments, independent commissions and a wide spectrum of food policy experts.

There is no mystery as to why mainstreaming has been difficult: in addition to the general barriers to sustainable procurement that I identified earlier, there are particular barriers to innovative *food* provisioning, not least the UK's low-cost catering culture, the lack of capacity in local authorities and the NHS and the chilling effects of austerity. Given all these barriers, the real wonder is that FFL emerged at all.

But the fact that some parts of the public sector have adopted the programme proves that these social innovators managed to overcome the barriers, proving beyond doubt that procurement regulations are not – and indeed were not – the impediments they were believed to be in so many parts of the British public sector. A cross-party parliamentary inquiry eventually acknowledged the truth of the matter when it addressed the vexed question of public sector food procurement:

> The Government has associated leaving the EU with the opportunity to encourage the public sector to 'buy British' and reduce environmental costs. It is, however, clear that even under EU rules, the UK already had opportunities to support British suppliers through proxy measures, such as specifying 'local' and 'seasonal' in procurement ... We are disappointed that those opportunities were not maximised before EU Exit and we expect the Government to make more effort in future.[53]

In the case of sustainable food procurement, the most important barriers are the same today as they were twenty odd years ago, namely lack of political leadership at the national level, weak institutional capacity at the subnational level and a woefully inadequate stock of whole-life procurement skills throughout the public sector. To remedy the situation, reformers need to craft a food system strategy in which *national* political leadership is calibrated with *local* capacity building on the part of local authorities and civil society organisations.

Reclaiming the public plate

Public procurement is now widely perceived as a panacea across the political spectrum in the UK, where conservatives and progressives alike tend to see it as a powerful policy instrument in and for itself. But the truth is that public procurement is being set up to fail if it is deployed as a solo policy instrument. To be effective, the power of purchase needs to be embedded in a suite of policies that integrates the purchasing process with supply-side policies on the one hand and demand-side policies on the other, enabling a more robust *food system* strategy to be designed and delivered. But here we come to what is arguably the single biggest barrier to the formation of a food system strategy in the UK: the dysfunctional nature of *food governance* in the multilevel polity.

The design and delivery of a sustainable food system strategy clearly requires a suite of policies that can be synchronised between national and subnational governments.[54] But with the creation of devolved governments in the Celtic nations in 1999, policy coherence has been conspicuous by its absence because successive Conservative governments have pursued an increasingly neoliberal policy path in contrast to the more social democratic policy paths embraced in Scotland and Wales.

Reclaiming the public plate

Compounding the problem of policy coherence is the fact that Conservative governments have also empowered themselves with new centralist powers that allow them to intervene in policy domains – such as agrifood, environment and regional economic development – that were devolved to the Celtic nations under their devolution settlements.[55]

Reclaiming the public plate – by which I mean the struggle to serve good food in public institutions – cannot be accomplished without a food system strategy that integrates the key domains of procurement, supply and demand. To appreciate the nature of the dysfunctional governance problem, let us briefly look at the track record of central government in each of these domains.

Although Conservative governments were in power continuously between 2010–24, this image of seamless stability is deceptive because, during these years, the UK has had five different Tory prime ministers, while the economy has been subjected to a triple shock in the form of Brexit, COVID-19 and the full-scale Russian invasion of Ukraine. Each of these shocks has had a big impact on the UK food system, as we will see.

From a food system perspective, the Tory track record leaves much to be desired because the positives have been grossly outweighed by the negatives. The positives would surely include the momentous net zero target, when the government committed the UK to a 100 per cent reduction in GhG emissions by 2050 compared to 1990 levels, a commitment that created new opportunities for the transition to a more sustainable food system from farm to fork. I would also include in the positives the two seminal reports that central government commissioned from Henry Dimbleby – the *School Food Plan* in 2013 and the *National Food Strategy* in 2021 – both of which offered a compelling analysis of the problems as well as a genuinely radical set of solutions from a food system perspective.

But these seminal reports were never acted upon in the manner envisaged. In fact, the government Food Strategy that finally emerged in 2022 was roundly criticised by Dimbleby himself for not being a strategy at all, 'merely a handful of disparate policy ideas, many of them chosen because they are unlikely to raise much of a media storm'.[56] A similar thing happened to the net zero target, when the government minister responsible for signing the commitment, Chris Skidmore MP, resigned from the government and the party in protest at its decision to issue a new set of oil and gas licences in the North Sea, part of a series of policy decisions that broke with what had hitherto been a climate change consensus in the UK. In his resignation letter, he said that the decision would send a 'global signal that the UK is rowing ever further back from its climate commitments'.[57]

Even in the domain of public procurement, where Tory ministers hoped Brexit would enable radical policy reforms, only modest change proved possible because independent WTO membership committed the UK to a free trade regime. In the event, the changes introduced in the 2023 Procurement Act may have created new purchasing opportunities, but they were constrained by the chilling effects of austerity and the drive to cut costs.

Procurement opportunities were also limited by the burgeoning supply-side problems of the domestic agrifood industry. Nothing illustrates these problems better than the travails of the horticulture sector, which provides the fruit and vegetables that are crucial to a healthy diet. In 2022 the government promised to produce a 'world leading horticulture strategy' but it abandoned the plan the following year even though the sector was beset by rapidly rising energy costs, acute labour shortages, environmental challenges and asymmetrical supply chains that offered prices below the cost of production. With food supply shortages exacerbated by Brexit, COVID-19 and the Ukraine war, the sector warned that, without urgent government intervention, 'the future of UK horticulture looks bleak ... leaving us vulnerable to political and climate induced food insecurity'.[58]

Reluctant to engage in food production issues, Conservative governments were even less disposed to intervene in food *consumption* issues because of a deep ideological aversion to the 'nanny state', a neoliberal confection that has been deployed to great effect by fast food industry lobbyists and right-wing media such as *The Sun* and the *Daily Mail*. The 'nanny state' theme resonates with two fast food industry tropes: (1) that there is no such thing as bad food, only bad diets; and (2) that food choice is a private choice and governments have no right to interfere with consumers' freedom of choice. A notable exception here was the mandatory Soft Drinks Industry Levy (SDIL) that was introduced in 2018, which proved to be very successful in reducing the sugar content of soft drinks, in contrast to the voluntary Sugar Reduction Programme (2015–2020), which merely encouraged businesses to reduce sugar in various food categories.[59] Though even here it is worth noting that the SDIL was primarily aimed at manufacturers, allowing the government to claim that it was not *directly* infringing the freedom of choice of consumers.

Aside from the SDIL, Conservative governments consistently rowed back on their commitments to introduce

Serving the public

healthier and more sustainable diets. The most glaring examples include the decision to delay the introduction of restrictions banning the advertising of unhealthy food and drinks on TV and online, and the ban on multi-buy promotions on unhealthy food and drink – two key commitments in the government's Obesity Strategy. Faced with escalating levels of childhood obesity since the pandemic, a newly installed Secretary of State for Health astonished and dismayed food policy campaigners when she vowed to avoid 'nanny-stateish' measures, preferring to focus on diet advice to counter obesity and promote healthy lifestyles.[60] But, as we'll see in Part II, the idea that reform should focus primarily on changing *behaviour* rather than the food *environment* has been totally discredited by a growing body of research in the social sciences, psychology and neuroscience, all of which confirms that information alone is not an effective way to change habitual behaviour.

Significantly, the Conservative stance on food policy is totally out of step with popular opinion. Polling by the Food, Farming and Countryside Commission (FFCC) shows that most citizens want the government to take more rather than less action on food to protect health, children and the environment: 75 per cent of the public think that the government is not doing enough to 'ensure that everyone can afford healthy food', compared to only 3 per cent who say that they are doing too much. Similar percentages applied across every government intervention that the FFCC asked about: 'protecting children from unhealthy food and drinks' (67 per cent/5 per cent), 'stopping farms from releasing animal manure and harmful chemicals into rivers and the sea' (62 per cent/6 per cent), 'minimising the environmental impact of the food we eat' (60 per cent/7 per cent) and 'ensuring that shops and public places (like hospitals) have healthy food options' (59 per cent/5 per cent).[61]

Public food provisioning may be a small niche in the UK food system but its problems and prospects need to be understood in the context of the larger system because, as we have seen, the domains of procurement, supply and demand are so inextricably connected. Clearly, public bodies cannot procure more fruit and vegetables for schools, hospitals and prisons if the horticulture sector is mired in a post-Brexit existential crisis.[62]

Reclaiming the public plate is part of the wider challenge of creating a fairer, healthier and more sustainable food system in the UK. The public sector ought to be in the vanguard of this process because the consumers of the public plate – such as children, patients and prisoners – are among the most vulnerable people in society. But a sustainable food system and a more empowered public sector are contingent on the same things – one of which is a multilevel polity in which central government is able and willing to work in a more concerted and collaborative way with the nations, regions and localities of Britain, a country that aspires to be a polycentric not a centralised polity. As the UK's leading food policy expert has said, 'food governance is itself a food problem, possibly even the fundamental one'.[63] The kind of governance that is needed to fashion a fairer, healthier and more sustainable food system, in which the public sector is a leader rather than a laggard, is addressed in Chapter 6.

This chapter has tried to sketch some of the wider pressures – national and international – that public sector catering is forced to navigate. Although I make frequent reference to the 'public plate' throughout this book, we should not think that the public sector is a homogenous entity. On the contrary, the chapters in Part II offer a more granular perspective on different parts of the public sector because schools, hospitals and prisons constitute very different institutional environments, their very own worlds of food.

Part II

Schools, hospitals and prisons

2

Food for life: the whole school approach

Introduction

The school meal is an infallible index of the values of a society. If that sounds too overblown, it's probably because we rarely think that a prosaic institution such as the school meals service can play such a grand role. Yet in its British guise, the school meal has proved to be a remarkably accurate reflection of the tectonic shifts in the political system: from being a pillar of the welfare state following its introduction in 1906, to being debased and marginalised by Thatcherism, and now, in its most recent incarnation, being a measure of a country's commitment to sustainable development.

But whatever the national context, the reform of school food raises some of the most compelling questions that a society can ask itself in the twenty-first century. Does the state have a duty to try to change the behaviour of its citizens for the better? Can a society truly claim to be sustainable if it fails to invest in nutritious school food for young and vulnerable people? What are the defining features of a sustainable school food service? And, as regards the provenance of the food, should societies seek to promote more 'localisation' of their food and farming sectors in the name of sustainability or more 'globalisation' in the name of fair trade? These are some of the questions that have been triggered by the school food reform movement.[1]

Creating a school food system that is fair, healthy and sustainable has proved to be a more challenging endeavour than reformers ever imagined. Reformers in the Global North as well as the Global South have grossly underestimated the complexity of the school food system. UN experts who designed the Home-Grown School Feeding System – so-called because it aimed to replace food aid from external donors with locally produced food in developing countries – spoke of 'quick wins' because they assumed that schools would provide a 'ready market' for local producers, an unwarranted assumption as it turned out because neither the indigenous supply chains nor the catering infrastructure was in place for a 'quick win'.

Reformers in the Global North have also been confounded by their preconceptions. This is especially the case in countries such as the UK and the US, where fast food culture is most advanced and where food provenance is more often associated with exclusive restaurants than school canteens. But the UK has an additional problem in taking the issue seriously because of a cultural stereotype that portrayed the school meal in film and literature in a comical light – as something to be endured rather than enjoyed, a character-forming rite of passage that did not merit serious attention from the political class. Fortunately, this cultural stereotype has withered in the UK because 'the humble school meal is now perceived to be a litmus test of the government's political commitment to sustainable development'.[2]

Food for life: the whole school approach

In this chapter I try to explain these shifting conceptions of the school meals service by calibrating them with tectonic shifts in the political system. The next section presents three models of school food provisioning, using the history of the British school meal service as an example, to illustrate how a society can treat the service in such radically different ways – *not* because the needs of children have changed but because the political landscape has changed.

The third section takes a different tack by sacrificing breadth for depth. Here I take a deep dive into what many reformers consider to be the gold standard of school food reform: the FFL programme. Designed by the Soil Association and its partners, FFL is a quintessential example of a phrase that I encountered time and again when talking to reformers: that a sustainable school food system is 'more than just a meal' on account of the multiple dividends that it generates.

The final section changes the focus by looking at what I call 'foodscapes of hope': the places that are trying to fashion sustainable school food systems in the real world. There are so many compelling examples that merit attention, but I focus on Malmö in Sweden because I have been engaging with the city's school food team for many years and because it has earned an international reputation for being a high-performing city in a country that is itself highly regarded in school food policy circles. This section also focuses on an exciting new trend in the UK: the Universal Free School Meals movement in which Scotland, Wales and some London boroughs have launched universal free school meals schemes for all primary school children, heralding one of the most important social policy innovations in the history of school meals provision in the UK.

Models of school food provisioning

Conventional histories of the British school food service tend to pay too much attention to the legislative milestones that mark new policy departures and too little to the myriad social struggles that prepared the ground for the legislation. As we will see later with hospitals and prisons, the cognitive landscape – which shapes the way issues are viewed and valued – begins to change long before the new legislative landscape takes shape. Each of the three models of school food provisioning considered below confirms this observation.[3]

The welfare model of collective provision

Although the universal welfare model formally begins with the 1944 Education Act, when all state schools were legally obliged to provide a school meals service, the preceding half century had spawned frenetic attempts to deliver free school meals to hungry children. Following the introduction of compulsory elementary education in 1870, which exposed the problem of hungry children unable to learn, philanthropic groups – such as the Manchester and Salford Ladies Health Association, the London Free Dinner Association and the Salvation Army – were the real pioneers of free school meals. Political parties took their cue from these civil society initiatives and, in 1879, Manchester became the first local authority to introduce free school meals for impoverished children, followed by Bradford. Such local policy experiments, together with the work of civic associations, helped to secure the passage of the 1906 Education (Provision of Meals) Act, which enabled (but did not compel) local authorities in England and Wales to supply meals for

Food for life: the whole school approach

'those unable by lack of food to take advantage of the education provided for them'.[4]

But warfare was as important as welfare in mobilising political support for school meals. The Army Medical Service had complained that, during the Boer War, almost two-thirds of recruits were 'physically unfit for military service'. To examine the problem the government set up the Inter-Departmental Committee on Physical Deterioration, which focused on the environmental conditions of 'certain classes' – a euphemism for the working classes – chief among which was found to be poor nutrition. When the committee reported in 1904, one of its most extraordinary conclusions was that poor nutrition was primarily caused, not by poverty, but by 'the ignorance of housewives who lacked knowledge of sound nutrition and efficient household management. The solution was to propose legislation that would provide the necessary "social education" for these women and school meals for children with mothers incapable of learning these lessons.'[5]

The interplay of warfare and welfare was also evident when the model of collective provision became codified in the 1944 Education Act. A war economy put the nutritional health of the nation at the forefront of the political agenda because the well-being of citizens and soldiers was paramount to a unified military campaign; and the mass employment of women raised questions as to how the nutritional needs of children would be met.

Rightly seen as a milestone in the history of the school meal, the 1944 Education Act placed a duty on local education authorities (LEAs) to provide school meals 'suitable in all respects as the main meal of the day'. The meals were based on specific guidelines drawn up by nutrition experts, with each

Serving the public

meal designed to provide one-third of a child's daily allowance of nutrients and energy according to the scientific knowledge of the day. The price of the meal was fixed and the meal consisted of meat, two vegetables and a pudding. Overall, the Act stated:

- All pupils attending a state school were entitled to a midday meal on every school day.
- The meals were to be free to those pupils whose parents were either unemployed or on low incomes. The price of the meal could not exceed the cost of the food.
- For other pupils, the parents were to pay.
- Each local authority was to report to the Ministry of Education on the quantities of ingredients used.[6]

Although the 1944 Act elevated the school meal to a central pillar of the emerging welfare state, one of the key aspects of the original welfare model was never actually realised. A parental guide to the 1944 Education Act, published in the same year, outlined a truly radical vision, saying 'when the School Meals Service is fully developed, school meals will be provided free of charge as part of the educational system'.[7] In this crucial respect, then, the new welfare model never realised its original design because the postwar Labour government jettisoned the most radical element of all: the commitment to free school meals for all.

Even so, the effects of the wartime policy were plain for all to see: 'Statistics from official records and surveys showed increased height, increased weight, faster growth and better dental health. The results were clearly visible in the general appearance of the children.'[8] A less tangible, but no less important, benefit was the cultural transformation of the school meals

Food for life: the whole school approach

service: 'School meals were no longer charity or "relief" for poor children only. After the war they became part of Social Welfare, a social service for all children, for the community. By 1950, school meals were the largest catering enterprise in the UK serving 2,750,000 children, i.e. 52 percent of the children in state schools.'[9]

The welfare model of collective provision peaked in 1966, when as many as 70 per cent of children in state schools were eating a school meal. A combination of political and cultural factors undermined the appeal of the welfare model. Under financial pressure to reduce public expenditure, the Labour government devolved financial responsibility for school meals from central to local government in 1967, leading to higher prices and lower take-up rates. Although the Thatcher governments of the 1980s are deemed to be solely responsible for dismantling the school meals service, one authoritative account rightly concluded that 'the seeds of its demise were sown much earlier'.[10]

The neoliberal model of consumer choice

Whatever the limitations of the welfare model, the fact that it would retrospectively appear as a 'golden era' spoke volumes for the neoliberal model that succeeded it after 1979. The preceding Labour government may have initiated the cuts to the school meals service in the 1960s and 1970s, but the Thatcher governments effectively eviscerated the welfare model under the banner of consumer freedom. Food culture was certainly changing beyond the school gate and the first Thatcher government sought to harness the new styles and tastes of cafeteria culture to justify a wholly new school meals service predicated on the two hardy perennials of Tory ideology: less public expenditure and more personal choice.

The neoliberal model was embedded in two radically new pieces of legislation. The first of was the 1980 Education Act, which transformed the school meals service from a compulsory national subsidised service for all children to a discretionary local service. The 1980 Act introduced four fundamental changes: (1) it removed the obligation on LEAs to provide school lunches, except for children entitled to free school meals; (2) it removed the obligation for meals to be sold at a fixed price; (3) it eliminated the requirement for lunches to meet nutritional standards; and (4) it abolished the entitlement to free school milk.[11]

Mark Carlisle, the Conservative chief education minister, identified three reasons why school meal reform was necessary:

- to make savings in public expenditure and to establish the principle of 'sound economics' for the parent, the taxpayer and the child;
- to ensure that the burden of education expenditure cuts fell on the school meal service and not the education service itself; and
- to give parents and children more freedom of choice.[12]

In the heated parliamentary debate on school meals, Carlisle and his junior ministers expounded their views and paraded their ideological prejudices in the process. To a startled House of Commons, Carlisle at one point said that the cuts had 'no implications for the classroom', as though hunger was no barrier to learning. His junior minister, Neil Macfarlane, went even further, saying that some parents had come to rely too much on the school meals service but in future they would have

Food for life: the whole school approach

to shoulder 'proper parental responsibility'. In other words, the state had no public duty of care for feeding hungry children, a task that was clearly deemed to be a purely private duty.

The neoliberal model was also aided and abetted by the 1988 Local Government Act, which introduced CCT into public sector catering. Under the CCT regime local authorities were obliged to subject their services, including school meals, to market competition. As bidders felt compelled to offer the lowest price, CCT fuelled a low-cost catering culture which induced major changes in the school meals service. The most destructive changes included: a less skilled workforce, a loss of kitchens as a processed food culture took root and a service ethos inimical to healthy eating. But of all the changes wrought by CCT, the most harmful was the debasement of the food itself, colourfully described by one school cook as 'cheap processed muck'.[13]

Secondary schools witnessed the most profound effects of the neoliberal model because:

> Children would spend as much, or as little, as they wanted, and there was no method of controlling what pupils ate. The school lunch service was very consumer-led and if a food sold well and was profitable, it was provided. If it did not sell, or was not profitable, it was not provided. Between 1980 and 1998 this strategy led to the current limited range of foods available in most secondary schools. Most caterers now provide the same food every day, of the school year and the stock items are chips, burgers, pizza, sausage rolls, sandwiches, doughnuts, cakes, fizzy drinks or variations on these foods.[14]

In retrospect we can see that the neoliberal model of school food provision was responsible for some monstrously myopic mistakes. The Thatcher government treated the school canteen as a crude extension of the high street, a space where consumers were deemed to be totally free to choose to eat as much and whatever they pleased. In this respect the neoliberal model fuelled the trends of unhealthy eating and childhood obesity, the costs of which are many times greater than what was saved by trimming the school food budget. Aside from the financial ledger, the most extraordinary aspect of the neoliberal model was undoubtedly the notion that the school meals service was not an intrinsically significant part of the educational system, a notion that is tantamount to saying that hunger is not an impediment to learning.

The ecological model of sustainable provision

Twenty-two years after the launch of the neoliberal model, a vision of the school food service appeared that could not be further removed from it. In the popular mind the sea change was due to the 'Jamie Oliver effect', a reference to the celebrity chef's popular TV series in 2005 that exposed the debasement of school food and highlighted its noxious effects on the health and well-being of children. While the celebrity chef certainly raised the profile of school meals, winning rapid political support from Tony Blair's New Labour government, the real origins of the new vision lay not in a TV studio in London but in an expert panel in Scotland which produced a highly significant report called *Hungry for Success*. The expert panel made a whole series of recommendations and three of its messages would resonate deeply throughout the UK:

- It called for a whole school approach to school food reform to ensure that the message of the classroom was echoed in the dining room.

Food for life: the whole school approach

- It called for better-quality food to be served in schools, supported by a combination of nutrient-based and food-based standards.
- It suggested that the school food service was closer to a health service than a commercial service.[15]

The Scottish report catalysed school food reform movements in England and Wales, both of which produced their own school food reviews. Because it appeared three years after the Scottish report, the School Meals Review Panel (SMRP) in England went furthest in promoting the ecological model, so-called because it emphasises the interconnections between diet, learning and behaviour.[16] The SMRP decided not to mince its words: 'There is both a public and a private responsibility to ensure that children are adequately fed ... The state of many school meals is an indictment of more than two decades of public policy which has in effect stripped nutrients off plates, removed skills from kitchen staff and seen the take-up of school meals drop precipitously.' Transforming school food, it said, was as much about people, skills and commitment as it is about nutrients and ingredients. It called for new forms of collaboration in the school food system because caterers will need to change their recipes and cooking practices; kitchen staff will need more time to prepare meals; local authorities, governors and school heads will need to prioritise food; parents and carers will need to support the changes; and children themselves will need to choose the new options. 'In short, it will require a whole-school approach.'[17]

The whole school approach referred to above is the ecological model in practice and the SMRP report was the boldest and most ambitious version of it that had ever been articulated in the UK to that point because it adopted a holistic food system perspective to school food reform. In operational terms this entailed new forms of collaboration among the different stakeholders in the school food system, especially between those who commission services (head teachers and governors), supply the service (catering staff), use the service (pupils and parents and carers) and educate children about food and nutrition (teachers). The SMRP also argued that the whole school approach should be extended to the sourcing of the food: 'The procurement of food served in schools should be consistent with sustainable development principles and schools and caterers should look to local farmers and suppliers for their produce where possible.'[18]

As well as calling for more resources, new skill sets and food standards that included both nutrient-based and food-based standards, the SMRP challenged one of New Labour's most cherished ideological concepts: choice. The reformers were unequivocal about the need to reverse the free-for-all that had characterised the previous twenty years in school canteens: 'A common thread in achieving change is controlling the range of choice, and we clearly and firmly advocate this. The SMRP standards are designed to drive the replacement of foods consumed at lunchtime which are low in nutritional value with foods which support children's health.'[19]

In policy terms, *Turning the Tables* remains the most radical school meals policy statement since the founding of the welfare state in the 1940s. As well as offering a devastating critique of the neoliberal model, citing the multiple health impacts as well as the financial costs of diet-related disease, its thirty-five recommendations offered a constructive, evidence-based alternative model predicated on the whole school approach – the antithesis of the neoliberal model.

Food for life: the whole school approach

Although most of its recommendations were accepted by the New Labour government, the deadline for secondary schools to comply with the new food and nutrient-based standards was 2009, twelve years after the Blair government was elected – a sobering reminder of the time lag between assuming office and enacting change. Translating the ecological model into practice was further stymied by the age of austerity in the decade after 2010, when local authority budgets were eviscerated by Tory governments in thrall to a pre-Keynesian creed designed to cut public expenditure and shrink the state sector.

This austere environment was one of the factors why the *School Food Plan*, a plan designed for England, was never fully implemented, even though it was another good example of the ecological model. Published in 2013, the *School Food Plan* conceded that the best schools did 'a brilliant job' of weaving good food education into school life and the curriculum. But other schools were lagging behind, it said, 'serving food that is much too bland, boring and beige', one reason why take-up was stubbornly low, at 43 per cent. The solution was clear: 'Increasing take-up is not something that can be done from the top-down. It requires a cultural change within each school. It means cooking food that is both appetising and nutritious; making the dining hall a welcoming place; keeping queues down; getting the price right; allowing children to eat with their friends; getting them interested in cooking and growing.'[20]

Food for life: more than just a meal

Reformers are wont to say that the school lunch is 'more than just a meal'. This is a shorthand way of conveying the multiple benefits of wholesome school food in terms of its positive

Serving the public

impact on health and well-being, educational attainment and social behaviour. Although the evidence base may not be as extensive as reformers would like – because successive governments in the UK have not invested enough in impact research, despite its manifest significance – both research and experience tell us that such benefits are real enough. Perhaps the most dramatic example of the beneficial effects of children's diet was the rationed diet during the Second World War, when official records showed the positive impact in terms of children's height, weight and dental health.

More recent research has been concerned to counter the epidemic of childhood obesity and burgeoning mental health problems among young people, both of which are strongly associated with obesogenic environments and the rapid growth of ultra-processed food and drink.[21] Over the past twenty years a growing body of evidence has demonstrated 'the remarkable role of nutrition in learning and behaviour' because of the potent effects of nutrients on brain function.[22]

An influential study was conducted in the London borough of Greenwich – the location of the Jamie Oliver TV series – because the local authority had introduced healthier menus and banned junk food in its schools. Since the meals were introduced in one local education area only at first, the researchers used 'a difference in differences approach' to identify the causal effect of healthy meals on educational performance. Focusing on Key Stage 2 test scores before and after the introduction of the new menus, and using neighbouring local education areas as a control group, they found that educational outcomes improved significantly in English and science and that authorised absences – which are most likely linked to illness and health – fell by as much as 14 per cent.[23]

Food for life: the whole school approach

Reformers in the UK are constantly under pressure to prove that good food has positive effects on health and educational attainment, as though the investment in good food for children can only be justified if it is *instrumentally significant* – a means to another, more important end – rather than it being intrinsically significant: an end in and for itself.

But school food reformers are not naïve. On the contrary, they are acutely conscious of the need for a robust evidence base to prove that good food generates multiple benefits for society, not least by promoting the health and well-being of people and planet and by reducing the spiralling costs associated with diet-related diseases and climate change. Capturing these multiple benefits would pose a challenge for any organisation, no matter how well resourced, so imagine how much more challenging it is for a non-governmental organisation (NGO) that depends on charitable funding. But this is precisely the task that the Soil Association and its partners set themselves when they launched FFL in 2003. Widely regarded as the gold standard in school food reform circles, FFL aims to fashion a sustainable school food system and capture its multiple benefits through independent third-party monitoring and evaluation. Let's examine the FFL system, warts and all, to assess the scope for systemic school food reform in the UK, the country with the highest rate of ultra-processed food consumption in Europe.

Food for Life: the scope and limits of systemic school food reform

The FFL concept was launched by the Soil Association in 2003 to support schools and caterers to provide healthier, tastier and more sustainable school food in a programme through which pupils learn about where their food comes from, how to grow their own food and how to acquire essential cooking skills. In 2007 it secured £17 million for a five-year pilot programme from the Big Lottery's Wellbeing Fund in which the FFL worked with 180 'flagship' schools, twenty in each region of England, based on their commitment to transform food culture in the school and the wider community and act as best practice exemplars to inspire other schools and communities. The goals of the programme were nothing if not ambitious, namely:

- to promote healthier eating habits among pupils;
- to improve pupil awareness of food sustainability issues;
- to influence food habits at home and in the wider community;
- to improve pupil attainment and behaviour;
- to increase school meal take-up; and
- to build the market for local and organic food producers.[24]

All schools in the programme were encouraged to work towards the FFLSH Award, which consists of a bronze, silver and gold system of awards based on four strands: (1) food leadership, (2) food quality and provenance, (3) food education and (4) food culture and community involvement. In parallel, the Soil Association operated a Catering Mark scheme for school caterers in which a traffic light system was designed to promote greater use of fresh, seasonal, local and organic ingredients, and high-welfare meat and sustainable fish, with increasingly challenging food-sourcing-related criteria attached to each award level.

Evaluating such a novel and ambitious programme poses a host of methodological challenges – far too many to delve into here. Perhaps the fairest thing to say is that the evaluation report

Food for life: the whole school approach

contained sufficient evidence to encourage school food reformers but enough caveats to fuel scepticism. Bearing in mind that 'school behaviour' reflects so many influences beyond the school, it proved impossible to attribute changes in food habits purely to school-based causes. The evaluation team was fully aware that socio-economic factors (e.g. the level of free school meal entitlement in a school and home background) appeared to be the main predictors of healthy eating behaviours.

But despite all the complicating methodological factors, the FFL programme generated a number of positives across its main goals. Two years into the programme, the evaluation found plausible evidence of an impact on year 5 and 6 students' consumption of fruit and vegetables and attitudes towards healthier eating and sustainable foods – and of all the findings, this was the one that attracted most attention from public health commissioners in local authorities.

As increased take-up of school meals is itself indicative of healthier eating, given the lower dietary value of packed lunches, it was encouraging that 17 per cent more children rated school meals positively, and over 24 per cent more children rated their dining room positively compared to baseline respondents. But the secondary school surveys with years 7 to 10 produced less conclusive results, possibly because these older groups are given more freedom, including the right to leave the school grounds at lunchtime.

While the desire to improve school meals and school food education primarily rests on health grounds, there remains considerable interest in whether such activities can also have a positive impact on behaviour, learning and performance – what I call the *instrumentalist* rationale for school food reform. However, the most the evaluation team could say here was that

Serving the public

Ofsted inspection reports were twice as likely to rate schools as 'outstanding' across ten areas of judgement on school performance for the period following FFL enrolment. School leads were certainly very positive about the impact of the programme across a wide range of domains of school life, but they were considerably less certain in their assessment of impact upon attainment and academic achievement. As one school lead put it: 'This impact on attainment is not quantifiable, however the contribution to the curriculum and family dining has increased enthusiasm and motivation.'[25]

Food sourcing proved to be the least successful part of the FFL programme. On the positive side, the flagship schools were spending significantly more on food ingredients as a result of FFL involvement. The rise from 70.1p to 78.8p represents a 12.4 per cent increase in food spend, in contrast to the national average of school meal ingredient costs at primary level of 68p at the time of the evaluation. Another positive was the fact that the number of local food suppliers increased by 73 per cent and organic suppliers by over 50 per cent after eighteen months' involvement in FFL. Overall, however, it proved too difficult to obtain sufficient data to draw any robust conclusions about the food-sourcing domain because caterers were either unwilling or unable to provide the necessary information, indicative perhaps of the low priority they assigned to monitoring the impact of their food procurement policies.

Perhaps the most interesting question about the FFL programme concerns the 'spillover' effect, or the extent to which new food habits in school ripple through to the home. Here the evaluation found that the degree to which parents responded to food messages from the FFL programme was largely a function of their own pre-existing beliefs and values, their financial

Food for life: the whole school approach

situation and general engagement with the school. Parents were asked about whether their child had raised discussions about healthier food choices at home with other family members. There was a very strong endorsement to this question, with 77 per cent reporting that they had, with 42 per cent reporting that their child had raised the issue of fair trade and 27 per cent had talked about locally grown food. From a parental perspective, children's involvement in the project had resulted in take-home messages that influenced food culture at home. For example, children's discussions had influenced cooking and food consumption, with 38 per cent reporting they either strongly agreed or agreed with a statement suggesting family attitudes to food had changed. In addition, 43 per cent reported changes in buying patterns and 45 per cent reported they were eating more vegetables as a result of the FFL. Primary school parents were generally much more engaged in the FFL programme than their secondary school counterparts, a finding the evaluators attributed to the greater reluctance of teenagers to discuss their learning at home.

By way of an overall conclusion, the evaluation team found that the key strength of the programme – namely the holistic focus of the whole school approach – was also a weakness in the sense that the multiple goals created problems of prioritisation and the wide range of activities placed extra demands on the participating schools. Even so, many positives emerged during the programme when we consider that the school catering service was still recovering from the noxious legacy of a neoliberal model of provision that had debased virtually every aspect of the service.

The Big Lottery's Wellbeing Fund was sufficiently impressed with the FFL results that it decided to invest £4 million in a

Serving the public

second phase of the programme covering the 2013–2015 period. One of the main novelties of phase 2 was the extension of the programme from its original niche in schools to include new settings, such as early years, care homes, hospitals, universities and workplaces.

Once again, the evaluation team found a mixed picture. Many positives were identified in schools and the other new settings, but food system reform faced serious challenges because:

> A legacy of catering systems driven by low-cost provision leaves an infrastructure – most notably in hospitals – which similarly inhibits a switch to models centred on freshly cooked local produce … It is difficult therefore, to demonstrate that actions – such as implementing Food for Life in a school – result in positive outcomes which contribute towards the desired change. An expectation of immediate, measurable impact can be to the detriment of initiatives with a long-term perspective and/or of complex nature.[26]

Although FFL has subsequently expanded to a wide variety of catering settings in the public and private sector, the school sector still accounts for the majority of its meals, as we can see from Exhibit 2.1.

One of the exemplars in the school sector is Leicestershire Traded Services, which serves around 35,000 meals daily at 240 schools. They currently hold the FFLSH Gold Award, the highest level of achievement in the FFL awards system.[27]

One of the challenges of the FFL awards system is not just attaining the Gold Award but *retaining* it. The case of Oldham is instructive in this respect, as we saw earlier. Once classed as 'the poorest town in England' by the Office for National Statistics, Oldham became the first local authority catering service to attain the FFL Gold Award in the north of England,

Food for life: the whole school approach

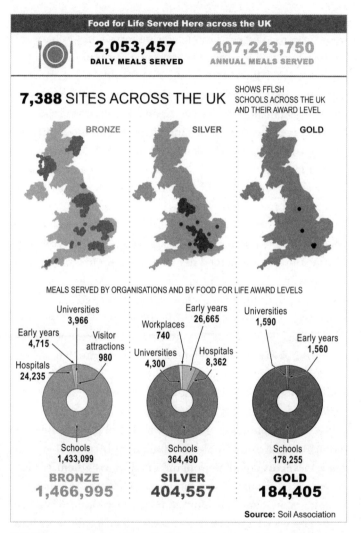

Exhibit 2.1 Food for Life meals by sector and award level (2021)

exploding the myth that services for the poor tend to become poor services. The education catering service in Oldham was led by a formidable woman called Anne Burns until her retirement in 2022. After they won their first Gold Award in 2014, I asked her how a poor borough had managed to become such an exemplary catering service. 'Everything depends', she said, 'on the people at the helm – the professional commitment of the catering manager, the skills and enthusiasm of the catering team and the sustained political support of local politicians.' What about the cost of FFL meals? Was it not prohibitively expensive for a cash-strapped council in a highly deprived local authority area? The cost was not prohibitive, she said, because sound menu planning and close working relationships with suppliers helped her catering team to win the Gold Award with a 60p cost of food on the plate. At the time of the Gold Award, Oldham was charging £2 per head for a school meal, one of the lowest charges in the region. When the Gold Award was renewed in 2019 – and the renewal cost of £11,000 a year is not easy to find in a poor local authority that has suffered a decade of austerity cuts – the cost of food on the plate had increased to 65p per plate, still one of the lowest in the region.[28]

But being a poor borough finally took its toll. After a decade of cuts to local authority budgets imposed by central government, Oldham could no longer afford to maintain its Gold Award and it was forced to relinquish it. The case of Oldham is a sobering reminder of the limits to progressive localism because, in the absence of a supportive *national* system, locally innovative policies will always remain fragile. I have always been struck by the contrast with Malmö, where the school meals service could draw on a more enabling national environment.

Food for life: the whole school approach

Foodscapes of hope: good food for all

The Swedish school meals system is one of the foundational pillars of the Swedish welfare state. A key turning point came in the 1930s, when the compulsory school system was transformed from a purely educational platform into an arena for social reform: the school was deemed an ideal means for fostering a strong and healthy nation and the school meal was perceived as a means of supplying 'food for future citizens'.[29] The celebrated free school meals system gradually emerged from this nation-building debate, a widely acclaimed social innovation that is now one of the most distinctive symbols of Swedish culture.

Far less well known is that a parallel debate occurred in the UK around the same time. In the 1930s and 1940s the school canteen was championed as a tool of social engineering, a laboratory for societal change. Reformers claimed that the school canteen should 'initiate children into a social life' by making them 'tolerant, self-reliant and easy mannered'.[30] And as we have seen, free school meals were part of the original design of the welfare model of collective provision in the UK, a pledge that was never honoured. But now, eighty years later, that free school meals pledge is being redeemed in parts of the UK for all primary school children, as we will see.

In this final section, I explore the 'foodscapes of hope' in Sweden and the UK in the hope they will inspire other places – countries, regions and municipalities – to follow their lead and provide good food for all.

Serving the public

Malmö: a beacon of good practice

Being embedded in a nationally supportive school meals system is one of the strengths of the school catering service in Malmö, a city that is widely regarded as a beacon of good practice in national and international school food circles. Although free school meals funded by central government grants began in 1946, it was not until 1997 that a national system was formalised by a law that stipulated that school meals were to be provided at no cost at the point of access. The funding of the free school meal (FSM) system has also changed in important ways since its inception because, in 1967, the central state devolved responsibility to the municipalities.[31]

Despite all these modifications, the underlying goals of the FSM system have remained much the same. In addition to health and well-being goals, a distinctive aspect of the Swedish FSM system is that it was also designed to promote gender equality by freeing women from the necessity of preparing packed lunches and enabling them to participate in the labour market. So much more than just a meal, the FSM system is a rich microcosm of national culture because 'the development of the school meal helps us understand the roots of the Swedish welfare system, the school system, the family institution, gender and power relations and the concept of childhood'.[32]

With a population of 350,000, Malmö is Sweden's third-largest city and it has been one of the pioneers of a sustainable FSM system. To overcome the recessions of the 1970s and 1980s that undermined its industrial base, it adopted sustainable development as a flagship strategy to reinvent itself. Subsequently the city sought to regenerate its economy and society through an environmentally friendly approach, a strategy championed by

Food for life: the whole school approach

a social democratic party that has governed the municipality since 1994. In 2009 the City of Malmö set itself one of the most ambitious climate targets in the world: it vowed to be climate neutral by 2020 and to be powered by 100 per cent renewable energy by 2030. Under this ambitious vision of developing a transition towards a sustainable city, the City of Malmö approved a Policy for Sustainable Development and Food in 2010.[33]

As the municipality aims to lead by example, it set itself two highly ambitious goals: all public food should be organic by 2020 and GhG emissions from food procurement should be reduced by 40 per cent by 2020 compared with the 2002 level. To meet these goals, Malmö's urban food policy drew on the 'S.M.A.R.T' model developed by the Institute of Public Health in Stockholm, which aims to provide health and environmental benefits without incurring higher costs. The model consists of the following principles: *S*maller amount of meat; *M*inimise intake of junk food/empty calories; *A*n increase in organic; *R*ight sort of meat and vegetables; and *T*ransport efficient. Alongside these core principles, Malmö also prioritised the purchasing of ethically certified products, reflecting its status as Sweden's first Fair Trade City in 2006.[34]

It's worth noting that the origins of Malmö's commitment to sustainable food procurement predated the formal strategy by more than a decade. In fact, the city began working on sustainable food in the early 1990s, animated by the UN Conference in Rio de Janeiro in 1992. The Agenda 21 action programme emerged from this conference with the aim of inspiring countries to work towards sustainable development and this was how employees in Malmö's school restaurants were introduced to sustainability thinking. The school chefs were determined

Serving the public

to reduce the spread of environmental toxins and protect Malmö's schoolchildren from exposure to chemical pesticides in their facilities. This was how, as early as 1996, Malmö School Restaurants started purchasing their first organic products: pickled cucumber and beetroot. It marked the beginning of their sustainability efforts.[35]

Although Malmö's twin policy goals – 100 per cent organic food and 40 per cent lower emissions – were challenging, they were also very clear and easily measurable. The main challenge with the fully organic food goal was that the organic supply industry was not well developed when the goal was set in 2010. Privately, however, the team knew that they were unlikely to meet the goal by 2020, but they thought it would incentivise the city administration to strive to do its best. The limited availability of organic products on the market meant that the catering team had to work very closely with the municipality's food procurement officers to seek out and nurture organic suppliers in a highly proactive fashion. So much so that by 2020, over 500 organic products had replaced commercial products in Malmö's procurement agreements and the proportion of organic food has increased more or less continuously since the policy was adopted, as we can see in Exhibit 2.2.

The 40 per cent lower emissions goal was equally important to the municipality, not least because the Greens had made headway at the political level in the city and because, at the officer level, the Environment Department was responsible for designing and delivering the sustainable food strategy. Reducing meat in the school menu was the top priority because it had by far the highest carbon footprint of all food product categories. The challenge here was how to present the new menu when many parents, fearing that less meat meant less

Food for life: the whole school approach

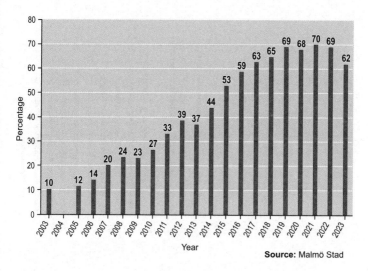

Exhibit 2.2 Amount of certified organic food served in Malmö

protein for their children, pushed back accordingly. The city's response was twofold: it went to great efforts to engage with parents and children to explain the food policy and it framed the new menus in positive rather than negative terms. As the municipality's internal assessment put it: 'instead of framing policy goals as "reducing the proportion of meat," which can be perceived as negative, we rephrased it as "increasing the proportion of plant-based foods." It is much easier to argue for an initiative than for a reduction.'[36] The results for the lower emissions goal have been broadly positive, as we can see in Exhibit 2.3, even though there is still some way to go.

Although Malmö is well on its way to meeting the twin goals it set itself in 2010, albeit a little later than originally planned, the city's Environment Department frankly concedes that there's no room for complacency because new challenges

Serving the public

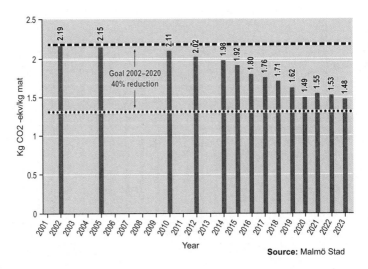

Exhibit 2.3 Greenhouse gas emissions from food procured by Malmö

are constantly arising. In its own internal assessment, the Environment Department identifies three major challenges that could threaten the integrity of the school meals service in Malmö: (1) food price inflation, (2) climate change and (3) the challenge of the pedagogical meal.

Food price inflation: in 2022, the school meals service began to feel the economic pressure from the increased food prices, with the result that only 11 of their 100 sustainable recipes could be accommodated within the budget and the proportion of organic food also began to decrease, as we can see from Exhibit 2.2. In response, the city had to urgently adjust its menus and use its power of purchase more robustly to secure quality ingredients at a fair price.

Climate change: ever since the mid-term evaluation in 2015, Malmö has used the metric 'amount of greenhouse gases per

Food for life: the whole school approach

kilogram of food' (kg CO_2e/kg) to calculate the climate impact of its food purchases. But this metric cannot solve the goal conflicts that are becoming common in climate-friendly food policies. As an example, the Environment Department poses the question: what do you do when the choice is between a product with low carbon emissions and a product with low water consumption? The city's procurement officers will need clearer guidance to manage these goal conflicts in the future.

Pedagogical meals: mealtimes can be pedagogical occasions when students learn about sustainable diets and healthy lifestyles, which is the philosophy of the whole school approach. But the pedagogical meal remains an untapped resource in the city's schools and the Environment Department would like to see even stronger links between curriculum, teaching and food to ensure that students have a sound knowledge of sustainable diets and why they are important for people and the planet.

Malmö's school meals service is not alone in facing these problems. Although it has an admirable capacity to be frank and self-critical about its own challenges, the Environment Department is also rightly proud of its achievements over the past thirty years. The internal assessment of the city's food policy concludes on a positive note: 'Malmö's Policy for Sustainable Development and Food has been a resounding success, positioning the city at the forefront of food and sustainability both nationally and internationally ... Malmö's dedication to sustainable development and food has made us a role model and innovator for future climate-neutral cities.'[37]

Malmö's status as a beacon of good practice in public food provisioning has been recognised by its peers in other countries. Over the years I have been personally involved in arranging for the Malmö team to speak at school food policy events in the UK. At a roundtable of school food stakeholders in Wales, hosted by Cynnal Cymru, Helen Nilsson from the Environment Department was invited to reflect on the Malmö experience. Among the factors that had contributed to the success of the policy (in Malmö) she stressed the following:

- *Clear aims*: the aims of 100 per cent organic food and 40 per cent lower emissions were both clear and measurable.
- *Dedicated leadership:* the political leadership had been steadfast and consistent since the 1990s and senior officers had the authority and the competence to deliver the strategy.
- *Engaged staff*: the main funding for the strategy was largely devoted to education and training for staff in many departments so that all employees across the municipality had a sound understanding of *what* was involved in a sustainable food strategy and *why* it was important to people and planet.
- *Tasting and engagement*: new recipes were subject to taste-testing sessions with children and scaled up if they were successful; and engagement with parents allayed their fears and misconceptions that plant-based diets meant protein-free food.
- *Supplier dialogue*: a close relationship with suppliers had been essential from the start, simply because organic food was scarce in the early days and the city had to nurture good organic suppliers.[38]

These factors may have been successful in Malmö but there is no guarantee they will work elsewhere. Research and experience tell us that, while social policies can be transferred from one jurisdiction to another, the *social context* in which they are applied is clearly not transferable because places and institutions are unique. Cloning other places may be a futile exercise, but learning from others is indeed possible and governments in the UK – national as well as local governments – have much to learn from Malmö.

Good food for all: the pioneers of free school meals in the UK

The devolution of power in the UK over the past twenty-five years has had a dramatic effect on food policy. As a result of devolution, new governments have been established in Scotland, Wales and Northern Ireland, creating a polycentric political system with multiple policymaking parliaments in place of the old centralised system in Westminster and Whitehall.[39] Food policy is one of the domains devolved to the Celtic nations, with the result that these new governments are largely free to develop policies that are attuned to their own circumstances and their own political priorities. The rise of the polycentric state helps to explain the growing diversity of food policies in the UK in recent years, especially with respect to FSMs, where Scotland and Wales are committed to universal provision for all primary schools, while England retains a means-tested national system except for five pioneering boroughs in London. To understand this patchwork quilt of food policies we need to delve into each component part, beginning with Scotland.

Since the new Scottish Parliament was created in 1999, Scotland has been the real pacesetter for food policy reform in the UK. It was the first nation in the UK to reframe the school meals service as a health service rather than a commercial service when it published *Hungry for Success* in 2002, a whole school approach to school meals in Scotland. It was also the first nation to commit to universal free school meals (UFSM) provision for

Serving the public

all primary school children. The UFSM commitment came not from the Scottish Labour Party, the source from which it might have been expected given its social democratic credentials, but from the Scottish National Party (SNP), though it took eight years before the manifesto commitment was put into practice.

When it was finally introduced, in January 2015, it was initially confined to Primary 1 to Primary 3 children in all local authority schools. Although this was a limited victory for the UFSM movement in Scotland, it was nevertheless an important breakthrough, not least because the Scottish Labour Party had been steadfastly opposed to the policy on the grounds that it preferred a means-tested policy. Without the new politics of devolution, it is doubtful if the UFSM policy would have emerged when it did. The SNP government made the original political commitment but it would never have been in power without the devolution settlement. The SNP was also fortified in its commitment by its political agreement with the Scottish Green Party, a party that claims the credit for keeping the SNP faithful to the UFSM cause as it was instrumental in persuading the government to extend universal provision to all primary school children by 2024.

Scottish political commentators have suggested that the extension of the UFSM commitment to all primary school children is on a par with the abolition of university fees and the smoking ban, all of which should be seen 'a true victory for devolution'.[40]

But the UFSM achievement is about so much more than party politics in Holyrood, the home of the Scottish Parliament. As with so many radical policy innovations, the cognitive landscape in which school food reform was debated had been totally reshaped by the concerted power of the Scottish Food Coalition,

Food for life: the whole school approach

which describes itself as a diverse alliance of civil society organisations working to achieve food justice in Scotland. Although many of its members campaigned for the UFSM cause, the latter was always part and parcel of a larger and more capacious campaign – the campaign for a Good Food Nation Bill, a groundbreaking piece of legislation that championed a sustainable food system for the benefit people and planet alike. The Good Food Nation (Scotland) Bill passed into law on 15 June 2022, the product of a decade of tenacious campaigning for a whole system approach to food policy reform.[41]

Some members of the coalition pressed for the UFSM commitment to be extended to all secondary schools, and for this to be part of the Good Food Nation Bill, but the SNP government and its Green Party allies refused to support this extension as they considered it too expensive when existing budgets were already under pressure. But this final stage of the UFSM campaign is only likely to gain momentum, fuelled by the growing evidence of poverty and hunger amid 'horrifying' food price inflation.[42]

The politics of devolution played an even more important part in food policy reform in Wales. Whereas the governing SNP was committed to the UFSM cause a decade before it was implemented, the Labour government in Wales had never espoused the cause in any of its party manifestos. The UFSM policy commitment in Wales was hastily fashioned in 2021 as part of a unique Cooperation Agreement between the Welsh Labour government and Plaid Cymru, the Welsh nationalist party, to secure a working majority in the Welsh Parliament. The Cooperation Agreement was presented as part of a new collaborative politics that aimed to be 'radical in content and co-operative in approach'. In total, the three-year agreement contained forty-six policy commitments covering social, economic, cultural and constitutional goals. But top of the list was the political commitment to:

> Free school meals – Extend free school meals to all primary school pupils, over the lifetime of this agreement, as a further step to reaching our shared ambition that no child should go hungry. We agree that universal free school meals will be a transformational intervention in terms of child hunger and child poverty, which will support educational attainment and child nutrition and local food production and distribution, benefiting local economies.[43]

The UFSM commitment is worth quoting in full because the headline policy clearly contains some very different goals, namely: (1) to combat child hunger, (2) to reduce child poverty, (3) to support educational attainment, (4) to promote nutritional health and (5) to foster local economic development by boosting the production and distribution of local food. The reason why so many goals were attached to the headline policy was partly because the Welsh government wanted the UFSM scheme to be aligned with the Well-being of Future Generations (WFG) Act, the most innovative legislation it had ever passed. The WFG Act obliges all public bodies in Wales to consider seven well-being goals and five ways of working in all their activities, a policy for which the Welsh government has earned plaudits from the UN for embedding well-being goals and the sustainability principle into the public sector in Wales. Passing legislation is one thing, but implementing it is quite another, especially when public bodies have been decimated by years of central government spending cuts. Capacity constraints, in other words, have stymied the implementation of the WFG Act to date.[44]

Food for life: the whole school approach

Despite the challenging climate, the WFG Act has undoubtedly helped to fashion a new, more progressive mindset in the public food procurement community.[45] Under the terms and conditions of the UFSM programme, for example, local authorities are obliged to ensure that they follow the Welsh government's procurement guidance for all food contracts to ensure compliance with the WFG Act, so that positive socio-economic, environmental and cultural outcomes are achieved. Among other things, this guidance aims to 'ensure a move away from lowest cost approaches in food tenders' and 'greater weighting on social/well-being objectives'.[46]

Like its food coalition counterpart in Scotland, the Food Policy Alliance Cymru aims to keep this progressive food policy agenda on track by monitoring progress on the UFSM front and by relentless campaigning for a whole system approach to food policy reform.[47]

While Scotland and Wales have been governed for many years by SNP and Labour governments respectively, England's national government was controlled by successive Conservative administrations from 2010 to 2024. The greatest food policy paradox in England is that the Conservatives commissioned the most comprehensive food policy review since 1945 – in the form of the NFS chaired by Henry Dimbleby – only to ignore most of its recommendations.[48]

Although the NFS championed a whole system approach to food policy reform to enhance the health of people and planet, one of its key recommendations was to 'extend eligibility for free school meals', for example by raising the household earnings threshold for FSMs from £7,400 to £20,000. Raising the threshold would have made a major impact on the problem of food-insecure households because it would guarantee an additional 1.1 million children from low-income families a lunch in school. To bolster its case, the NFS stressed that FSMs are extremely popular with the public, citing a poll in which 89 per cent of respondents agreed that: 'Every child has the right to have a healthy meal at least once a day.'

Unless eligibility was extended, the NFS said, children in England were in danger of being disadvantaged compared to those elsewhere in the UK because Scotland and Wales had embraced UFSM for all primary schools, while Northern Ireland's eligibility threshold was already £14,000, almost double the English threshold. But Dimbleby's pleas fell on deaf ears because, when Boris Johnson's government issued its formal response, it totally ignored the FSM recommendation. Reflecting on his chastening experience, Dimbleby dispensed with diplomacy: 'The so-called "government Food Strategy" that was unveiled in June 2022, in response to my review, is not a strategy at all. It is merely a handful of disparate policy ideas, many of them chosen because they are unlikely to raise much of a media storm.'[49]

In the absence of a national response, the UFSM cause in England has been pioneered at the *local level* by five London boroughs – Newham, Islington, Southwark, Tower Hamlets and Westminster – and they have done so in the face of unprecedented financial pressures imposed by central government's spending cuts. Take Newham as a case in point.

Newham was part of an official FSM pilot study (along with Durham and Wolverhampton) in 2009–2010 to assess the costs and benefits of universal entitlement in primary schools versus other, more limited forms of extended entitlement (a study which found that only the universal entitlement approach had positive impacts on children's diet and attainment). An earlier

Food for life: the whole school approach

FSM pilot study had been conducted in Hull between 2004 and 2007 but this was discontinued on cost grounds despite a very positive evaluation.[50]

While Durham decided against adopting the UFSM policy on cost grounds, Newham chose to continue it as its Eat for Free scheme. After running the scheme for ten years, however, Newham considered shelving the scheme in 2020 because of financial pressures. But in the face of a local public outcry, the £6 million a year Eat for Free scheme was retained, benefiting 14,000 children annually and saving families £500 per child in food costs per year. For the second poorest borough in England, where half the children are in poverty, Newham's decision to retain the Eat for Free scheme was a truly momentous political decision. Local MPs wrote to Rokhsana Fiaz, the Newham mayor, to say the scheme was needed more than ever given the cost-of-living crisis: 'We are proud that Newham will continue to set a positive moral and political example of excellence, especially in the context of stretched finances.'[51]

The pioneering boroughs set a precedent for the London mayor. In a one-off measure to deal with the cost-of-living crisis, mayor Sadiq Khan committed £135 million to fund a UFSM scheme for *every* London borough for the 2023–2024 academic year. Announcing the policy, he called for central government to fund a national scheme for England beyond the limited scheme that already existed for infant school children.

In the meantime, the UFSM cause is gaining momentum. Although it is the poorest borough in England, Tower Hamlets has nevertheless become the first local authority in the country to extend UFSM provision to all its secondary schools and other boroughs are considering following its lead.[52] But as things stand, a third of school-age children in England (900,000) living

Serving the public

in poverty remain ineligible for FSMs, a sobering reminder that England lags behind Scotland, Wales and Northern Ireland.[53]

Not surprisingly, political support is growing for campaigns in England such as Feed the Future, which is calling for two major reforms: an immediate extension of FSMs to all children in families in receipt of Universal Credit as a prelude to the ultimate goal of UFSM for *all* school children. It is testament to the power of the Feed the Future coalition – which is led by influential civil society organisations such as the Food Foundation, Sustain and the Soil Association – that UFSM has become such a compelling moral cause, and political parties will ignore it at their peril.

3

Catering for health: the quest for good food

Introduction

Writing a healthcare manual without mentioning nutrition is akin to writing *Hamlet* without the Prince. At least that's how it felt to two young medical students who wrote to the *British Medical Journal* to complain about the shortcomings of their educational curriculum. In a survey of professional training, they said, more than 75 per cent of American junior physicians felt inadequately trained to counsel patients on diet and physical activity and this picture was similar in the UK. The General Medical Council in the UK requires qualifying medical students to understand the role of diet in health promotion and disease prevention, which includes being nutritionally competent.

But nutrition education was conspicuously lacking in the curriculum, they said, and this neglect was attributed to a wider and deeper problem about the hierarchy of status and knowledge in the medical establishment. 'Nutrition science', they argued, 'suffers from an image problem in medical practice. This starts with its subordination in curriculums and qualifying exams. Dietary interventions are considered to be outside of the evidence base, unscientifically "fluffy", and the domain of dieticians rather than doctors ... In later clinical years, the details of healthy diets, ways to assess malnutrition or specific food requirements for particular diseases in hospital or community settings are glossed over.'[1]

The *British Medical Journal* article triggered a lively response, with a wide range of medical professionals confirming the marginal status of nutrition in healthcare and its total subordination to pharmaceutical treatments. A good illustration of this reaction came from a fellow student, Chloe Hall at University College London Medical School, who said that in her experience of consultations with type 2 diabetic patients, the discussion revolved almost entirely around upping their Metformin dose, or trialling them on another anti-diabetic drug, even though National Institute for Health and Care Excellence guidelines advise 'lifestyle and diet' as the first line of treatment.

This exchange helps us to understand that the professional culture of healthcare in and beyond the UK is overwhelmingly framed in terms of drugs, devices and diagnostics, the three Ds of the medical-industrial complex. Although diet and lifestyle factors have begun to assume more importance in medical practice in recent years, they are still the poor relations of the NHS in the UK and health services in other countries, and this explains why the odds are stacked against campaigns to serve good food on the public plate in hospitals.

The paradox of the hospital

Hospitals in fast food cultures are being set up to fail because they confront the Sisyphean task of trying to provide a *clinical*

Catering for health: the quest for good food

solution to a *societal* problem – the problem of diet-related diseases associated with the rapid growth of cheap, ultra-processed food. Concerned healthcare professionals, such as the Medact health advocacy group, fully acknowledge the problem and present it as a paradox of the hospital: 'It is difficult to reconcile the paradox of hospitals that are administering life-prolonging operations and medications to patients while fuelling them, and their staff, with unhealthy food.'[2]

Sadly, hospitals in fast food nations are condemned to live with this paradox until the societal food problem is resolved. But resolving it is no easy matter because, among other things, it requires two parallel cultural shifts: a shift in mainstream *food culture* from ultra-processed diets to more sustainable diets; and a shift in *healthcare culture* from treatment to prevention, a transition in which nutrition is fully integrated into a holistic approach to health and well-being. What are the prospects for these twin cultural shifts in the UK?

Reforming food culture

Reforming food culture must surely begin with a full reckoning of the real costs of the conventional food system. British consumers have been subjected to so many food crises – foot and mouth in 2001, the horse meat scandal of 2013 and the cost-of-living crisis in 2023 – that they have become accustomed to food shocks. But the most shocking thing of all is that ill-health due to unhealthy diets is many times greater than ill-health due to food-borne diseases. Nearly twenty years ago researchers argued that the burden of food-related ill-health had been grossly underestimated by food and health policymakers and they concluded by saying: 'The cost to the NHS is twice the amount attributable to car, train, and other accidents, and more than twice that attributable to smoking. The vast majority of the burden is attributable to unhealthy diets rather than to food borne diseases.'[3] In other words, 'safe' food, in the form of mainstream diets, harms more people than 'unsafe' food, a truly shocking idea that is hard to comprehend.

But this brings us to one of the key questions, which is how to establish the real costs and benefits of the food system. The central problem is twofold: many of the costs of harmful foods are externalised (i.e. not factored into market prices) while the benefits of healthful foods are not fully appreciated by either policymakers or the market. Estimating these externalised costs – the 'hidden costs' – is a notoriously difficult exercise, which is one reason why they tend to vary so much. Estimates of the externalised cost of food in the UK, including to the health service and the environment, range from £40 billion per year in some studies to £94 billion per year in other studies. If these external costs were factored into the price of food, 'the price of the average weekly shop could double'.[4]

The escalating costs of diet-related diseases are the most tangible sign that all is not well with the food system. Many chronic conditions – notably obesity, coronary heart disease, type 2 diabetes and certain cancers – are linked to poor diets, and diet-related disease costs are becoming unsustainable for the NHS. The costs of obesity alone seem to grow inexorably by the day. A path-breaking Foresight study in 2007 found the cost of obesity to the economy and society could escalate to £49.9 billion a year by 2050, a sum that would threaten the viability of the NHS. But a more recent study of the costs of obesity, combining direct costs to the NHS and indirect costs to economy and society, found that the cost of obesity in the UK

Catering for health: the quest for good food

had already reached £58 billion a year, equivalent to 3 per cent of gross domestic product in 2020.[5]

Nothing better illustrates the paradox of the hospital than obesity. While the health service is equipped to treat the *clinical* symptoms of the condition, it is powerless to deal with its *societal* causes. This is especially apparent in the UK, where there is a marked disconnect between the scientific evidence and the political readiness to address the problem. The Foresight study is widely believed to be one of the most robust scientific studies ever conducted into the causes and consequences of obesity, a study that demolished the idea that the condition was attributable to lack of willpower on the part of feckless individuals: 'People in the UK today don't have less willpower and are not more gluttonous than previous generations. Nor is their biology significantly different to that of their forefathers. Society, however, has radically altered over the past five decades, with major changes in work patterns, transport, food production and food sales.'[6]

As we can see from Exhibit 3.1, the Foresight study concluded that obesity needs to be understood as a complex bio-social system, since it was essentially the outcome of an obesogenic environment that exploits our biological propensity to accumulate energy and conserve it because of genetic risk, the influence of early life experiences and the sensitivity of the appetite control system. In the face of a powerful obesogenic environment, a strategy that places the main burden of responsibility on individuals to change their eating habits is doomed to fail.

To counter obesity, and the junk food culture that fuels it, Foresight proposed a comprehensive long-term strategy that needed to work in two complementary ways: (1) to fashion an environment that supports healthy food choices and (2) to

'Taken together, the evidence presented in this report provides a powerful challenge to the commonly held assumption that an individual's weight is a matter solely of personal responsibility or indeed individual choice. Rather, the evidence supports the concept of "passive obesity" (where obesity is encouraged by wider environmental conditions, irrespective of volition). As society has changed over the last three decades energy expenditure on physical activity has declined. Today, the majority of people in the UK are sedentary when at work and at home. Most are car owners. Patterns of food consumption have also changed markedly. Eating habits have become more unstructured, and low-cost, energy-dense "food and drink on the go" is widely consumed. For a multitude of reasons, healthy lifestyles may be less available to those on low incomes.

Therefore, as a general rule, people do not "choose" to be obese. Their obesity is mainly driven by a range of factors beyond their immediate control that in practice constrain individual choice ... Strategies based on personal motivation and individual responsibility alone do not provide an adequate response to the obesity problem.

To be successful, a comprehensive long-term strategy to tackle obesity must act in two complementary ways to achieve and maintain a healthy population weight distribution. First, an environment that supports and facilitates healthy choices must be actively established and maintained. Second, individuals need to be encouraged to desire, seek and make different choices, recognising that they make decisions as part of families or groups and that individual behaviour is "cued" by the behaviours of others, including organisational behaviours and other wider influences.

The strategy needs to be planned and co-ordinated effectively by Government and must involve multiple

Exhibit 3.1 Tackling obesities: building a sustainable response

Catering for health: the quest for good food

> stakeholders. The role of non-governmental organisations – businesses, employers and voluntary organisations – is also critical and in some cases may be the dominant influence. National strategic action must be coherent, with local strategies that reflect local conditions, needs and aspirations. In particular, the role of local bodies such as local government and local health authorities must be clearly defined and linked to sufficient resources and the necessary skills to implement effective responses.'
>
> **Source:** Government Office for Science (2007) *Foresight: Tackling Obesities*, London: HMSO, p. 122.

Exhibit 3.1 continued

encourage individuals to make different choices, recognising that individual behaviour is 'cued' by the behaviour of family, peers and institutions. Although every societal actor had a role to play in countering obesity, Foresight was unequivocal that government ought to take the lead in reforming the obesogenic environment, particularly in the early years of childhood, because there is evidence that 'the period soon after birth is a time of metabolic plasticity. Factors in the environment, such as nutrition, can have long-lasting consequences in that they appear to set the baby on a particular developmental trajectory.'[7]

But even when governments take the initiative, public health policies can vary enormously in efficacy and equity, depending on the degree of agency that is required of individuals. Successive governments in the UK have met the challenge of unhealthy diets and obesity with policies that focus on providing advice, guidance and encouragement. Public health researchers refer to such policies as 'high-agency interventions' because recipients must use their personal resources or 'agency' to benefit. In contrast, 'population interventions that require recipients to use little or no agency to benefit may be more effective and equitable ... The amount of agency individuals must use to benefit from an intervention is a fundamental determinant of how, and for whom, it will work.'[8]

If low-agency interventions are likely to be more effective and more equitable in tackling diet-related disease and fostering more sustainable diets, why are so many public health and food policy interventions in the UK predicated on *high-agency* interventions? The answer would seem to be that low-agency interventions are resolutely opposed by neoliberal politicians and the junk food industry on the grounds that such interventions restrict 'free choice', even though food choices are largely determined by habits, affordability and availability. And as we know from the Foresight evidence, choices are anything but free given the bio-social dynamics of the obesogenic environment.

Promoting healthier, more sustainable diets will need a population-based approach that uses low-agency interventions to a much greater extent if public policies are to be effective and equitable in reforming mainstream food culture. But low-agency interventions that work 'behind our backs' are not sufficient because, as Hilary Cottam reminds us, what all societal problems have in common today is that their solution requires our participation. Whether we think about diabetes or climate change, she says, 'we have to be active agents of change'.[9]

While consumers and citizens need to be actively involved in changing their food culture, the transition to healthier and sustainable diets is just too complex and too daunting for it to be left to individual choice. One of the biggest barriers

Catering for health: the quest for good food

to this transition is the growing divide between the scientific evidence and the political capacity to act on the evidence. As regards the science, there's a growing consensus about what constitutes a healthier, more sustainable diet. All the evidence suggests that the diets that are healthier for people and planet alike consist of a diverse range of tubers, whole grains, legumes and fruit and vegetables, with animal products consumed more sparingly.[10]

However, the transition to healthier and sustainable diets faces an enormous political barrier: 'Because many governments have adopted laissez-faire approaches to consumer choice, the leadership required by governments and food system actors is considerable. This leadership demands coordination, consultation, and good policy facilitation by important policy actors.'[11]

The EAT–Lancet Commission refers to this transition as the Great Food Transformation, a goal that will only be achieved through widespread, multisector, multilevel action on the part of a new 'alliance of forces'.[12]

Reforming healthcare culture

The NHS marked its 75th anniversary on 5 July 2023. Marked being the operative word rather than celebrated because the health service was widely deemed to have reached a crisis point, which was exacerbated but not created by the COVID-19 pandemic. Although the NHS is the largest employer in Europe, with some 1.9 million employees, it still has more than 100,000 unfilled vacancies, a sure sign of an organisation in crisis. In international comparisons of healthcare systems, the UK fares poorly on many indicators: low numbers of doctors and nurses;

low numbers of beds; and low levels of investment in scanning technology and in capital investment generally. Not surprisingly, therefore, 'the UK performs poorly on health care outcomes across several different major disease groups and health conditions'.[13]

There's no real mystery as to causes of the crisis. A lack of capital investment in staff, technology and the NHS estate, together with politically sponsored reorganisations that diverted energies from healthcare provision and the cumulative effects of Conservative-led governments since 2010 that have been in thrall to a pre-Keynesian creed of austerity. The impact of austerity had a perverse effect by inadvertently increasing demand pressures on the NHS from within the service and without. Within the health service, public spending had been biased towards hospitals rather than primary care and community services, where some 90 per cent of healthcare activity occurs in the UK, so the *preventive* work of public health in the community suffered as a result.

But demand pressures were also fuelled by the fact that austerity-driven spending cuts outside the health sector – in social care, housing, leisure, local government – indirectly created more pressure on hospitals because these constitute the wider determinants of health. As a result, 'improvements in population health stalled or went into reverse during the 2010s at the very time when risk factors such as obesity – for which the UK has the highest rates in Europe – were having an increasing impact'.[14]

The perverse effect of austerity provides yet another illustration of the paradox of the hospital because, by focusing almost entirely on the supply of hospital services, successive governments neglected the *demand* side – the domain of public

Catering for health: the quest for good food

health – which was transferred out of the NHS and into local government in England, where it withered under a series of severe public spending cuts. By neglecting the demand side, the hospital sector is locked into an ever-growing and never-ending spiral that will always overwhelm its supply-side capacity.

Reforming healthcare culture in the UK needs to begin with a renewed political commitment to public health as part of a new emphasis on *prevention* to reduce the demand pressures on hospitals in the healthcare ecosystem. Sustainable diets need to be part of this transition to a more holistic healthcare system for the sake of NHS staff as well as patients.

The quest for good food

Nutrition may have been the poor relation in the medical-industrial complex in the UK until recently, but its effects were readily apparent in the statistics of patients and staff in NHS hospitals. Nearly a third of patients admitted to hospital are at risk of malnutrition and the number of admissions for malnutrition is rising rapidly. This problem is especially acute for older patients because, in a survey by Age Concern, six out of ten older people are at risk of becoming malnourished in hospital and this has ripple effects on the hospital economy: 'Malnourished patients stay in hospital for longer, are three times as likely to develop complications during surgery and have a higher mortality rate than well-fed patients.'[15]

Concerns about the health and well-being of NHS staff have also increased in recent years, concerns that were dramatically amplified by the trauma of the COVID-19 pandemic. As many as one in four nursing staff is obese and this has been attributed to the growing pressures on their time and the difficulties of eating healthily at work.[16]

Simon Stevens, the former CEO of NHS England, was the first chief executive to take this problem seriously when he launched a major drive to improve health and well-being in the NHS workplace in 2015. Staff absence was judged to cost NHS England around £2.4 billion a year, which was a serious underestimate because this figure did not take account of the extra cost of agency staff hired to fill in the gaps or the cost of treating absent staff. 'When it comes to supporting the health of our own workforce', Stevens said, 'frankly the NHS needs to put its own house in order ... Equally, it's time for PFI [private finance initiative] contractors and catering firms to "smell the coffee" – ditch junk food from hospitals and serve up affordable and healthy options instead. Staff, patients and visitors alike will all benefit.'[17]

While the rhetoric around this initiative sounds promising, we need to remember that campaigns to promote good food in UK hospitals have a long and woeful history. So much so that the prior decade was described as 'a decade of hospital food failure'. In a study conducted by Sustain, the authors summarised their findings by saying: 'Not a single scheme over the past decade has succeeded – however famous the celebrity chef – precisely because the initiatives were voluntary. Government has failed to send a clear message to hospital caterers that the quality of their food is critical to patient health and to the sustainability of our food system.'[18]

Perhaps the most notable failure was the Better Hospital Food initiative that was launched with great fanfare in 2001. Loyd Grossman, then BBC *Masterchef* host, was commissioned to lead a food team for a £40 million revamp of NHS catering by harnessing the collective talents of a group of celebrity

Catering for health: the quest for good food

chefs. Together they created 300 restaurant-style recipes for use in hospitals. Although the new-style menus may have been perfectly at home in exclusive restaurants, Age Concern feared that 'Navarin of lamb with couscous and grilled vegetables' may have been too challenging for sick and frail patients 'looking for something with which they are familiar'.[19] But patients who preferred more traditional fare need not have worried because, within five years, the Better Hospital Food initiative was scrapped as ineffective.

The popular image of hospital food has not been helped by persistent media coverage about poor quality and unappetising meals generating high levels of waste. A poll by Unison, which represents nurses and healthcare assistants among other NHS staff, found that more than half would not eat the food they serve to patients.[20]

What gives hospital food an even worse reputation in the eyes of the public is when it is unfavourably compared to prison food. But this was the conclusion of a comparative study of hospital and prison food systems in the UK. In both systems the food was organised centrally and transported to a remote location for service. Food leaving kitchens in both institutions had adequate nutritional and sensory quality. However, in prison the system was managed more effectively, transport was rapid and food quality was maintained up to the point of service. But in the hospital setting:

> [T]he system was less effective, and delays in the delivery of meals meant that the sensory quality of food reaching patients was poor. The demands of ward rounds, tests and treatments compounded delays, compromised the environment in which the food was eaten and meant that individuals' food requirements might be missed or forgotten. Many of these issues can

be traced back to a general perception that nutritional intake is incidental to clinical concerns and is therefore approached as an 'afterthought'.[21]

The independent review of hospital food

A crisis often triggers a new direction in policy and practice, and this is exactly what precipitated a major review of hospital food in the NHS in England. A serious outbreak of listeriosis in 2019 claimed the lives of seven patients after they had eaten hospital sandwiches contaminated with *Listeria monocytogenes*. In response, the government announced a 'root and branch' review of food served and sold in hospitals, focusing on the safety, nutrition, quality and production methods of food for patients, staff and visitors in NHS hospitals. Chaired by Philip Shelley, a former National Chair of the Hospital Catering Association, this was an *independent* review conducted by senior people (medical staff, dietitians, caterers and administrators) working in the NHS, many of whom had already made successful changes in their own hospitals; a sharp contrast, in other words, to the use of celebrity chefs who were strangers to the world of hospitals.

Although the Shelley review tried to be agnostic as to which hospital food system was best, it acknowledged that hospitals that outsourced their catering had, on average, slightly worse satisfaction ratings in surveys than those who do their own catering. Among its main conclusions it found that all the best-performing hospitals had four things in common:

- They adopt a 'whole-hospital approach'. This means integrating food into the life of the hospital – treating the

Catering for health: the quest for good food

restaurant as the hub of the hospital, where staff and visitors eat together; the chef and catering team are as important as other staff members; and food is considered as part of a patient's care and treatment.
- They have a chief executive who leads the change and understands the value of food and nutrition.
- They concentrate on the things patients and staff care about – good food, an attractive environment and a belief that the hospital they are in serves nutritious food at the best available quality.
- They have integrated multidisciplinary working, bringing together catering, dietetics and nursing to help improve nutritional outcomes for patients, and ensuring that staff well-being is prioritised with nutritious food and drink available on site at all times.[22]

The review panel had two major advantages over the celebrity chefs who preceded it. First, its intimate knowledge of the hospital food environment meant that it was fully aware of the organisational complexities of the NHS. Better hospital food, it said, requires both national focus and local leadership, 'but it is hard to deliver from the centre when power is devolved to individual trusts. We also need trusts to lead the change.'[23]

The second advantage was that it adopted a holistic food system perspective rather than focusing on one particular issue (e.g. the hospital menu) because it recognised that the lack of coordination within the food chain system was the source of so many food quality problems. The review highlighted three key problems of the NHS hospital food system – procurement, catering and waste – that had hitherto been treated separately even though they are all highly interconnected and interdependent.

Procurement

The hospital food chain begins with the procurement process, the values that inform it and the weightings that are attached to these values when contracts are designed. Sustainable food procurement was attracting growing interest in the NHS, the review claimed, because it could deliver social, economic and environmental benefits in addition to the obvious health dividend. But it conceded that good intentions on this front had proved difficult to translate into good practice at local level and it urged commissioners and procurers to adopt a more holistic value-for-money approach in assessing food contracts and 'not prioritise the lowest cost over quality'.[24]

Such concerns were well founded because, for many years previously, the NHS had displayed a disturbing delivery gap between rhetoric and reality with respect to food procurement. In fact, the NHS had a lot of ground to make up according to the King's Fund. In 2004 the Better Hospital Food programme commissioned the King's Fund to identify opportunities for managing food procurement sustainably and promoting healthy eating in acute hospitals. The analysis was deeply revealing because it exposed the shortcomings of food procurement policy at both the national level, where the Purchasing and Supplies Agency (PASA) was in charge, and at the local level, where NHS trusts were the key players.

Although PASA had adopted a sustainable development policy in principle in 2003, its food procurement policy was found to be highly restrictive in practice. The King's Fund

Catering for health: the quest for good food

researchers said: 'PASA believes that EU procurement rules would interpret local preference contracts as discriminatory, and domestic policy would regard restricted competitive tendering as compromising of best value for money.'[25] Neither of these things was true at the time as many public bodies in Europe were already practising local food sourcing in all but name and domestic UK policy was more permissive than conventional wisdom allowed, especially when public bodies had the capacity to design creative food procurement policies.[26]

If PASA left much to be desired at the national level, the performance of the local trusts was even worse. The King's Fund revealed that the trusts had little or no knowledge of sustainability policies, and menu design and food sourcing were purely cost driven, resulting in 'a food system that favours standardised meals, and ingredients that are sourced internationally with little awareness of the potential economic, social, and environmental and health impacts'.[27]

Although some progress was made, both nationally and locally, in the subsequent years, the review panel was sufficiently concerned to say that NHS trusts needed to use independent accreditation (like the Soil Association's FFLSH Award) to demonstrate that they were meeting strong sustainability criteria and complying with the relevant mandatory standards. It was also concerned about the low-cost procurement culture in the NHS; so much so that it recommended that a 40 per cent cost/60 per cent quality split be mandated across the NHS for the procurement of food and all catering services.

Mandating rigorous standards is one thing, but compliance is another matter, especially when there are no systems in place within the NHS to monitor compliance.

Serving the public

Catering

Of all the professions involved in the hospital food chain, catering is by far the most amorphous, the least well organised and the least professionalised. The hospital catering workforce straddles a wide array of people, including chefs, food service dietitians, catering assistants, nurses, hosts and hostesses, drivers, healthcare support workers, housekeepers, porters and supervisors. Aside from nurses, who tend not to see themselves as part of the catering team, chefs are perceived to be the highest-skilled members of the team, though this is not always the case because many chefs actually acquire their kitchen skills on the job. For all these reasons, the Shelley review said that hospital caterers are the poor relation of the catering trade, so it recommended new professional and vocational training routes to raise the status and skills of chefs and other members of the hospital catering team. But it recognised that a new catering culture would be challenging because, 'with the years of assembling premade, often prewrapped items, real chefs are a thing of the past in many hospitals and will need to be recruited and trained'.[28]

Upskilling the hospital catering profession may be a steeper challenge than the review panel implies because an earlier survey of hospital catering and facilities management in the UK found a parochial and insular labour market, where staff teams are perceived to have 'low skills with limited commitment and poor motivation'.[29] When asked about the main challenges of hospital catering, respondents spoke of workplace tensions between clinical and support staff, while a catering services manager said the main challenge was 'losing control after the food leaves the kitchen'.

Catering for health: the quest for good food

These two challenges – professional tensions between clinical and non-clinical staff within the hospital and the lack of control of food quality – were uppermost in the minds of the review panel because their recommendations sought to resolve these problems.

To overcome workplace tensions – and improve nutrition for hospital patients, staff and visitors – the Shelley review said that 'a strong relationship between the "Power of Three" (caterers, dietitians and nurses) was vital'.[30] Forging cross-disciplinary teams will require hard work and goodwill on all sides because the review panel said it had heard from dietitians that they struggle to liaise with catering due to caseload pressures, and there is a lack of recognition and value for catering dietitians within trusts who feel that they are valued less than clinical dietitians. Clinical dietitians, it said, 'are sometimes seen as having little to do with the food service'.

To ensure food quality is maintained from kitchen to plate, the review focused on the final step in the process, what it called the 'Last Nine Yards'. Central to good service, it said, is having the right staff, trained appropriately on the ward. At this point the review addressed the thorny issue of who is ultimately responsible for ensuring that patients actually eat the food on the plate, and its answer was unequivocal: 'Nurses are accountable for the nutritional care of patients and this has been an explicit responsibility in the Nursing and Midwifery Council's code since 2015.'[31]

Perhaps to placate the nursing profession, the review conceded that nurses often feel that they lack the time to ensure that patients eat their food because they have so many other responsibilities. To address this problem the review panel called for a major cultural change in the way that nurses and doctors are trained about the role of nutrition in healthcare: 'We want nutrition to become a mandatory part of all health professionals' training, including existing nurses' and doctors' continuing professional development.'[32]

Waste

The weakest part of the independent review was its treatment of waste. Drawing on a Waste and Resources Action Programme analysis, it said that food waste represents a cost to the UK healthcare sector of £230 million each year. But this figure was based on data from 2012 and the review made no attempt to update the estimated cost of food waste in NHS hospitals. The review panel could be forgiven for not offering a new estimate because, shocking as it sounds, there is no mandatory framework to record plate waste in the NHS. Given the dearth of data, the review was forced to conclude that: 'Food waste data is currently underreported. In 2018 to 2019, 81 per cent of hospital sites that provided food service did not report their food waste data and there is significant regional variation.'[33]

Quite apart from its financial costs, a high level of plate waste can mean hidden health problems because uneaten food implies malnourished patients. It also carries significant environmental costs if wasted food is not properly recycled. All the review could do to improve matters was to call for NHS trusts to agree a common method of recording and monitoring food waste and for waste minimisation plans to be rolled out in conjunction with a campaign to raise awareness.

Monitoring and measuring are necessary but not sufficient. Studies of hospital food waste suggest that the source of the problem lies in the fragmented nature of the hospital food chain. While most food waste research tends to focus on its

Catering for health: the quest for good food

contribution to climate change, through landfill methane emissions, very few researchers have utilised hospital food waste as a prism to explore the interlinkages between different stages of the food chain. A fascinating and instructive study of food waste in the NHS in Wales set out to plug this research gap by asking: how does food become wasted, and why, and which practices and food chain actors are responsible for the generation of waste?

The research was carried out in three hospitals in the Cardiff and Vale University Health Board (UHB), which delivers specialist medical services to 2.5 million people. Most of the hot main meals for the UHB are made by in-house staff in the Central Processing Unit, which is also in charge of day-to-day food procurement. The research showed that there was a strong and direct correlation between the general quality of the hospital meal service and the high amount of food wasted. One of the key factors responsible for plate waste was the lack of staff capacity to interact with patients, especially with respect to their menu choices and their ability to eat the food. Plate waste was especially high for meals and wards where ward-based caterers would automatically serve vegetables – even when they had not been ordered. Most staff on the ward lacked a sense of ownership of the problem of food waste, a problem that was widely seen as the preserve of the catering department that covered the costs of the food. What was needed, the researchers concluded, was 'a more joined-up approach to hospital food policy that brings together procurement officers, officials responsible for facilities, food and physical activity and nursing services and that creates arenas where knowledge can be exchanged and best practice can be disseminated'.[34] This conclusion anticipated the Shelley review, which called for a more holistic approach to hospital food policy, where nutritional care is best served in teams and where diet is afforded parity of esteem with medicine.

Although it was the most thorough review of hospital food in living memory, the reviewers were clearly too optimistic about its political prospects. Philip Shelley and Prue Leith, respectively the chair and advisor, wrote in their foreword that all previous efforts to improve the quality of hospital food had run into the sand. But this time is different, they said, because they could count on the leadership of the Secretary of State for Health and Social Care (Matt Hancock) and the backing of the Prime Minister (Boris Johnson). In the event, Hancock was forced out of office within twelve months and Johnson followed suit the year after; a sobering reminder that reformers need to place less faith in the fickle world of high office and invest more energy in forging durable alliances for change.

Catering for health: agents of change

As we have seen, crises can trigger new directions when new ways of working are deemed to be utterly imperative, a case of 'needs must' as it were. There was no better illustration of this reaction than the NHS response to the COVID-19 pandemic, when managers and clinicians agreed that new practices should be introduced in a matter of weeks when they would normally have taken years to implement. But short of an existential threat such as a pandemic, it is never easy for novel or radical ideas to gain traction because habits and routines are so deeply engrained in the prosaic practices of all organisations. Even when novel ideas do emerge, they are tolerated so long as they remain on the margins. New work is often 'allowed',

Catering for health: the quest for good food

says Hilary Cottam, while the numbers are small: 'Innovation that does not encroach on the existing system and can be contained as an interesting pilot, or published as an inspirational case study, is usually celebrated … Later, as the work becomes more successful and therefore more challenging, the system reasserts itself.'[35]

Although Cottam was referring to her work as a social innovator trying to reform welfare services, the point is equally applicable to the realm of public food provisioning, where good practice has been a bad traveller.[36] Novel ways of working have indeed emerged in hospital food provisioning but they tend to remain isolated examples; so we need to understand how and why these novel developments emerged and what prevented them becoming the mainstream food system in the NHS. In other words, we need to address two different but equally important questions here: first, how does change happen; and second, what prevents change becoming contagious?

Duncan Green has been exercised by these questions for many years in his capacity as a strategic advisor at Oxfam. In *How Change Happens* he distils the lessons from Oxfam's work, highlighting 'the importance of unpredictable events and accidents: the arrival (or loss) of champions in positions of power, unexpected changes in laws and policies, crises, and scandals'.[37] While these unforeseeable things can trigger a change of direction, they do not of themselves dictate the new course of action – the *what* rather than the how so to speak. In the case of hospital food provisioning, a food-poisoning incident triggered a health crisis and the crisis bequeathed an independent review of the entire food system.

But what's missing from this linear sequence is the changing cognitive landscape in which the review panel conducted its inquiry. The cognitive landscape in the NHS is the prism through which healthcare issues are viewed and valued and it defines what matters, what counts and what gets measured. Although the cognitive landscape is largely fashioned by government policies and regulations, the latter are often the culmination of many years of campaigns spearheaded by NGOs working in concert with pioneering trusts and hospitals.

Two of the most influential NGOs in the UK food space are the Soil Association and Sustain. In their different ways they have been important agents of change in reshaping the cognitive landscape around hospital food provisioning. If NGOs have helped to change the hospital food agenda, by highlighting the multiple benefits of sustainable food systems, the role of pioneering hospitals and trusts has been even more important in trying to put sustainability ideas into practice. Agents of change, in other words, come from two distinct directions – from outside the NHS, in the form of NGO-sponsored campaigns, and from within the healthcare system, in the form of good food pioneers. Let's take a brief look at each of these agents.

Agents of change: how NGOs shaped the cognitive landscape

NGOs rarely get the credit they deserve in shaping the healthcare policy agenda in the UK, a field where government initiatives tend to monopolise the media's attention. But some NGOs have had a disproportionate influence given their limited size and resources in setting the agenda for hospital food provisioning. Here I focus on two such organisations – Sustain and the

Catering for health: the quest for good food

Soil Association – each of which has its own distinctive policy agenda.

Sustain is an alliance of NGOs devoted to the cause of better food and farming. Based in London, it builds networks and platforms to design and deliver projects that seek to catalyse permanent change in policy and practice, and it advises and negotiates with government and other public bodies to ensure that policies on food and agriculture are publicly accountable and socially and environmentally responsible. Sustain began working on enforceable public sector food standards in 2008, after running practical projects for nearly a decade to demonstrate what is possible. Its campaign for Better Hospital Food has been the main advocacy vehicle for its work in hospitals, where it focused its argument on two key targets: to demonstrate the failure of voluntary targets and to advocate for legally binding food standards.

In 2009 Sustain published a highly influential report, *A Decade of Hospital Food Failure*, which documented the rise and fall of innumerable governmental initiatives to improve the quality of food, some of which we encountered earlier. 'Not a single scheme over the past decade has succeeded – however famous the celebrity chef – precisely because the initiatives were *voluntary*. Government has failed to send a clear message to hospital caterers that the quality of their food is critical to patient health and to the sustainability of our food system.'[38] Among other things, the report argued that more than £53 million had been wasted on these voluntary schemes and it was time for government to change tack and adopt mandatory standards.

An even more influential report was published in 2016 based on a survey of food standards in NHS hospitals, using London as a test case. Thirty of the capital's thirty-nine acute hospitals

Serving the public

responded and the findings revealed the wide variation in food policy and practice across the city:

- Only 50 per cent of hospitals surveyed met all five hospital food standards required in the NHS Standard Contract for hospitals.
- 67 per cent of hospitals reported that they have already met the health and well-being Commissioning for Quality and Innovation (CQUIN) food targets or were working towards meeting them by the March 2017 deadline.
- Twenty-four-hour access to healthy food for staff is the CQUIN target where most hospitals were lagging behind (only 40 per cent had met this target at the time of the survey).
- 60 per cent of trusts surveyed reported their NHS trust had a food and drink strategy (a requirement in the NHS Standard Contracts), but only 25 per cent covered all the required criteria.
- 75 per cent of trusts reported they had CEO buy-in to improve food standards.
- 30 per cent of hospitals surveyed cooked fresh food for adult patients.
- 42 per cent cooked fresh food for paediatrics patients.
- 77 per cent of hospitals cooked fresh food for staff.
- 10 per cent of hospitals had a Good Farm Animal Welfare Award for staff and visitor food.
- 21 per cent of hospitals had signed up to the London Healthy Workplace Charter.[39]

The foreword to the report was written by the highly influential Prue Leith (hospital food champion, broadcaster and journalist)

Catering for health: the quest for good food

who complained that, unlike the situation in schools and prisons, there are no minimum legal protections for hospital food. 'This means', she said, 'hospital food is uniquely vulnerable to a race to the bottom in terms of food quality, and patient care'. She also noted that the general quality of food across most London acute hospitals is highly variable, 'due to the lack of legal standards for hospital food, and the light touch regulation that leaves hospital food improvements open to the initiative of each hospital. There is now a strong argument for a new legal approach. A holistic legislative framework would provide direction to improve the whole food environment in hospitals, whilst also getting tougher on compliance with inspections and regular reporting.'[40]

To be endorsed by someone of the calibre of Prue Leith was a real coup for Sustain because, as we have seen, she would eventually become the chief advisor to the independent review of hospital food. Significantly, the review's recommendations included measures that were closely aligned with Sustain's long-running campaign for Better Hospital Food, such as:

- *Enshrining hospital food standards in law* – like the school food standards are already – and ensuring that standards for quality, health and sustainability apply to patient, staff and visitor food, food manufacturers and food retailers within hospitals, including vending machines.
- *Enhancing the role of the Care Quality Commission to better monitor and enforce standards.* The review had said that the current monitoring process – self-reported survey data – had become a 'tick-box' process for some trusts and may not accurately reflect reality.

Serving the public

While Sustain focused most of its energies on campaigning, the Soil Association has mixed its campaigns with standards-setting work for organic certification. Although it is best known for being the standard-bearer for organic food and farming, the Soil Association long ago diversified its activities into a broad array of sustainable food campaigns and certified assurance schemes. Perhaps the best example of this broader food policy work is the FFL Sustainable Catering Standards, which have two schemes:

- FFLSH supports public and private sector caterers to serve food that is fresh, local and sustainable. FFLSH standard meals are designed to have a positive impact not only customers eating the meals but also the organisations they are prepared for, the teams involved in cooking them and the local economy.
- The Green Kitchen Standard was created in partnership with the Carbon Trust to acknowledge innovative organisations making a positive environmental impact through their catering practices. Certification is awarded to caterers who are taking positive steps to sustainably manage their water, energy and waste.[41]

Created in 2007, the FFLSH scheme is the more established of the two and it's a tribute to the Soil Association's creative campaigning that it was strongly endorsed by the two most important food policy reviews of recent years. In the NFS, published by the government in 2021, FFL was cited as the model to emulate. For its part, the Shelley review suggested that NHS trusts should acquire a suitable accreditation, such as the FFLSH certification scheme, to demonstrate their commitment to food quality and sustainability standards.

Catering for health: the quest for good food

Both Sustain and the Soil Association clearly 'punch above their weight' because, despite their meagre resources, they managed to translate their priorities and targets into the highest levels of food policy discourse. But discourse is not the same as actual government food policy, and successive governments, Labour as well as Tory, have resisted demands for legally binding hospital food standards. If the cognitive landscape highlights the success of NGOs as influential agents of change, the actual policy landscape reveals the limits of that influence.

Agents of change: local food experiments in the NHS

The cause of sustainable food provisioning in the NHS was pioneered not by national-level initiatives from on high but by individual hospitals and trusts working in a learning-by-doing mode through local experiments. The local experiment that attracted most national attention was the Cornwall Food Programme (CFP). A notable feature of the project was that it was funded by external sources and involved working in concert with the NGO that was most closely associated with the cause of sustainable food systems: the Soil Association.

The CFP was triggered by a very prosaic event: a patient's complaint about the provenance of a sandwich that was sourced from the other end of the country, from a company in the north of England. In response, the catering manager at the Royal Cornwall Hospital Trust (RCHT), Mike Pearson, began a search for a local source of supply to enhance the freshness of the offer, and the sandwich contract became the template for a wider programme of local sourcing of meat, dairy and vegetables, where the trust worked directly with suppliers rather than working through PASA, the national NHS procurement system. Pearson said: 'I came here six years ago and I saw farmers producing meat and dairy, fishermen bringing in their haul every day, people growing abundant vegetables and fruit. Almost all the food needed for our hospitals was being produced here in Cornwall. Yet we were getting fish from Grimsby, tomatoes from Bristol, milk from Scotland and so on. It was incongruous.'[42]

When it was eventually formalised, the CFP had three key aims: (1) to scale up the RCHT's cook-freeze operation in order to accommodate the food supply needs of all five NHS trusts in Cornwall; (2) to increase the amount of locally and sustainably sourced food in Cornwall NHS; and (3) to address the food supply needs of all five Cornwall NHS trusts by scaling up and relocating the RCHT's cook-freeze operation to accommodate the increased capacity.[43]

Following a feasibility study, it was decided to build a Central Production Unit on a dedicated site which would provide for the needs of the entire NHS in Cornwall through a cook-freeze facility, whereby the food would be procured from local sources and cooked in a central kitchen. One of the many challenges facing the CFP was the weakness of the local supply chain, without which it was impossible to purchase more local produce. To bridge the gap between demand and supply, a sustainable food development manager was appointed in 2004, a post that was wholly funded by Organic South West (OSW), a Soil Association project jointly funded by DEFRA and the EU's regional development fund.

The strategy of a Central Production Unit serving all the NHS trusts in the region looked compelling on paper, but in practice it required all the trusts to source their food from the

Catering for health: the quest for good food

facility, an idea that ran foul of EU procurement regulations that required public contracts to be open, transparent and non-discriminatory. Other problems quickly emerged, not least the demanding targets for sourcing local organic food, which was one of the conditions for the OSW funding.

One of the perennial problems facing all sustainable food experiments in the NHS revolved around personnel change. The researchers who tracked the Cornish experiment were fully alive to this danger because they concluded their analysis on a prescient note, saying: 'The success of this project so far has to a notable extent been down to the enthusiasm and commitment of the individuals involved ... So far there has been a continuity of staffing which has contributed to the strength of the project, but there is a chance that the network could be vulnerable to a change in the personnel involved.'[44]

And so it proved. The Central Production Unit never managed to cater for all the food requirements of the NHS in Cornwall and, slowly but surely, the talented team behind the project began to fragment, as most of them were funded on a temporary basis, and the key architect of the Cornish project, Mike Pearson, eventually retired.

There is a pattern here. Every sustainable food project I've ever encountered in the NHS runs into the same gamut of problems that eventually smothered the CFP vision. If we look at the history of the Soil Association's FFLSH Award since 2009, when they were first introduced, we can recognise a familiar pattern: senior management scepticism, supply chain challenges, the spectre of prohibitive costs and the final coup de grace, the fragmentation of the team behind the local experiment. To highlight this pattern in more detail, let's look at the experience of North Bristol NHS Trust (NBT), because

Serving the public

it illustrates the scope for local experimentation as well as the limits to what can be achieved at a purely local level.

NBT has over 12,000 staff delivering healthcare across Southmead Hospital Bristol, Cossham Hospital, Bristol Centre for Enablement and within the local communities of Bristol and south Gloucestershire. It's worth remembering that its location helps to explain its food trajectory because Bristol is one of the greenest cities in the UK, being the first city to win the EU's Green Capital Award and the first city in the UK to create a Food Policy Council to promote good food throughout the city and its regional hinterland. Bristol also hosts the headquarters of the Soil Association.

But the origins of NBT's sustainable food journey began in a rather unlikely place: Clarence House in London, the home of HRH Prince Charles (or King Charles as he is now). As Patron of the Soil Association, and a lifelong champion of sustainable food and farming, Prince Charles was fond of using his 'convening power' to persuade chief executives over dinner to support his favourite causes. One of these Clarence House dinners was convened in 2007 to mark the launch of the Soil Association's report on the CFP, to which Prince Charles penned the foreword, where he said: 'I hope the lessons of this remarkable and innovative project will soon come to influence the quality of food in every hospital in the land.'[45]

One of the participants at the Clarence House dinner was the chief executive of NBT, Sonia Mills, who became enthused by the local and sustainable food agenda discussed at Clarence House. On her return she discussed the new food agenda with Simon Wood, NBT's director of Facilities and Estates, who was receptive to the new direction as he believed it was part of the zeitgeist sweeping the country and the sector.

Catering for health: the quest for good food

Already we can see that NBT avoided the problem of a sceptical senior management, the problem faced by many sustainable food experiments. As well as having a supportive chief executive, Simon Wood was also in an influential position because he was a member of NBT's main board, which at the time was very unusual in NHS management culture. But the new food strategy only began in earnest in 2008 when the head of catering, Gary Wilkins, was asked to explore the prospects for local food sourcing.

As the Soil Association was based in Bristol, Gary began working with the NGO on an FFL pilot project, which proved more difficult than he imagined. For a start, many of his traditional suppliers showed little or no interest in supplying local or sustainable products. But he eventually convinced existing wholesalers, who were already NHS accredited, that the trust was serious about procuring more local food – working within a fifty-mile radius wherever possible. The wholesalers were invaluable in finding local producers and they were also able to deal with many of the contract and accreditation requirements.

One of the early breakthroughs was a locally produced ice cream that came from Marshfield Farm near Bath. The wholesaler identified the farm and assisted in negotiations, helping the farmer to cut prices by using plain boxes and packaging. The new ice cream also proved to be a higher-quality product, with no chemical colours or flavours and the same price as the previous product. NBT staff as well as patients liked the fact that the new ice cream came from a local source near Bath, whereas the former ice cream had come through a highly circuitous route from Belgium via Bolton.

Sourcing other products that complied with FFL standards proved more challenging. Farm Assured Meat, for example, was £30,000 a year more expensive, but the catering team presented this additional cost to senior management as a worthwhile investment as it translated into just a few pence per meal, and it was largely secured from a local butcher. Procuring a jelly that was free of additives presented another challenge because 'virtually all jellies on the market were full of Es' according to Gary Wilkins. In the end he had to source an additive-free jelly from Germany.[46]

The local food pilot project at NBT had to be conducted within a strict budget – around £2 per patient per day – which convinced the catering team that it was possible to make significant changes to local sourcing through the careful benchmarking of food costs. In Gary's view, the new food strategy made catering staff more knowledgeable about local sustainability, procurement and working with seasonal produce. Because the NBT board was served the same food as the patients, the profile of the catering team within the trust increased from senior managers to front-line ward staff, all of whom showed a new interest in more localised food menus.

The new food strategy rapidly won recognition beyond the trust. In 2009, NBT achieved the FFLSH Bronze Award and in 2013 it became the first NHS Trust in the UK to win the FFLSH Silver Award. But the Silver Award proved to be the high point of NBT's sustainable food journey. The trust decided against seeking a Gold Award because buying more organic meat, a condition of the top FFLSH Award, was deemed to be too prohibitive as it would have cost an additional £250,000 a year.[47]

NBT's food journey is instructive because it illustrates the scope for local innovation, especially when the chief executive and the board are committed to sourcing and serving good

Catering for health: the quest for good food

food to patients and staff, and when the catering team are energised and empowered to deliver the strategy. But it is also a sobering story because, when the senior management team retired, the trust lost its Silver Award for the simple reason that the new team did not share the same commitment to sustainable food provisioning. Although NBT avoided some of the problems associated with the forlorn pattern of local food experiments – since its chief executive fostered the good food trajectory rather than being sceptical of it – it nevertheless fell prey to a change of personnel, which tends to be fatal for such novel experiments.

NBT is not the only hospital trust to have lost its FFLSH status. An even more dramatic example is Nottingham University Hospitals (NUH) NHS Trust, which became the first trust in the UK to achieve the FFLSH Gold Award in 2014 for serving fresh, healthy meals made with local, seasonal and organic ingredients at City Hospital and Queens Medical Centre, with a guarantee that all the food was free from harmful additives and trans fats. Chris Neale, central food production manager at NUH, said that switching to local suppliers had been a cost-neutral exercise, itself a major achievement. 'As a result', he said, 'NUH are able to provide patients, staff and visitors with quality meals at an ingredient cost price of £4.53 per patient per day – which is below the national average for patient day costs.'[48]

But the Gold Award was lost within a few years, undermined by the trust's disastrous partnership with Carillion, the UK multinational that had been awarded a £200 million facilities management contract in 2014. Within two years the trust had terminated the contract, due to poor hygiene in wards and kitchens, and then Carillion went bankrupt in spectacular fashion in 2018. Elior, the French multinational, took over the facilities management contract and NUH catering staff were transferred to the company in an outsourcing deal. But this move also proved damaging for the trust because catering workers accused the company of underpaying them, provoking a rancorous round of pay disputes and industrial action.[49]

Looking back on the local food experiments in the NHS trusts in Bristol and Nottingham, we can see that the real challenge lies not in attaining a standard of good food provisioning but of *retaining* it in the face of personnel change and organisational upheaval, when new priorities displace old priorities. The problem, in other words, is how to embed the values of sustainability in the warp and weft of the organisation, enabling the cause of good food to be something more enduring than an ephemeral priority of animated individuals who are committed to catering for health.

4

Doing time: food behind bars

Introduction

The most serious prison riot in British penal history occurred at Strangeways Prison in Manchester in April 1990 and lasted for twenty-five days. The Strangeways riot triggered rioting in at least five other prisons, resulting in fifty-one criminal trials and a public inquiry that proved to be the most thorough review of penal policy in a century. The public inquiry identified a cocktail of factors at work: oppressive behaviour on the part of some prison officers, inadequate redress for grievances, poor hygiene, a lack of clean clothes and the quality and timing of meals. Lord Woolf, who chaired the inquiry, highlighted the pervasive importance of food, saying: 'The poor quality of prison food was the most common complaint from prisoners. It was said to be monotonous, inedible, cold and insufficient in quantity … There is also a problem over the timing and serving of meals, which are often crowded into a short period.'[1]

The quality of the carceral diet turns out to be one of the perennial complaints of prisoners throughout the world. 'Food', said one prison governor, 'is one of the four things you must get

Serving the public

right if you like having a roof on your prison' (the three other things being mail, hot water and visits).[2]

It is hard to exaggerate the significance of food in prisons. Our diet affects our physical, mental and emotional well-being whoever we are and wherever we live. But eating assumes even more importance for prisoners as they may be confined to a cell for twenty odd hours a day – even during mealtimes – and meals help to punctuate a day that otherwise consists of hours of mind-numbing tedium. Eating in prison is a unique experience because prisoners have limited capacity to choose what, where and when they eat, with the result that they lose control over key aspects of their health, their self-esteem and even their sense of identity.[3]

This chapter explores the unique context of food in prisons. It begins by examining the condition of prisons and prisoners in the UK, with reference to their counterparts in the US, the two countries with the highest incarceration rates in the Global North. The following section focuses in more detail on the carceral food system and its discontents, along with the struggle to leaven prisoners' diets by serving more nutritious food and furnishing less alienating eating environments. The final section explores one of the most important social innovations in the British penal system today: the training and rehabilitation of prisoners through the medium of food service in the Clink.

Prisons and prisoners

British citizens can be forgiven for not knowing that the UK has the highest incarceration rate in western Europe because prisons and prisoners are literally invisible in public life. As prisons are a devolved matter in the UK, prison statistics are

Doing time: food behind bars

published separately for England and Wales, Scotland and Northern Ireland. As of June 2023, the UK had a total prison population of approximately 95,526 people, comprising 85,851 in England and Wales, 7,775 in Scotland and 1,900 in Northern Ireland. When these figures are expressed in terms of prisoners per 100,000 population, they reveal different rates of incarceration: 159 prisoners per 100,000 of the population in England and Wales; 162 per 100,000 in Scotland; and 97 per 100,000 in Northern Ireland. The profile of the UK prison population can be summarised as follows:

- The prison population is ageing: in 2002, 15 per cent were under the age of twnty-one compared with 4 per cent in 2023 and the number over the age of fifty went from 7 per cent in 2002 to 17 per cent in 2023.
- In 2023, 4 per cent of the prison population was female, down from 17 per cent in 1900.
- Prison sentences have been lengthening, with 56 per cent of determinate prison sentences being over four years compared with 40 per cent in 2013.
- Foreign nationals made up 12 per cent of the prison population, with Albanian, Polish and Romanian being the top three nationalities.
- People of minority ethnicities made up 27 per cent of the prison population compared with 13 per cent of the general population.
- 61 per cent of prisons in England and Wales were classified as crowded in 2023.
- The average cost per prison place was £31,476 in England and Wales in 2021–2022, £39,350 in Scotland in 2020–2021 and £44,868 in Northern Ireland in 2021–2022.

Serving the public

- The prison population in England and Wales is projected to grow to between 93,100 and 106,300 by 2027, to 7,800 in Scotland by 2022, and to 2,251 in Northern Ireland by 2022.[4]

As we can see from Exhibit 4.1, the prison population in England and Wales has grown steeply since the 1990s, a trend that seems set to continue. The projected growth in the prison population in England and Wales is one of the most worrying trends, not least because ten of the most overcrowded prisons are all in this jurisdiction. A prison is classified as overcrowded if the number of prisoners held exceeds the establishment's Certified Normal Accommodation (CNA). The CNA is the Prison Service's own measure of accommodation and represents the decent standard of accommodation that the Prison Service aspires to provide for all prisoners. As of June 2023, 61 per cent of prison establishments in England and Wales were overcrowded. In total, 'overcrowded prisons held 10,000 more prisoners than the CNA of these establishments.'[5]

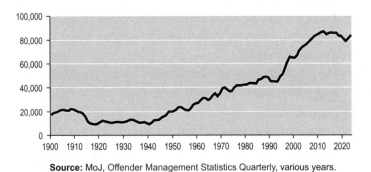

Source: MoJ, Offender Management Statistics Quarterly, various years.

Exhibit 4.1 Prison population of England and Wales since 1900 (annual average population)

Doing time: food behind bars

Up to 90 per cent of prisoners are thought to have mental health issues and many of them are also functionally illiterate, with 57 per cent of adult prisoners having literacy levels below those expected of an eleven-year-old. According to His Majesty's Chief Inspector of Prisons, Charlie Taylor, it is 'a serious indictment of the prison system that so many prisoners are no better at reading when they leave prison than when they arrived'.[6]

Reading the annual reports of the Chief Inspector of Prisons must rank as one of the most depressing reads of any official publication, a modern equivalent to reading the annual reports of the factory inspectors in the nineteenth century or the reports of the special area commissioners in the interwar period of the twentieth century. All these reports have one thing in common: they document the wretched plight of the most marginalised people and places in the country.

Take the annual report for 2021–2022 for example. Here we see the same sad catalogue of problems as its predecessors: a vicious cycle of prison overcrowding, an inability to recruit and retain staff, too many prisoners locked up in their cells for up to twenty-two hours a day, escalating rates of self-harm, poor nutrition, few opportunities for education and training, and 'purposeful activity' being the exception rather than the rule. It begins with a quote from the first annual report that documented all these problems, adding ruefully: 'It is 40 years since this passage was published in the first annual report from HM Chief Inspector of Prisons and it remains as relevant now as it did in 1982.'[7]

Frances Crook, the former chief executive of the Howard League, the prison reform charity, retired in 2021 after a thirty-five-year career devoted to reforming prisons, her life's mission. In a poignant valedictory address, she said:

Serving the public

> I will leave my work with one sad but inescapable conclusion: prisons are the last unreformed public service, stuck in the same cycle of misery and futility as when I arrived. If a time traveller from 100 years ago walked into a prison today – whether one of the inner-city Victorian prisons or the new-builds where the majority of men are held – the similarities would trump the differences. They would recognise the smells and the sounds, the lack of activity and probably some of the staff. It is not only the buildings that have stayed the same – it is the whole ethos of the institution.[8]

How does the condition of prisons and prisoners in the UK compare with other developed countries? While the UK compares unfavourably with its west European neighbours, it clearly fares better than the US, the world leader in mass incarceration. What complicates comparisons is the fact that the US system has multiple criminal justice systems, with more than two million people incarcerated in thousands of federal, state, local and tribal prisons and jails.[9]

The key feature of the US carceral system is its racialised character. While white people are under-represented, almost every other racial and ethnic group is over-represented. Racial inequalities are most acute for Black Americans, who make up 38 per cent of the incarcerated population but only 12 per cent of the residential population. Most shocking of all, perhaps, is that most Black people in prison were first arrested as youth, with over three in four (76 per cent) reporting a first arrest before age nineteen. The incarcerated population is a tragic testament to the noxious connections between adverse childhood conditions relating to housing, poverty, education, family history of incarceration and eventual incarceration in a state prison, leading to the inescapable conclusion that 'the US criminal justice system targets the least powerful people in society'.[10]

Doing time: food behind bars

Racial injustice was at the root of the most notorious prison revolt in US penal history, when prisoners rioted at the Attica Correctional Facility in New York State in September 1971. Earlier that year, prisoners had sought to improve their lot through negotiation by drawing attention to deep-seated grievances, including poor medical care, unappetising and unhealthy food and the racist and oppressive behaviour of prison officers. Having taken over the prison, the Attica uprising lasted for four days before the State Police were allowed to use gunfire and tear gas to retake the prison, resulting in thirty-nine deaths: twenty-nine prisoners and the ten guards who had been taken hostage. The immediate result was a state-sponsored cover-up of the evidence and political deception at the highest levels, involving the state governor (Nelson Rockefeller) and the White House (Richard Nixon), who claimed that the prisoners had killed the hostages by cutting their throats. It later transpired that the hostages had all been shot by the 'friendly fire' of the State Police.[11]

More than fifty years later, the Attica prison uprising remains the most potent symbol of a racialised and brutalising mass incarceration system. The historical significance of the uprising was immediately recognised in the preface of the official report, which said: 'With the exception of Indian massacres in the late nineteenth century, the State Police assault which ended the four-day prison uprising was the bloodiest one-day encounter between Americans since the Civil War.'[12]

That 'the explosion' occurred first at Attica was probably chance said the McKay Commission, but it clearly saw the uprising as a microcosm of the US carceral system because it noted ominously: 'Attica is every prison; and every prison is Attica.'[13]

Serving the public

Continuity in change is what we see in the US and the UK because their mass incarceration systems are still dealing with profoundly vulnerable people, many of whom continue to suffer from high rates of mental illness, low rates of educational attainment and impoverished lifestyles. Conditions in US and UK prisons are still doing too little today to ameliorate these problems because of chronic overcrowding and the limited opportunities for education, training and gainful employment. In addition to these well-known problems, there is the less visible but no less important problem of poor nutrition, which exacerbates mental and physical health problems to a greater extent than we might imagine.

Before we look at the carceral diet it is worth asking why the UK and the US have such high rates of incarceration compared to other developed countries. If we dig deeper than the conventional wisdom – which fixates on the role of intolerant public attitudes and a punitive right-wing media – we find more interesting and certainly more instructive perspectives involving types of welfare states and high levels of social inequality.

Countries with 'liberal' welfare states, where benefits are minimal and beneficiaries are stigmatised, tend to have high rates of incarceration, a correlation that seems to fit the cases of the US and the UK. Countries with 'corporatist' welfare states, such as Germany, France and the Netherlands, tend to have mid-range levels of incarceration, while 'social democratic' welfare states, such as Finland and Sweden, have the lowest levels of incarceration. Although there is a lively debate about the nature of causality involved in these correlations, the main claim of these researchers is that there is a strong association between a country's political economy and its penal system; so much so that the more developed the welfare state, which fosters communitarian rather than atomistic norms, the more it exhibits a less punitive penal culture.[14]

Another compelling perspective, and one that complements the political economy approach, highlights the strong association between relative income inequality, on the one hand, and a range of social problems, such as high rates of mortality, morbidity and incarceration, on the other.[15] The greater the degree of inequality, the argument runs, the higher the level of incarceration as a result of a society that is more stressful, more punitive and less cohesive. These perspectives are more persuasive when taken together. What they have in common is that they locate the source of the problems in the power dynamics of the larger society rather than seeking the primary causes in the behaviour of the individual. If the problem of mass incarceration originates in power dynamics beyond the prison gates, in other words, then so does the solution. This is confirmed by a study of the causes and consequences of prison growth in the US, which concludes by saying that any movement for reduced incarceration 'will need to develop a clear analysis of the role of politics, race, media and coalition building in order to succeed'.[16]

The carceral diet and its discontents

In the history of penal reform, the name of John Howard (1726–1790) looms large because he was one of the early pioneers. Having visited prisons in England and Wales and abroad, he published his findings in a path-breaking book, *The State of the Prisons*, in 1777. What he found horrified him. 'Many who went in healthy', he wrote, 'are in a few months changed to emaciated dejected objects.' In virtually every jail he found the same complaint, namely 'want of food'. To ease the wretched plight of prisoners, he urged the authorities to provide the bare necessities: a proper diet to support health and strength for labour.[17]

Despite Howard's humanitarian pleas, the debates around the carceral diet during the following 120 years were dominated by the principle of *less eligibility*, which cautioned that prisoners should on no account receive better-quality food than the very poorest labourers, otherwise the latter might be induced to commit crime to secure a better diet in prison. In other words, the carceral diet was *designed* to be part of the penal system, even though reformers sought to exempt it from the punishment regime. By the end of the nineteenth century, however, a new consensus had begun to emerge: the carceral diet should be sufficient to maintain health, but the authorities should be alive to 'the grave dangers which would accrue should the lowest scale be unduly attractive'.[18]

The early years of the twentieth century in the UK were known as the 'golden age of nutrition' as vitamins began to be discovered in plant foods, creating new knowledge about the links between diet and health. This set the stage for one of the twentieth century's landmark reports on the carceral diet that was published in 1925 by the Prison Commission. Among its key recommendations it said: 'Our first and most important recommendation relates to fresh vegetables. We desire to urge, as a matter of paramount importance, that every inch of available ground should be cultivated and used for the production of vegetables (more particularly of green vegetables) and of herbs for flavouring.' A nutritious diet was now deemed to be part of a prison regime to enable prisoners, at the end of their sentences, to 're-enter the world in as good a physical condition as possible'.[19]

Doing time: food behind bars

Whatever its shortcomings, the 1925 report was enlightened in two respects: (1) it championed the cause of a nutritious carceral diet as part of a prison regime designed to rehabilitate prisoners rather than merely punishing them; and (2) it advocated a localised system of in-house production of fresh vegetables to enhance the nutritional quality of the carceral diet. But, as we will see, the subsequent history of penal food policy failed to develop these enlightened recommendations.

On the procurement side of the prison food system, the main trend over the past twenty years has been to aggregate demand to negotiate better deals and create economies of scale. Following a review of its food procurement methods in 1999, the Prison Service has progressively reduced the number of its contracts, a process that has been driven by constant pressures to make cost savings in prison catering.[20]

Aggregating demand often leads to the aggregation of supply, and this is what has happened in the prison food system, where a low-cost procurement culture favours the largest food service suppliers: the likes of Compass, Sodexo and Bidfood. Prison farms have been sold off, denuding the Prison Service of the in-house food production capacity that was extolled in the enlightened Prison Commission report on diets in 1925. Bidfood holds the largest national contract to supply prisons in England and Wales, but the Ministry of Justice contract does not require the company to provide data on the provenance of the food, such as the proportions of local or organic produce.[21]

On the consumption side, successive surveys by the National Audit Office have found that the quality of prison food has steadily improved over the years, though it is difficult to generalise too much because catering budgets are devolved to individual prison governors and their commitment to healthy

Serving the public

eating is highly variable, notwithstanding the introduction of uniform standards. A major survey of food in prisons conducted by Her Majesty's Inspectorate of Prison (HMIP) in 2016 presented a much less sanguine assessment.[22] Among other things it found:

- Overall spending on food was in decline; so much so that as little as £1.87 per prisoner per day was spent. This compared to the average daily spend per patient on in-patient food service in hospitals of £9.88, which was almost five times higher.
- Only 29 per cent of prisoner survey respondents described the food they received as 'good' or 'very good' and many complained of the lack of variety of fruit and vegetables as well as insufficient food.
- Mealtimes were another source of complaint because, as dinner was served so early (4.15 pm) and breakfast was so meagre, there could be a gap of twenty hours before prisoners received another substantial meal.
- Being forced to eat in cells was deeply resented. As one prisoner commented: 'I feel no one should be forced to eat their food a couple of feet away from their toilet. Some sit on their toilet as a seat to eat. This is degrading and totally unhygienic.'

HMIP concluded its survey by saying that, while many prisons make commendable efforts given the low level of resourcing,

> too often the quantity and quality of the food provided is insufficient, and the conditions in which it is served and eaten undermine respect for prisoners' dignity. This does little to improve

Doing time: food behind bars

what for many prisoners, is a history of an unhealthy lifestyle. It also potentially jeopardises prisoner and staff safety. Food budgets are very low, and we have consistently found that this is a major barrier to improving food in prisons.[23]

The HMIP assessment resonates with prisoner feedback in *Inside Time*, the national newspaper of prisoners, where letters complaining about the quality and quantity of food are regular features. In a typical letter one prisoner said:

> To those outside of prison who think here goes another whining prisoner, it is very difficult to keep healthy in prison and on a poor diet and with very little exercise it is even more difficult. You are what you eat. I want to be as healthy as I can when leaving prison and not just for myself, I don't want to be a burden on the NHS, and I want to be a positive member of society. How can I manage any of that by eating poor quality food or very small amounts of nutrition? Can we have less carbs and more healthy stuff please.[24]

The history of the carceral diet has been a perennial struggle between cost and quality: prison governors face a daily challenge of keeping catering costs as low as possible while ensuring that prisoners receive food that is sufficiently nutritious and wholesome that it is consumed without provoking too much protest. This is a difficult balancing act because, even when the food meets the nutritional standards of the day, prisoners often choose the less healthy options on account of the dietary habits they acquired prior to prison. To illustrate some of the nutritional challenges, it is worth reflecting on two campaigns that sought to enrich the carceral diet in the UK and the US.

Serving the public

The road not taken: the Aylesbury mystery

One of the greatest nutritional experiments ever conducted in a British prison was launched at the Aylesbury Young Offenders Institution, the results of which were published to critical acclaim in 2002.[25] The aim of the study was to test empirically if physiologically adequate intakes of vitamins, minerals and essential fatty acids cause a reduction in antisocial behaviour. Such a controversial study clearly had to be based on a robust scientific methodology, and consequently the researchers opted for what is widely regarded as the gold standard – namely an experimental, double-blind, placebo-controlled, randomised trial of nutritional supplements on 231 young adult prisoners, comparing disciplinary offences before and during supplementation.

The results were truly remarkable and sent shock waves through the criminal justice system. Compared to the placebo-controlled group, prisoners whose diets were supplemented committed an average of 26.3 per cent fewer offences, while the most violent offences decreased by 37 per cent. These results appeared even more remarkable when compared to the placebo results, which showed no notable changes in behaviour. Despite the significance of the results, the researchers concluded their study on a modest note, saying: 'This research strongly suggests that the effect of diet on antisocial behaviour has been underestimated and more attention should be paid to offenders' diets.'[26]

Although the results were largely replicated in similar trials in California and the Netherlands, the Home Office remained highly sceptical, despite the fact that its own independent assessor said: 'This is the only trial I have ever been involved with

Doing time: food behind bars

from the social sciences which is designed properly and with a good analysis', a verdict that was amplified by other eminent scientists.

Further support was offered by the deputy governor of Aylesbury Young Offenders Institution, Trevor Hussey, who was personally responsible for implementing the nutrition study. Although he admitted to some scepticism at the outset, he said it was difficult to remain sceptical as the study progressed because 'the particular decrease in offending among the group receiving the dietary supplements could not be ignored. Something significant did seem to be occurring ... From a prison governor's perspective, the results of the trial do seem to demonstrate the link between diet and behaviour. The experience at Aylesbury demonstrated that.'[27]

Although it reluctantly conceded the need for a follow-up study, which failed to materialise as planned, the Home Office never showed any enthusiasm to act on the revolutionary findings of the Aylesbury study, hence the mystery.

At least three explanations have been used to explain the mystery since the Aylesbury results were published in 2002. First, there is the punitive factor, a modern equivalent of the less eligibility principle: that prisoners are simply undeserving of special treatment because poor diets are common in society and the penal system, faced with declining catering budgets, has no incentive to provide above-average nutritional care. Second, there is the overt political explanation which prison reformers describe as the 'enormous amount of resistance to any effort to improve prisons, in part because of simple-minded, "get tough on crime" politics'.[28]

But there is a third explanation for the lack of official action which is more profound in its societal implications because it challenges the conceptual foundations of the way the criminal justice system frames volition and culpability. Drawing on the Aylesbury study, Bernard Gesch, the principal author of the study, and Lord David Ramsbotham, the former chief inspector of prisons, called for a total rethink of the real causes of crime because the criminal justice system presumes that behaviour is entirely a matter of free will, a presumption that makes it easy to establish culpability.

However, in a provocative but prescient article, 'Crime and Nourishment', they posed a question that seriously irked the criminal justice system: what happens if there are factors – such as poor nutrition– that affect behaviour without even the offender's knowledge? Nutrition, they argued, will 'interact with important social factors such as poverty, stress, the fragmentation of family, but unless we know better, we will interpret these events entirely in terms of what we can see. Yet physiological factors may be important in understanding tragic and irrational acts which defy a rational explanation. Nutrition is not the only explanation of antisocial behaviour, but it might form a significant part.'[29]

Far from being mutually exclusive, these three interpretations provide a more credible explanation of the Aylesbury mystery when they are combined because each offers an important reason as to why the Home Office failed to act on the findings of a social experiment that had manifestly reduced the violent behaviour of young prisoners. Apart from alleviating the human costs on malnourished prisoners, the Home Office could have also secured major financial savings had they acted on the Aylesbury findings. When the Home Office learned that the financial cost of the nutritional approach was estimated to be just £3.5 million per year to reduce violent behaviour across

Doing time: food behind bars

the entire prison estate, they privately conceded that 'they had nothing as remotely cost efficient'.[30]

The Aylesbury study continues to resonate today because it was the first study to demonstrate the causally significant links between nutritional deficiencies and antisocial behaviour among prisoners. Although the health consequences of ultra-processed diets are becoming all too visible in some respects – such as obesity rates – we are only beginning to appreciate the implications of diet for brain chemistry, mental health, cognition and behaviour. The Aylesbury researchers used food supplements because it allowed the use of a placebo control group and because the nutrient content of food supplements could be defined with precision. For the principal researcher, however, food supplements were simply a proxy for a better diet and the main implication of the study was the need for the Prison Service to enhance the nutritional quality of prison food.[31]

Although the Aylesbury study is more than twenty years old, it continues to inspire researchers working on the causal linkages between nutrition, health and behaviour.[32] But then as now, researchers face a common problem in the form of official indifference to their work. 'Hardly anyone', writes Kimberley Wilson, 'especially those in positions of power and influence, is paying attention to the clear link between what we eat, how we feel, and who we are ... Some researchers have been ringing the early warning alarm bell on food and the brain for 50 years. It's time we started listening.'[33]

But the carceral diet may be the last public plate to benefit from any improvements in the quality of public sector catering for the simple reason that prisoners, given their marginal social status, are deemed unworthy of good food. As one compelling analysis said of the carceral diet: 'It is the principle of less-eligibility which endures, as if enjoyment of food is tantamount to a travesty of social justice.'[34]

Food as punishment: the nutraloaf controversy

It's difficult to compare prison food systems in the UK and the US, not least because the American system is so fragmented across federal, state and local jurisdictions. But if prisoner satisfaction is the yardstick, then the US lags way behind the UK in terms of the quality of the carceral diet. Although the size of the prison population is so much larger in the US, this alone cannot explain the poor quality of its prison food. A more important explanation is the way that mass incarceration has been accompanied by the industrialisation, concentration and standardisation of the American prison food system, all of which is designed to reduce costs through economies of scale. A brief history of this process is illustrated in Exhibit 4.2.

Mass incarceration and mass production are two sides of the same coin, evolving together to the benefit of large firms and to the detriment of prison diets. Although only 9 per cent of the incarcerated population in the US is housed in private prisons, many more are served meals that are provided by a small number of large companies, the most important being Aramark, Trinity, Compass and Sodexo. While some states have outsourced their food service to these companies, others have maintained the service in-house to retain control over both costs and quality and to avoid the food service crisis that engulfed Michigan, which hired Aramark in 2013 on the promise of $16 million in annual savings (mostly achieved by replacing unionised state employees with contract workers). The results were disastrous: kitchens regularly ran out of ingredients,

Doing time: food behind bars

A brief history of prison food in the United States

Early 20th century

The emerging science of nutrition leads to a more diversified diet and standard portions in many prisons. Prison plantations (large farms worked by incarcerated people for little or no pay) spread across the south – a practice that continues to serve as a source of food for prisons today – as convict leasing is phased out.

Mid 20th century

Individual prisons have near complete control over what to buy, cook and serve, with quality ranging from meals that are relatively good – in the otherwise notorious Alcatraz prison, for example – to those that are inedible. Instead of withholding food, prisons are more likely to intentionally overfeed people to make them lethargic and docile, and more compliant.

1970s

Towards the middle of the decade, the shift to a punative mindset emphasizing retribution over rehabilitation coincides with the beginning of mass incarceration and the routine dehumanisation of incarcerated people. State departments of correction begin to centralise food procurement and menu planning to follow nutritional guidelines and control costs.

Late 20th century to present

With well over one million people to feed every day, state prison systems allocate fewer resources per person, rely heavily or exclusively on factory-produced and ultra-processed food, and in many cases outsource food service to large corporations – policies and practices that produce the declines in food quality, quantity and essential nutrition that are documented in this series. Poor nutrition and a degrading relationship with food compromise the health and well-being of individuals while they're incarcerated and often long after their release, consequences that disproportionately affect people of colour and the low-income communities to which they return.

Source: L. Soble et al. (2020) *Eating behind Bars: Ending the Hidden Punishment of Food in Prison*, Impact Justice, impactjustice.org.

Exhibit 4.2 Mass production for mass incarceration

meals were routinely served late and lacked the required calories and prisoners were served rotten food, provoking maggot infestations and outbreaks of food-borne illness.[35]

But unhealthy food is not the preserve of the private food service companies. Many state-run correctional services are equally guilty of serving ultra-processed meals that undermine the health of the prisoners in their care. Washington State, for example, is widely cited as a microcosm of the nutritional crisis in state prisons throughout the country. Thirty years ago, Washington State's Department of Corrections (DOC) could legitimately take pride in its food services menu, which at that time was not fundamentally different from ordinary household food. Prisons grew their own food and maintained dairies and bakeries, and the food was cooked locally.

But this traditional model of food provisioning changed radically after 1995, when the food service was centralised, industrialised and transferred to Correctional Industries, the DOC's state-owned business arm. In the following years,

> it substituted 95 per cent industrialized, plastic-wrapped, sugar-filled 'food products' for locally prepared healthy food. This has resulted in a vast state-sponsored food desert, with drastic reductions in fresh produce, lean protein, and whole grains in the diet of incarcerated people. This unhealthy diet encourages disadvantaged populations to eat poorly, disproportionately impacts the health of people of color, and leads to increased health-care expenditures on preventable diseases such as diabetes, hypertension, and heart disease.[36]

The food justice movement in the US has highlighted the perverse economics of this relentless drive to serve ever cheaper food. Considering the additional costs of serving poor-quality food, campaigners have shown that this policy is fiscally perverse

Doing time: food behind bars

because the $2.1 billion that is collectively spent on food costs in the mass incarceration system is dwarfed by the £12.3 billion spent on health costs.[37] These additional costs would also need to include the security costs of prisoner protests. A dramatic example occurred in September 2016, when tens of thousands of prisoners staged a coordinated strike around the country to mark the 45th anniversary of the riot at Attica prison. One of the common demands of the national prisoner protest, as it was at Attica in 1971, was the demand for 'a balanced and proper diet'.[38]

The nutraloaf controversy needs to be understood in the context of growing protests about the quality of the carceral diet, especially when food is weaponised as a disciplinary tool. Food has been used to discipline and punish prisoners throughout the history of prisons, ranging from the withholding of food to the use of parsimonious bread-and-water rations. Nutraloaf is arguably the most egregious example of food as punishment in the US carceral system and, not surprisingly, it's the subject of burgeoning litigation efforts as prisoners try to render it unconstitutional under the Eighth Amendment.[39]

Although the nutraloaf recipe varies from state to state, it is essentially an amalgam of totally unrelated foods – for example blended bread, pineapples, potatoes, non-dairy cheese, beans, fruits and vegetables baked into a loaf – and it is universally regarded as a repulsive concoction. Nutraloaf is usually given to prisoners as punishment for misbehaviour and it is often the only item on the menu for prisoners held in solitary confinement. Several lawsuits have challenged the use of nutraloaf, many claiming that it caused vomiting, diarrhoea, gastrointestinal bleeding and distress, significant weight loss and other adverse health outcomes. The fact that the American Correctional Association discourages it, and fourteen states have already banned it, illustrates that the use of nutraloaf is a totally unethical practice. For all these reasons, prison reformers argue that the use of nutraloaf runs counter to the Eighth Amendment of the US Constitution, which prohibits 'cruel and unusual punishments'.

As Jackie Cuellar has shown, the current framework for assessing Eighth Amendment claims in confinement conditions utilises a two-part test in which the plaintiff is required to show that: (1) conditions were objectively cruel and unusual and (2) the corrections staff acted with the requisite subjective intent of deliberate indifference to serious harm or injury. This two-part test sets a high bar for plaintiffs who allege Eighth Amendment violations because they must first show that they suffered a deprivation that is sufficiently serious, satisfying the objective prong; then they must also demonstrate that the official responsible for imposing that deprivation acted with a sufficiently culpable state of mind of deliberate indifference, satisfying the subjective prong. While many prisoners have brought legal challenges regarding the quality of food in prisons, the vast majority are unsuccessful, leaving correctional facilities with few incentives to improve the prison food service.

As an example of a hostile judicial system, Cuellar cites the famous nutraloaf case of *LeMaire v Maas* in 1993, where the court stated that the Eighth Amendment requires that prisoners need only 'receive food that is adequate to maintain health; it need not be tasty or aesthetically pleasing'. Despite a history of hostile court judgements that have all deemed nutraloaf to be constitutional, Cuellar concludes her review by arguing that the judicial system is increasingly out of tune with changing professional and public attitudes. To prove her point, she cites mounting evidence from social psychologists and corrections experts who claim that nutraloaf is an ineffective punitive measure that

Doing time: food behind bars

does not promote safety in prisons; public attitudes also strongly support criminal justice reform and alternatives to mass incarceration, while human rights organisations say that the use of nutraloaf is 'a disgusting, torturous form of punishment that should have been banned a century ago'.[40]

Growing opposition to the use of nutraloaf has led to it being banned in at least fourteen states. Even so, to focus exclusively on nutraloaf because it is the most egregious example of food as punishment runs the risk of diverting attention from the punishing effects of the *mainstream* carceral diet in US prisons, which is summarised in Exhibit 4.3.

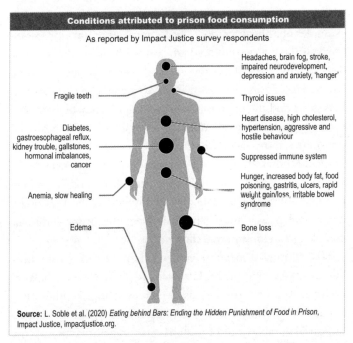

Exhibit 4.3 The punishing effects of the mainstream carceral diet

Serving the public

Prison abolitionists are the most radical critics of the mainstream carceral diet, arguing that there can be no real food justice within the carceral system. They make an important distinction between reformist and non-reformist reforms: while the former take the current carceral system for granted, the latter aim to transcend the system by abolishing the prison-industrial complex. Mass incarceration is facilitated, they argue, by *carceral nutrition*, 'ideologies of food and eating that reduce complex relations of nourishment to biopolitical calculations of nutrition in the interests of discipline, punishment, control, and confinement'.[41]

Inspired by the abolitionist ideas of Angela Davis and Ruth Wilson Gilmore, the prison abolition movement is changing the climate of opinion by refusing to focus on particular examples of unhealthy food – be it nutraloaf or ultra-processed breakfast boats – and instead advocates a focus on the systemic discrimination that links the carceral diet, mass incarceration and racialised American capitalism. Its agenda for the abolition of prisons and the prison-industrial complex may be idealistic, even utopian, but its compelling analysis is inspiring a non-reformist reform agenda in the here and now.[42] For example, 'instead of advocating for "kinder, gentler" prisons – even in the short term – we ask how addressing the role of food in confinement can ultimately advance an abolitionist vision that builds communal power and helps tear down the prison-industrial complex in all of its manifestations'.[43]

Like all radical social movements, however, the prison abolitionist movement in the US needs to strike a better balance between its long-term agenda, which aims to substitute more benign community-based solutions for the punitive prison-industrial complex, and the short-term imperative to improve the quality of the carceral diet because, as well as being

Doing time: food behind bars

dehumanising, daily exposure to ultra-processed food imposes lifelong health problems.

Serving time: rehabilitation through food service

Prison regimes vary enormously with respect to where they sit on the spectrum between retribution and rehabilitation: in democratic societies the prevailing stereotypes would suggest that the US sits closer to the former, while Norway is closer to the latter, with the UK occupying an intermediate position. While these stereotypes contain a good deal of truth, they also conceal as much as they reveal because they elide the internal nuances within each country. In this final section I try to tease out these nuances by focusing on the social innovations that are underway in UK and US prisons, where sustainable food projects are being used to infuse dignity and hope in prisoners who plan to find gainful employment on release.

As we might expect, there's a strong correlation between low-quality rehabilitation regimes and high rates of recidivism or reoffending. In England and Wales, 49.2 per cent of prisoners reoffend within a year of release, compared to a reoffending rate of just 20 per cent in Norway and 52 per cent in the United States.[44] High rates of incarceration and recidivism impose enormous burdens on the public purse, to say nothing of the human costs involved. In the case of the UK, for example, the total economic and social cost of reoffending has been estimated to be as high as £18.1 billion a year.[45]

Although prisons are duty bound to provide some form of *purposeful activity*, in the form of work, education or training for example, the reality leaves much to be desired, as we saw earlier. The reason why prison regimes in the UK and the US are unable to deliver purposeful activity is because they are mired in a vicious cycle of prison overcrowding, chronic staff shortages and a carceral culture that sets a low premium on rehabilitation.

Chinks of light in the US carceral system

Despite these vicious systemic pressures, social innovations can and do emerge, and this is invariably down to the talent and tenacity of local institutional leadership taking advantage of chinks of light in the hierarchical carceral system. One of the most celebrated examples of local innovation in the US carceral system is in the state of Maine. According to Impact Justice, the Maine DOC is at the leading edge of better practice, not least because it gives facility food service managers considerable local autonomy over menu planning and food purchasing, which is perhaps easier to do in Maine because it has one of the smallest prison systems in the country, with just six facilities and some 3,000 prisoners.[46]

The leading-edge facility is the Mountain View Correctional Facility in Maine, where Mark McBrine, the food service manager, has spent years cultivating relationships with local producers to source grains, dairy, eggs and other products at locally agreed prices. An organic farmer himself and a veteran of the hospitality industry, McBrine's work demonstrates that a willingness to innovate and advocate for better food not only benefits people in prison, by boosting health and morale, but also pays off economically. In recent years, Mountain View's kitchen has averaged over 30 per cent local food purchases while coming in more than $100,000 under budget. These local innovations were rendered possible by regulatory reform at the state level, where two significant changes occurred. The first change came in 2014, when the state of Maine passed

Doing time: food behind bars

legislation to increase the consumption of Maine food in its state institutions, such as universities, hospitals and correctional facilities, and this bill also established a minimum percentage of Maine foods that must be purchased by 2026.

The second change came in 2019 with the arrival of a new commissioner of corrections, Randall Liberty, who was personally committed to local food sourcing and food-based training as a form of rehabilitation, a professional commitment inspired by his personal experience of growing up with an incarcerated parent and being a master gardener and beekeeper. He used his position as commissioner not only to expand the gardening programmes but also to increase the amount of food that all state prisons are required to purchase from local producers to serve fresh, whole foods to prisoners, saying: 'Our job is about rehabilitation, redemption, and getting busy healing those wounds. Our job is to reduce the frequency of future victims. Our job is to help these men and women back to society.'[47] These are not the words we normally associate with the US carceral system.

Social innovations in the prison regime are also underway in California. One of Governor Gavin Newsom's key campaign pledges was to transform California's incarceration system from a punishment regime to a rehabilitation system, a reform inspired by the Norwegian prison ethos. The state's most notorious prison, San Quentin, is being converted from a maximum-security prison into a rehabilitation and education facility and renamed the San Quentin Rehabilitation Center. Announcing the policy shift, Newsom said: 'We hope this will be a model for the nation, a model for the world. This is about stretching people's minds about what we're capable of doing and reducing recidivism in the state.'[48]

Rehabilitation schemes – involving gardens, food growing and a host of liberal arts programmes – are encouraging signs of change, but they are dwarfed by the chastening challenges in California, where the massive prison system was famously branded a 'Golden Gulag' on account of its punitive environment.[49]

The Clink model of rehabilitation

One of the boldest social innovations ever undertaken in the UK prison system is the Clink Integrated Rehabilitation Programme (CIRP), which aims to design and deliver accredited training to prisoners in the food and hospitality sectors within prisons *and* after their release. The original concept of the Clink restaurant was created by Albert Crisci in 2009, when he was the catering manager at HMP High Down in England. A highly unusual catering manager in the prison environment, Crisci earned a national reputation when he won the coveted Cook of the Year prize in the annual BBC Food and Farming Awards in 2005. He used his newly acquired celebrity status to launch the first prisoner-run restaurant within a prison, the aim being to help inmates acquire accredited skills and to reduce high rates of recidivism. The following year the Clink charity was created to develop and extend the concept to other prisons throughout the UK to ensure it did not remain a purely local innovation.

The CIRP model involves an integrated programme of training and support which is illustrated in Exhibit 4.4. One of the unique features of this model is the emphasis placed on 'through-the-gate' support: the critically important post-release period when employment opportunities and new social networks need to be in place to help trainees make a successful

Doing time: food behind bars

Training and qualifications

The Clink charity delivers a structured, integrated and unique training model that focuses on through-the-gate support for all students, starting from three months before release and ending, on average, around twelve months after release from prison.

People in prison volunteer to be trained in a Clink project and will be considered once they have completed all other restorative courses during their sentence. Students are registered to train and work towards gaining their City & Guilds National Vocational Qualifications in a real-life working environment that doesn't look or feel like a prison. Chef and garden trainer assessors guide students through their training and rehabilitation alongside resettlement support workers who aid each student on an individual basis, helping them to reintegrate back into society.

The charity works with multiple local and national employers who are willing to employ Clink graduates based on satisfactory interviews. The support workers encourage students and graduates by advising on employment, including best interview practice and writing CVs as well as ensuring they have simple logistics in place such as accommodation, bank accounts and strong links into their probation service.

Clink works in partnership with City and Guilds and delivers their qualification training courses.

City and Guilds National Vocational Qualifications delivered by The Clinic:
- Food and Beverage Service levels 1 and 2
- Food Preparation and Cookery levels 1 and 2
- Diploma Food Production and Cooking level 2
- Food safety level 2
- Barista level 2
- Diploma in Horticulture levels 1 and 2
- Level 2 General Patisserie and Confectionary
- Level 2 Professional Patisserie and Confectionary

Source: The Clink Charity (2023) *Funders Update*, London: The Clink Charity, p. 3.

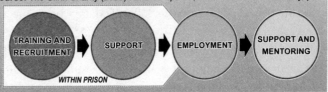

Exhibit 4.4 The Clink Integrated Rehabilitation Programme

transition from life in prison to life in society, thereby reducing the incentive to reoffend. The Clink's full-time support workers provide an intensive package of support before and after release into the community, including help with accommodation, debts, substance misuse, employment, budgeting and life skills.

Although the COVID-19 pandemic arrested the development of the Clink network, the charity managed to extend its activities across a wide range of projects, from restaurants to gardens, kitchens and events. At the end of 2022, the first Clink bakery was opened in HMP Brixton, where two chef trainer pâtissiers were recruited to train the first students in specialist patisserie and baking qualifications. Despite two years of lockdown, the charity still managed to train 500 people in 2022 and, thanks to its support staff, 72 per cent of all Clink graduates were placed into employment, compared with just 16 per cent of the prison population overall.[50]

A cost–benefit analysis found that the Clink delivered at least a fourfold return on investment based on the following analysis:

- *Impact*: the rate of proven reoffending among Clink graduates is lower than a comparable control group, at 0.46 reoffences per individual versus 0.63 in the comparison group, for the period 2010–2016, the full period for which data are available.
- *Societal benefit*: the reduction in reoffending can be converted to estimates of economic and social benefit. Using Home Office figures on the costs of crime, the saving from the reduction of reoffending was estimated as at least £111,000 per reoffence. When combined with the reoffending reduction impact from

Doing time: food behind bars

the Clink, this converts to an estimate of 'per individual benefit' of at least £18,900.
- *Costs of running the scheme*: using management accounts from the Clink, the costs of running the scheme work out at £3,900 per individual.[51]

Considering that every cost–benefit analysis leaves some room for debate – especially regarding the counterfactuals associated with what would have happened in the absence of the intervention – there seems to be a rare consensus among all political parties about the positive impact of the Clink. Despite the consensus, however, successive Conservative governments have been unwilling to put the Clink on a sustainable financial footing, even though it would help to reduce the UK's annual £18.1 billion reoffending bill. Time and again, says Yvonne Thomas, the Clink's chief executive, 'the government refuses to fund a sensible, provably effective solution to a problem in society that it says it cares about'.[52]

As things stand, the Clink's funding model comes largely from charitable donations, foundations and revenue from its restaurants, with just 15 per cent from government grants. The fact that the government is not more supportive of the Clink suggests that the punitive principle of less eligibility continues to cast its shadow over the contemporary prison regime, even though it stymies a rehabilitation programme that has demonstrated its worth in reducing the costs of recidivism. Current capacity constraints mean that the Clink has the resources to train around 750 prisoners a year, a modest number that makes little impression on a prison population that is predicted to be more than 100,000 in England and Wales by 2027.

Serving the public

Apart from the funding constraint, the growth potential of the Clink also depends on finding fully engaged operational leaders in each prison, where the two key players are the prison governor and the catering manager. The governor needs to be fully committed to the programme, otherwise trainees can be moved without notice to other prisons, with the result that their training is terminated. In some prison kitchens the Clink's curriculum is not integrated into the production process and attempts to nudge the kitchen culture away from mass pre-prepared food has been resisted by the catering manager. But to deliver proper training, the Clink insists that 'students need to cook not simply heat up prepared meals'.[53]

Prison governors can make or break the best-laid plans of the Clink charity – as the premature closure of the Clink restaurant at HMP Cardiff demonstrated. After a highly successful decade, Cardiff's Clink restaurant was unceremoniously closed in 2022, ostensibly because the prison wanted to use the space for other purposes. The closure was a blow to the charity and the city because it was the largest single training site in the Clink network and one of the highest-rated restaurants in Cardiff. But it was also a blow to the prisoners themselves because, according to the first ever ethnographic study of a Clink restaurant, the Clink at HMP Cardiff helped 'the boys' in multiple ways. Among other things, it helped them develop their human and social capital, it supported their family ties and its through-the-gate support in the community was widely considered to be 'the best of the best'.[54]

The Clink charity is one of a number of food-focused social innovations in UK prisons. Other initiatives include Food Matters, Food Behind Bars and Think Through Nutrition.

The Food Matters Inside and Out Programme aims to change food systems and enable prisoners to make healthier

Doing time: food behind bars

food choices through a prison-wide approach. It has been piloted at HMP Wandsworth and HMP High Down and facilitates participatory healthy eating courses and cooking workshops, peer mentor 'Food Champions', staff training sessions and consultancy to catering and food procurement services.

Food Behind Bars uses professional chefs who work with catering managers and people in prison to improve the food in prisons and provide employment training, for example developing an existing in-house bakery with catering staff at HMP Wealstun and teaching cooking skills to men in the wing kitchens at HMP Manchester.

Think Through Nutrition translates nutritional research into clear information and seeks to empower individuals to think about their nutrition and make positive changes by understanding the importance of a healthy diet and how nutrition impacts the brain. It has developed a digital educational pilot programme which will be delivered to 5,000 people in prison at HMP Berwyn, HMP Wayland, HMP Newhall and HMP Askham Grange in 2024.[55]

The impact of all these initiatives is limited by the fact that funding is typically localised, short lived and project based. The lack of continuity and longevity means that 'there is not sufficient momentum to progress our collective understanding of the benefits that a greater focus on food and nutrition could offer to people in prison, to prison environments and for prison reform'.[56]

To overcome this constraint, the Clink aims to generate more of its funding from commercial activities, especially through its large events business and by securing prison food contracts. These commercial activities will be complemented by its work in education, training and mentoring, all of which will need to

Serving the public

be supported through a combination of external and internal reforms.

Externally, the key challenge is how to put the Clink programme of training and rehabilitation on a sustainable financial footing. If the UK government refuses to help the Clink meet this challenge, then it is being doubly negligent: not only is it failing to discharge its *ethical* duty of care to prisoners who are paying their dues to society but it is also abdicating its *fiscal* duty to reduce the costs of a burgeoning carceral system.

Internally, the Clink's culinary ethos needs to infuse the mainstream food culture within each prison so that all prisoners can take advantage of the multiple benefits of the good food revolution. Since most prisoners will eventually be released into civil society, the Clink's innovative model of community support should inspire prisons to engage more effectively with their host localities to create employment opportunities for the men and women who, having served their time, need a little help to redeem themselves.

Part III

Foodscapes of hope

5
The Good Food movement

Introduction

Having looked at the prospects for good food in the public sector, this chapter shifts the focus from institutions to *places* by looking at local interventions to reform the food system in various localities in the UK and the US. What I think emerges is an extraordinary story of a social movement that has never received the attention it deserves. When all its component parts are considered together, the Good Food movement is far larger than we think. From the standpoint of progressive food politics, this story contains two instructive messages. The first, an encouraging message, is that there is a tremendous appetite for reform on the part of localities throughout the UK and the US, and the rapid growth of the movement is one of the most tangible signs of this public mood. It is where civic energy and municipal activism meet that this appetite for change has been most successfully mobilised, when the good food issue becomes a prominent item on the local political agenda.

The second message is more discouraging, because it highlights the fragility of local food policy groups. In both the UK and the US, many of these local groups are operating with scant resources and are desperately short of finance and (paid) staff. Although the lack of financial autonomy is a serious barrier to progress, this problem need not be fatal if local groups can forge national networks to share resources and if they can form public–social partnerships in their localities with municipal governments and health boards with a view to generating revenue streams from the delivery of good food services to deprived areas for example, which have been ruthlessly targeted by the fast food industry.

There is a great irony here. While local food groups are struggling to survive on the margins of financial viability – many of them highly reliant on charities and foundations – they are nevertheless addressing some of the greatest societal challenges of the twenty-first century insofar as their good food interventions are on the front line when it comes to combating climate change, food insecurity and the double burden of malnutrition. In this chapter I examine the scope and limits of these local food policy alliances in the UK and the US.

A quiet revolution

A quiet revolution is underway in the Anglo-American world and its aim is pure and simple: to make good food more readily available and affordable to all. The unassuming agents of this revolution come from many walks of life and collectively they constitute a rapidly growing social movement: the Good Food movement. In the broadest sense of the term, they are *consumers* who are becoming ever more conscious of how and where their food is produced. They are *public health professionals* who want to see more nutritious food served in public institutions

The Good Food movement

and retail stores. They are *campaigners* who want to reform the conventional food system to replace it with a fairer, healthier and more sustainable system. They also include *municipal leaders* who want their towns and cities to foster health and well-being rather than the obesogenic environments that so many places have become today.

Curiously, the scale of this social movement has never been fully registered in political circles. We have failed to recognise the significance of food, says Carolyn Steel, 'because it is too big to see'. But when it is viewed laterally, she says, 'it emerges as something with phenomenal power to transform not just landscapes, but political structures, public spaces, social relationships, cities'.[1]

The fragmentation of the food system is another reason why the scale of this social movement has eluded us. Yet if all the food-based movements across the globe were stripped of their single-issue status and assigned a common designation – such as the Good Food movement – the latter would probably be the largest social movement in the world today. But most food-based movements are dedicated to a single purpose, such as hunger relief, urban agriculture, sustainable diets, economic regeneration, land access, fair trade, organic food, local food, animal welfare, school meals, food sovereignty, food worker rights, climate change mitigation, agroecology and so forth. The single-issue focus of these movements helps to explain why we often fail to recognise that food is the common denominator of so much social and political activity around the world, particularly at the local level.[2]

In towns and cities in the Global North, the visibility of the food system has been further obscured by a curious omission in the municipal landscape. The essentials of everyday life – air, water, shelter and food – have all been addressed by urban

Serving the public

planners with the conspicuous exception of food. This was the 'puzzling omission' that provoked the American Planning Association (APA) to produce a radically new policy guide on Community and Regional Food Planning in 2007, a belated attempt to make amends for the fact that the planning community, academics and professionals alike had signally failed to engage with the food system. The APA's epiphany was triggered by the work of two pioneering planning experts, Kami Pothukuchi and Jerry Kaufman, who had concluded that the food system was 'a stranger to the planning field'.[3]

Whatever the reasons for it, the 'puzzling omission' is now merely a matter of historical interest because the food system has become an important and legitimate part of the urban planning agenda in developed and developing countries alike. Planners now find themselves addressing multiple food policy issues for one very simple reason: their political masters have been forced to treat food policy more seriously because of the *new food equation*. The new food equation refers to a confluence of new and highly complex developments, the most important of which are the following:

- *The food price surge of 2007–2008*, when global wheat prices nearly doubled and rice prices nearly tripled, forcing hitherto secure social classes into food insecurity, a condition which already afflicts some two billion people. The full Russian invasion of Ukraine in 2022 fuelled another food price surge.
- *Food security has become a national security issue* after the food price surge triggered food riots in more than sixty countries around the world, forcing the G8 leaders to convene their first ever Food Summit in 2009.

The Good Food movement

- *Climate change effects*, in the form of water and heat stress, damaged ecosystems and rising sea levels, for example, are expected to be worse in the poorest countries, the very countries that have done least to cause the problem of global warming, and the food system is responsible for about a third of global GhG emissions.
- *The epidemic of obesity and other diet-related diseases* makes the food system a prime target for campaigners who want to transform healthcare from a treatment service to a health-promoting and prevention service.
- *Food poverty* is increasingly visible in the cities of the Global North, as we can see from the explosive growth of food banks, making food a social justice issue as well as a human and planetary health issue.
- *Land conflicts are escalating* as rich but food-stressed countries (e.g. Saudi Arabia and South Korea) seek to buy up fertile land in Africa and Asia to ensure their own food security, fuelling charges of a new colonialism.
- *Rapid urbanisation* means that cities are becoming more conscious about how they feed themselves because, given their sensitivity to food shortages, they are the most politically combustible areas in every country.[4]

One of the most dramatic developments in food politics in the Anglo-American world over the past twenty-five years has been the growing visibility of local governments and their civic partners – in towns, cities and other localities – in public debates about food system reform. As national governments have been unable or unwilling to address the noxious effects of the industrial food system, and the obesogenic environments it has spawned, *subnational* actors have been forced to fill the

Serving the public

vacuum, being compelled to act as they are on the front line of dealing with these effects. This signals a big shift because the food policy landscape has hitherto been the exclusive preserve of a tightly knit corporatist alliance of nationally based players – governments, farmers, processors and manufacturers – an alliance with a strong producer bias. But the advent of the Good Food movement suggests that the traditional corporatist food agenda is coming under pressure from new players who are trying to fashion a more holistic and more sustainable foodscape in which consumption, public health, ecological integrity and social justice are the primary concerns. At the heart of the Good Food movement is a network of local alliances that fuses municipal activism with civic engagement, an alliance that is dedicated to reframing the foodscape for the sake of people and planet.[5]

Municipal governments in Europe and North America have struggled to accommodate a food policy function for many reasons. Apart from falling outside the conventional municipal policy repertoire, food policy had no obvious departmental home, given the multidimensional nature of food, so the question often arose as to where it should be located and who should take the lead. One of the most inspirational food policy activists that I ever worked with was the late Wayne Roberts, the former director of the Toronto Food Policy Council, who resolved this conundrum by showing that a food policy perspective could contribute to virtually *every* municipal department because 'the choices we make around food affect the shape, style, pulse, smell, look, feel, health, economy, street life, and infrastructure of the city ... Given the over-arching importance of food in urban life, planners need to put food closer to the top of their planning menu.'[6]

The Good Food movement

Crafting place-based food alliances is rarely a smooth or seamless endeavour, however, because the bureaucratic culture of municipal governments and the activist grassroots culture of civil society groups are so radically different. But there seems to have been something of a rapprochement between the two sides since the turn of the millennium as many civil society groups shifted their tactics from contesting the local state to collaborating with it in jointly created food policy councils or partnerships. As we will see in the following sections, the form of these food-based alliances varies a good deal from one place to another, reflecting local political relationships and local food priorities. Let's begin by focusing on the Good Food movement in the UK before exploring the US scene.

The Good Food movement in the UK

For more than a century the only food voices that seemed to command attention from the mainstream media and the political class were from the agrifood industry – farmers, processors and manufacturers – and the government department responsible for food and farming. A radically new voice emerged with the advent of local food movements, perhaps the most distinctive feature of the UK food policy landscape in the past twenty-five years.

A combination of global and local factors triggered the growth of these place-based food movements. Globally, Local Agenda 21 was a product of the 1992 Earth Summit in Rio and it sought to encourage locally based initiatives to promote sustainable development. Locally in the UK, the noxious effects of the industrial food system were becoming ever more apparent in the form of diet-related diseases and ecological damage.

Although these local food movements emerged slowly and unevenly across the country, around ninety of them are now affiliated to the Sustainable Food Places (SFP) network, the main forum for local food movements in the UK today. To give a flavour of what they are and what they do, let's look at Brighton and Bristol, two of the most prominent local food partnerships in the UK and (thus far) the only winners of the SFP Gold Award for their contributions to the good food cause.

Brighton and Bristol: pioneers of the Good Food movement

Conceived in 2003, the Brighton & Hove Food Partnership (BHFP) owes its origins to the combined efforts of three distinct organisations: civil society groups that wanted to see a more localised and sustainable food system, the health promotion unit of the local NHS trust and the city council's Sustainability Commission. Following a series of public engagement exercises, the Spade to Spoon food strategy was launched in the summer of 2006. The opening sentence captured the main focus of the strategy when it referred to 'our health and our environment' as the two dominant themes that were chosen to frame the local food strategy. Equally significant, the audience to which it was addressed was quite consciously broad and inclusive and in no way confined to the stereotype of middle-class locavores. Spade to Spoon, it announced, 'aims to develop an integrated, cross-sectoral approach to food policy, which links initiatives within public health, environmental sustainability, community development, education, agriculture, cultural and economic development, waste management, urban planning/land use, and tourism.'[7] In other words, it adopted a

The Good Food movement

whole system approach to food policy and practice under the banner of 'healthy, sustainable, fair food for all'.

Local food partnerships come in many shapes and sizes; some are located within municipalities while others are formal joint ventures between municipalities and their civil society partners. One of the distinctive features of the BHFP is that it was adamant that it needed to be a fully independent body from the outset if it was to be a credible and forceful champion of good food for all in the city. Being independent has proved to be an asset rather than a liability when it comes to crafting partnerships with public, private and civic sector organisations because BHFP now has more than fifty local partners in its local food alliance. Crafting such a broad and inclusive local food alliance was one of the reasons why, in 2020, Brighton and Hove became the first city in the UK to win the prestigious SFP Gold Award. In making the award, the SFP network said that Brighton and Hove is 'the first city in the UK to create a citywide food strategy, the first to have food growing written into planning guidelines for new residential developments and the first to require all council food procurement to meet minimum health and sustainability standards. Brighton and Hove's approach to food poverty is widely recognised and is now a model for other places.' Tom Andrews, the convenor of the SFP network, underlined the wider significance of the city's achievement when he said that the 'Brighton and Hove Partnership are leading a vanguard of more than 50 pioneering local food partnerships and creating one of the fastest-growing social movements in the UK today'.[8]

Although the work of the BHFP extends across the entire food system, from spade to spoon as they say in the city, three of its local initiatives merit particular attention. First, the Good

Serving the public

Food Procurement Group (GFPG) was established in 2012 and hosts all the major public sector food procurement bodies in the city, including local NHS trusts, universities, the city council, primary and secondary schools, community meals provider ('meals on wheels'), care homes, workplaces and major venues. The Food Partnership role has been to act as a hub, bringing together catering managers and chefs from different organisations to share good practice, to make new contacts and to learn about the benefits of buying and serving good food. The GFPG organisations represent all the major public sector food purchasers from across Brighton and Hove, and they collectively serve over a million meals a month. As BHFP says: 'Some of the most vulnerable people in the city are served by these organisations, so it is vital that quality food is provided.'[9]

Second, the Planning Advice Note (PAN) project brought together BHFP with the city's Planning Department, supported by Sustain, with funding from the Esmée Fairbairn Foundation. The project has integrated food into the planning system in three ways: (1) a revised and improved PAN on Food Growing was adopted in September 2020 and its development included consultation with developers, planning agents and front-line planners – the PAN provides technical guidance to encourage the inclusion of food growing spaces in new developments; (2) a new Health Impact Assessment checklist which developers are required to complete incorporates food growing, access to food shops and control of fast food outlets; and (3) a new Urban Design Framework Supplementary Planning Document that is underway will incorporate provisions for food growing and food access.

Third, an agile and resilient local food movement that showed its worth in response to the COVID-19 pandemic,

The Good Food movement

when the Emergency Food Network became the vehicle for an astonishing citywide crisis food response to the lockdown that was led and coordinated by BHFP in conjunction with its partners and the city council. BHFP set up a central food-processing hub where wholesale purchased food and surplus food was organised and distributed by a team of volunteers to food banks and meal projects. This central hub supported a citywide network of fifty neighbourhood food hubs to coordinate the sourcing and delivery of essential food to vulnerable families.

These three initiatives are part of a wide array of activities managed by the BHFP and its local food alliance partners in the city. I've often thought that it's a minor miracle that BHFP has been able to provide such vitally important services when it operates on such scant financial resources. Although it can count on scores of highly committed volunteers, BHFP has around twenty full-time staff and its funding model consists of a combination of grants, from the likes of the Big Lottery and the Esmée Fairbairn Foundation, and revenue-earning services from the public health arm of the local NHS trust. One of the challenges facing BHFP, and every other local food partnership for that matter, is how to put such essential food services on a more sustainable financial footing – for example by nurturing the kind of public–social partnerships that Robin Murray advocated in his radical prospectus for public service reform.[10]

The Bristol Food Network is another local food movement that has acquired a national profile. Bristol was the first city in the UK to create a Food Policy Council (FPC), the first city in the UK to win the European Green Capital Award and the second UK city (after Brighton) to win the SFP Gold Award for its contributions to the Good Food movement. The creation

Serving the public

of the FPC in 2011 was the culmination of many years of local food activity in a city that boasts a very active civil society and an environmentally conscious city government. The civil society food groups had organised themselves under the common banner of the Bristol Food Network to enhance their profile and their voice in urban politics.

The city council and the NHS also played innovative roles by making joint appointments to develop a food and health strategy for the city. Within the city council an informal cross-departmental network called the Food Interest Group played an important silo-busting role in raising the profile of food across all council departments and policy domains. It was against this background that Bristol City Council and NHS Bristol commissioned *Who Feeds Bristol?*, which is thought to be the first local food audit ever conducted in the UK. One of the distinctive features of this food audit was that it embodied and championed a *food systems planning* approach that treated food in a fully integrated fashion to illustrate the interconnections in the food system.[11]

In 2011, Bristol City Council created the UK's first FPC to implement the recommendations of *Who Feeds Bristol?* and to develop the local food agenda, the aim being to raise its profile with politicians and the public.[12] In organisational terms the Bristol FPC was a very fragile concoction because, unlike the BHFP, it had no full-time staff, no formal powers and no dedicated budget. While city officers were seconded to provide administrative support, the entire board consisted of unpaid volunteers, creating a clear discrepancy between the ambition and the capacity at the heart of Bristol's FPC.

In recent years the FPC has evolved into new forms – initially into the Going for Gold Steering Group and more recently into

The Good Food movement

the Bristol Good Food 2030 Partnership, which has developed a sophisticated local food strategy that identifies not just priorities but concrete frameworks for action.[13]

The achievements of the local food movement in Bristol might seem intangible and inconsequential if they only amounted to putting good food on the political agenda (though that's not a trivial achievement). But the local food movement can point to more tangible achievements that would not have happened without its resolute campaigns on public food procurement. For example:

- Bristol City Council adopted a Good Food and Catering Procurement Policy in March 2018, introducing minimum standards and requiring standardised criteria across all the council's catering and food provision contracts. The standards are based on the Soil Association's FFLSH Silver Award criteria and the policy requires caterers to be part of the Bristol Eating Better Award (BEBA) scheme, encouraging them to achieve Silver or Gold status.
- The tender specification for the school's procurement contract specified an FFLSH Gold Award for primary schools and an FFLSH Silver Award for secondary schools. This contract covers fifty-nine local schools. The current contractor (Chartwells) achieved the BEBA in September 2020, which gives each school in this contract an individual good food accreditation.
- Contracts to supply city venues and museums must hold an FFLSH Silver Award as a minimum.
- Part of the Bristol city food supply contract is a dynamic purchasing system, which makes supplying the city more accessible for small and medium-sized enterprises (SMEs).

Serving the public

This has resulted in them supplying twelve schools, numerous care homes and the city park cafés.

With its six themes – eating better, the local food economy, urban growing, food waste, food justice and good food governance – Bristol Good Food 2030 is one of the most ambitious strategies ever designed by the local food movement in the UK. When I discussed the pros and cons of the new strategy with Joy Carey – the author of *Who Feeds Bristol?* and one of the most experienced members of the city's local food movement – she thought the biggest challenges were twofold. First, the lack of funding meant that it was difficult to support a cross-sectoral systems approach to the six themes identified in the strategy. Second, the dependence on volunteers led to the problem that stymies local food movements everywhere: the burnout of activists.[14]

Sustainable Food Places network: the social infrastructure for a national movement

Another problem facing all local food movements is the inherent limits of localism, a problem that led to the formation of the Sustainable Food Cities (SFC) network. Launched in Bristol in 2011, the network was fashioned and sponsored by three prominent food policy NGOs – the Soil Association, Sustain and Food Matters – who had realised that localised action needed to be supplemented and supported by a social infrastructure that straddled the whole country if local food partnerships were to find a *national* voice in the food policy arena. One of the biggest hurdles at the outset, however, was how to fund the launch of the network, a problem that was

The Good Food movement

eventually solved thanks to the enlightened support of the Esmée Fairbairn Foundation, a progressive charity which aims to 'improve our Natural World, secure a Fairer Future and nurture Creative, Confident Communities'.[15] Foundational support is often the unsung hero in the history of local food movements, but the SFC network would never have got off the ground without the resolute support of Esmée Fairbairn, which loyally supported the network through three successive funding rounds between 2011 to 2024.

The growth of the network has been little short of remarkable when we remember the inhospitable climate of these years, marked by unprecedented public expenditure cuts imposed on local government and many other public bodies in the UK in the name of austerity. Despite the cold climate, the network has grown to such a point that it now boasts over ninety members and these local food partnerships have established themselves in a wide range of jurisdictions, so much so that in 2019 the network felt obliged to change its name from Sustainable Food *Cities* to the Sustainable Food *Places* network to accommodate the diversity. Although these local food partnerships come in many shapes and sizes, there are basically three main organisational forms:

- *Housed by a public sector organisation*, such as public health, environment or the economic development department of the local authority. These are funded or staffed by government employees.
- *Housed by a third-sector organisation*, such as an environmental or community development organisation or charity. Funds are secured by the third-sector organisation to support the set-up, running costs and staff.

Serving the public

- *Fully independent.* These are likely to have minimal resources, and be staffed entirely by volunteers initially, but over time develop into fully fledged organisations, when they secure their own funds and employ their own staff to administer the partnership.[16]

Reflecting on its rapid growth, the SFP network had noticed common challenges that were confronting many partnerships whatever their organisational form, and three particular challenges tend to arise. First, it was proving difficult to work in a holistic, cross-sectoral way when local authorities worked in silos, with the result that many partnerships ended up working almost exclusively with the public health department, where the food poverty agenda was particularly strong. Second, the SFP network had initially assumed that the independent organisation was the ideal organisational form, but experience seemed to suggest that this should not be idealised because many partnerships were not mature enough to manage all the administrative and financial responsibilities of going it alone. But perhaps the biggest challenge of all was the challenge of sustaining engagement over time:

> The levels of engagement tend to wax and wane over time. At the outset there is excitement and eagerness of new partners to engage and take part in discussions that have perhaps never been held about a town or city's food system. As the quick wins are achieved and the focus shifts to particular themes and perhaps longer-term issues, SFP Members have found it difficult to keep the agenda relevant for the original wide range of partners.[17]

The Good Food movement

But, overall, the SFP network has proved remarkably adept at helping the established partnerships to navigate these common challenges without neglecting to nurture the less mature partnerships, enabling the latter to learn from the mistakes of the pioneers. Among the most useful support services on offer from the SFP network are the thematic guides. The guide on how to engage with local authorities, for example, is a treasure trove of judicious advice as to why a newly established partnership needs to engage with its local authority, especially if it is housed outside the authority. Even though they may not know it, local authorities are well placed to influence the local food system because they have a wide range of policy levers, including:

- *Planning.* Local authorities can promote and protect land for food growing in the Local Plan, including allocation of land for 'starter farms' (e.g. London, Manchester, Sheffield); the use of leases to enable food growing to take place when development is stalled; and the promotion of food growing in public places. Planning advice notes can illustrate good practice, including food-growing space in new developments, while the Core Strategy can include provision for the protection of high-grade agricultural land. Supplementary planning documents can restrict the development of fast food near schools. Healthy food shops and markets can be protected and encouraged in the Core Strategy and through street trading policies, while Section 106 agreements can be used to request funds from fast food outlets to contribute to tackling obesity.
- *Land ownership.* Some local authorities own large areas of land, including farms, allotments and housing estates. These can be managed in a way that enhances their contribution to a sustainable local food system. This might include

encouraging organic or pesticide-free production, protecting grade 1 and 2 agricultural land or mapping green and brownfield sites and making them available to local communities.
- *Procurement.* Local authorities procure large quantities of food across their settings, including schools, parks, nurseries, care homes, community meals and leisure centres. This amounts to substantial buying power. With the adoption of minimum buying standards, this can drive demand for locally sourced, sustainable, healthy food.
- *Food system infrastructure.* Local authorities can maintain or create infrastructure such as processing facilities, storage facilities, wholesale markets, street trading and slaughterhouses, which can contribute to short food supply chains. Local authorities are responsible for waste management, including food waste collections.[18]

While local authorities do indeed have these powers, often such powers have not been applied to the food system because the latter has been a neglected policy domain for municipalities; so much so that one of the main tasks of a local food partnership is to help its local authority to use its influence to fashion a healthier and more sustainable food system. To this end the SFP network has identified as many as twenty-nine local authority food policy levers that local partnerships can utilise to inspire and enable their municipal partners to build food policy capacity at the local level.[19]

An evaluation of the network in the period 2011–2019 identified a number of strengths and weaknesses. On the positive side, the national network had clearly created a social infrastructure that enabled a collective learning process to take root that could disseminate knowledge and good practice. As well as helping

The Good Food movement

local partners to frame a local food strategy, it also helped them to design and implement 'a set of approaches for *how* change can take place in the food policy field'.[20] Assessing the most popular local food policy goals during this period, the study found that the top three goals in descending order of popularity were: (1) the development of a local authority food charter and food action plan, (2) public sector food procurement and (3) addressing food poverty and insecurity.[21]

On the negative side, the network had emerged in the context of the worst macro-economic environment in living memory – and local authorities were one of the biggest victims because they saw their central government grants cut by nearly 50 per cent in some cases during the decade of austerity after 2010. Apart from austerity, another key problem facing the network was the total absence of a national food policy framework, although this vacuum created opportunities for local governments to enter the field of food policy planning. Because of these problems, the network faced what is perhaps the single biggest challenge facing all local food movements, namely 'the gulf between aspiration and capacity at the local level'.[22]

The Good Food movement in the United States

The food movement was well underway in the US long before it had even started in the UK. The different starting point is usually attributed to the fact that the welfare state is much less developed in the US, with the result that hunger is a more visible and widespread problem. So much so that many social movements sprung up to champion the anti-hunger cause, or what became known as community food security, an idea that played 'a pivotal role in building today's food movement'.[23]

From a European perspective, however, it is difficult to appreciate the societal implications of a minimalist social safety net in the US, which must surely count as one of the darker sides of American exceptionalism. Whatever the pros and cons of this minimalist system, its effects are all too clear in terms of poverty, precarity and the associated 'deaths of despair' from suicide, drug overdose and alcoholism.[24]

A movement of movements: the rise of food policy councils

Fighting hunger was the main reason why some FPCs emerged in the first place. FPCs are the most tangible sign of the rapidly growing food movement in the US, where their number swelled from just eight in 2000 to 301 in 2020 (see Exhibit 5.1). The Knoxville FPC in Tennessee is generally believed to be the first council of its kind in the US. It formed in 1982 at a time when the city was hosting the World Fair and when millions of visitors were attending the event. A Community Food System Assessment study conducted by the University of Tennessee had found there was limited access to nutritious food in the inner-city and the study broke new ground by championing the idea that a community's food system deserved the same attention and treatment as the transport and housing systems. The combination of inner-city hunger and the lack of food system planning capacity persuaded the mayor, Randy Tyree, that an FPC could help to address both problems and the Knoxville FPC was duly founded, garnering national and international praise.[25]

The geographic focus of FPCs has remained fairly stable over time. According to a 2020 survey, 68 per cent operated at the local level (e.g. county, city or municipality), 19 per cent

The Good Food movement

> Food policy councils work to address food systems issues and needs at the local (city/municipality or county), state, regional or tribal-national levels. They represent multiple stakeholders and may be sanctioned by a government body or exist independently of government. They address food systems issues by advising, shaping and helping enact policies that further their goals.
>
> **Source:** Center for a Livable Future (2020) *Pivoting Policy, Programs and Partnerships*, Baltimore: CLF, p. 3.

Exhibit 5.1 What is a Food Policy Council?

at the multi-county level, 11 per cent at the state level and 2 per cent worked within tribal nations. The two most popular organisational structures were for councils to be housed either in a non-profit organisation (34 per cent) or within government (25 per cent). Most FPCs reported some type of relationship with government; most commonly, government employees were members of the council or participated in meetings, and 37 per cent received some form of support from the government, either financial or in-kind.[26]

Although the policy priorities of FPCs will inevitably reflect their local circumstances, a good deal of commonality has developed over the years and this convergence process has been accelerated by the COVID-19 crisis, which forced councils to pivot towards the most pressing priorities. As a result, the top three policy priorities in 2020 were:

- *Healthy food access*, which includes healthy food financing, food and nutrition incentives at farmers markets and school wellness policies, and has consistently remained the most common policy priority since 2014.

- *Anti-hunger and anti-poverty work* – which includes outreach and enrolment for the federal Supplemental Nutrition Assistance Program (SNAP, the former food stamps programme) and other federal social assistance programmes, as well as support for food banks, summer feeding programmes, senior hunger, and poverty reduction – has gradually risen to the second highest policy priority, with 53 per cent reporting it among their top three priorities in 2020 compared to 19 per cent in 2014.
- *Food production and transportation and distribution* gained renewed interest in 2020, while there was decreased prioritisation of food procurement, land use planning and food waste reduction and recovery compared to previous years.[27]

Regarding the key challenges facing FPCs, the survey confirmed that *funding* was the most significant challenge and the most highly cited problem for all councils. But a problem not addressed in the survey – a problem that haunts food movements in every country – is the inherent tension between equally compelling goals, such as anti-hunger versus the more capacious goal of addressing hunger alongside the other goals of food system reform – such as health, poverty, racial equity and the environment – in the name of sustainability.

Where structural racism has seriously disfigured the local food system, some councils have identified this as the overriding problem to be addressed. The Detroit FPC, for example, has made racial disparities in food access, retail ownership, food sector jobs and control over food-producing resources the cornerstone of its policy platform and its way of combating 'structural racism inherent in the food system and creating space for greater economic democracy and food justice'.[28]

The Good Food movement

Even from this brief sketch we can see that FPCs fulfil a unique role in the US food system because, in contrast to single-issue special interests – such as the farm lobby, manufacturers, processors and retailers – they aim to be multistakeholder bodies that take a holistic and integrated approach to food policy reform. Their agendas will differ as their areas differ and, while their composition has been criticised for being too white and too middle class, as we'll see later, their unique quality is that they aspire to be 'democratic spaces for convergence in diversity' along the lines outlined in Exhibit 5.2.

The new urban foodscape: New York City as a pacesetter

While FPCs campaign for healthier and more sustainable food systems, cities are rapidly becoming the places where good food policies are enacted or – just as likely – defeated by the awesome power of Big Food, the colloquial term for the industrial food system. New York City (NYC) can rightly claim to be in the forefront of both these trends. First, under the banner of its public health mandate, NYC has been a pioneer in the design and delivery of good food policy, illustrating the potential of city governments to refashion the urban foodscape through their urban policy repertoires, especially through their powers of purchase and their land use planning powers. Second, NYC's pioneering healthy food policies have been subjected to the most concerted backlash as Big Food has mobilised its formidable resources to defeat policies that threatened its profits, demonising the city government as a threat to consumer freedom and an affront to the American way of life. In this section I look briefly at both these developments, because the NYC case

Serving the public

> 'What many people refer to as the "food movement" is actually a collection of social movements: food justice, fair food, fair trade, organic food, slow food, food security, food sovereignty, family farms ... and local folks just trying to make things better. The list is extensive because the problems with our food systems are systemic, increasing, and acute. While these groups have much in common, it would be naïve to think that they coordinate their actions. Food Policy Councils are just one expression of this "movement of movements." Nevertheless, FPCs have a unique quality within this wide array of activists, advocates and practitioners: they create democratic spaces for convergence in diversity. The power of informed, democratic convergence – especially when linked to the specific places where people live, work and eat – has an additional, emergent quality: it can change the way we – and others – think. This is social learning; the basis for social change. Food Policy Councils hold great potential as action-centers for the social learning needed to build democracy into the food system. By helping communities exercise agency over the parts of the food system that people do have the power to change, and by building political will for deeper, systemic change, Food Policy Councils are "making the road as we travel" towards better local food systems.'
>
> **Source:** A. Harper et al. (2009) *Food Policy Councils: Lessons Learned*, Oakland, CA: Food First, p. 48.

Exhibit 5.2 A movement of movements

highlights not only the scope for reforming the urban foodscape but also the political forces arrayed against reform.

NYC is widely regarded as one of the front-runners in framing the new terrain of urban food policy through its innovative food programmes to improve nutritional well-being, support community and economic development, promote

The Good Food movement

food security and encourage more sustainable food production, distribution and consumption practices.[29] Although many US cities have developed local food strategies, what is distinctive about NYC is that it was one of the first to fashion a holistic *food systems* approach to its urban food strategy, the product of a collaborative endeavour between the city council and a rich array of food policy advocacy groups in civil society which are in the vanguard of the emerging food justice movement in the US.[30]

The first example of this food systems approach was *FoodWorks*, a new vision of the city's food system that was unveiled by city council Speaker Christine Quinn in 2010, which was described as the most comprehensive report on the NYC food system that the city had ever seen, even though it echoed many of the proposals published earlier that year by Manhattan borough President Scott Stringer in the *FoodNYC* report.[31] Quinn and Stringer were vying to succeed Mayor Bloomberg and their food policy reports were taken as evidence that the urban food question had finally come of age as a mainstream political issue in the city.

The great merit of *FoodWorks* was its systemic focus on the key stages of production, processing, distribution, consumption and post-consumption and the need for a more integrated food policy to align supply and demand in the city and the state. To take just one example: while New York State was a major producer of apples, and produced enough to support its entire demand, it imported apples from Washington State and apple juice from China. The report stated that: 'These kinds of practices are not sustainable and can create environmental and economic inefficiencies in our food system. By making a conscious effort to support our regional farmers through developing infrastructure, programming and procurement change, we can ensure they are competitive at home and nationally.'[32]

Although these initiatives were warmly welcomed by the food policy community in the city, an influential assessment by food policy experts in City University New York concluded that the successes of the past decade were hampered by serious shortcomings. While *FoodWorks* presented an ambitious list of policy proposals, it 'did not include a governance plan, budget allocations, or measurable goals – essential prerequisites for fair and effective food governance'.[33]

In response to such criticisms, the mayor's Office of Food Policy orchestrated a comprehensive ten-year food policy plan, *Food Forward NYC*, that it published in 2021 while the city was mired in the COVID-19 crisis. The plan said that it was based on decades of work and learning by communities, food policy advocates and city staff and that it was 'shaped by what the city heard directly from New Yorkers about how they want their food system to work for them'.[34] *Food Forward NYC* is organised around five goals and fourteen specific strategies and the city aims to work in concert with its food system partners to accomplish the goals and strategies summarised in Exhibit 5.3.

Running through the whole of the ten-year plan was a major commitment to leverage the power of the public sector to fashion a fairer, healthier and more sustainable urban food system. City government, it said, had used its public health mandate to improve the food system for more than a century, starting with the distribution of pasteurised milk to address infant mortality in the early 1900s, to the first school lunch programmes during the Great Depression, to the rollout of food stamps in the 1960s. But the ten-year plan aimed to address multiple goals, not just public health, and it planned to use all the powers of the

The Good Food movement

GOAL	DESCRIPTION
1	All New Yorkers have multiple ways to access healthy, affordable and culturally appropriate food. The city faces an unprecedented food insecurity crisis, affecting nearly one in five New Yorkers, that requires a focus beyond traditional emergency food systems. NYC will: **A.** Expand food benefits to reach more New Yorkers in more places. **B.** Distribute food more equitably. **C.** Reconfigure how the City sources food.
2	New York City's food economy drives economic opportunity and provides good jobs. NYC's extraordinarily diverse food system depends on tens of thousands of small and micro businesses and the hundreds of thousands of workers who make them run. NYC will: **A.** Protect food workers, improve pay and benefits, and support ownership. **B.** Support small food businesses by cutting red tape, protecting data and promoting innovation. **C.** Train the next generation of food workers for high-quality jobs.
3	The supply chains that feed New York City are modern, efficient and resilient. The plan is committed to securing and improving our critical infrastructure and recognises that strengthening regional connections is critical to that end. NYC will: **A.** Strengthen the City's food infrastructure. **B.** Improve regional coordination and sourcing. **C.** Support increased urban farming.
4	New York City's food is produced, distributed and disposed of sustainably. Our food system has profound impacts on the local, regional and global environment, as well as animal welfare. NYC will: **A.** Integrate sustainability and animal welfare into City food programmes. **B.** Reduce in-city air pollution and greenhouse gas emissions from the food system. **C.** Promote innovation around food and sustainability.
5	Support the systems and knowledge to implement the ten-year food policy plan. Few systems are in place, whether in City government or outside of it, that have the capacity and the knowledge to alone implement a comprehensive food policy. NYC will: **A.** Strengthen community engagement and cross-sector coordination around development and implementation of food policy. **B.** Create and share knowledge about the food system.

Source: Food Forward NYC

Exhibit 5.3 Goals for NYC's food future

Serving the public

municipality to do so. The main powers in the city's food policy repertoire were defined as follows:

- *Food assistance programmes*: the city provides a lifeline to food-insecure New Yorkers, dispensing over $2 billion in SNAP, operating the largest school-feeding programme in the country and funding the City's Emergency Food Assistance Program.
- *Business regulation*: NYC regulates food businesses, directly through planning permits and licences and indirectly by setting policy for land use, transportation and labour practices.
- *Food infrastructure*: NYC manages critical food infrastructure, including the Hunts Point Food Distribution Center in the Bronx as well as vital industrial sites in all five NYC boroughs that house supply chain businesses.
- *Power of purchase:* NYC is a major food purchaser, spending about $500 million annually on food across all municipal departments, from schools to public hospitals to senior centres, making up about 2.5 per cent of total food sales.
- *Convening power:* NYC has a unique power to convene, plan and advocate. Because the urban food system is so complex and distributed, no single entity has a complete picture of what's needed or a platform to plan ahead. The city plays an important role in convening experts, sharing data and knowledge, leading efforts to change state and federal policy.
- *Mayor's Office of Food Policy* (MOFP): the MOFP is now enshrined in the City Charter, with a mandate to lead city food policy and coordinate multi-agency initiatives. This provides the city with the structures to leverage all the tools mentioned above and pursue ambitious, multi-sectoral policy.

The Good Food movement

The concerted use of these powers certainly enhances the public sector's capacity to shift the urban food system in a fairer, healthier and more sustainable direction. But there are limits to what the public sector can realistically expect to achieve, especially when its own purchasing power accounts for less than 3 per cent of total food sales in the city. To conclude this NYC vignette, it's worth focusing on the strengths and weaknesses of the city government's role, beginning with what is generally believed to be its most direct and consequential role: public food purchasing.[35]

NYC has become one of the main 'living labs' for the Good Food Purchasing (GFP) programme, a procurement framework I examine later, which helps public institutions to better understand the source of the food they purchase along with a methodology to quantify the impact of that food along five core values: nutrition, local economies, valued workforce, environmental sustainability and animal welfare. But long before the city adopted the GFP framework in 2018, it already enjoyed a strong reputation for using the public plate to deliver health and social justice benefits, especially through its school meals programme. In 2017, NYC became one of the first US cities in the country to offer a free lunch to all children in public schools thanks to its Free School Lunch for All programme. To fund the programme, the city used a new data-matching engine to identify which families were eligible, and this enabled NYC to qualify for the highest level of reimbursement from the federal government through the Community Eligibility Provision, a programme that allows school districts to provide meals free of charge to all enrolled students.[36]

NYC officially adopted the GFP framework in 2018, working with the Center for Good Food Purchasing to collect data and

Serving the public

establish a baseline assessment. At first only two city agencies were involved, the Department of Education and the NYC Health and Hospitals, but then it was later extended to seven agencies. Launching the framework, the executive director of MOFP, Kate MacKenzie, said:

> Today we establish a transparent, clear foundation for tracking The City of New York's food purchasing: who supplies our food, what we serve and to whom, and how we are performing against 5 key values each tied to clear data and metrics: nutrition, support for local economies, a valued food production and delivery workforce, environmental sustainability and animal welfare ... Institutional food purchasing is an enormous lever for change and a critical tool for equity. Together, we can deliver higher-quality food and make progress on climate, animal welfare, workers' rights and supporting minority and women owned businesses. We value your partnership and feedback as we strive to feed New Yorkers and bring a dynamic new value system to The City of New York's procurement of food and ultimately meals for our residents.[37]

Serving healthier meals on the public plate is perhaps the easy part of a sustainable food strategy because the city has a direct role in fashioning the market for institutional meals. What is far more difficult is the regulation of the *private* market, which is where the problem of unhealthy food and drink is most acute. A notorious example of this problem in NYC occurred when Mayor Bloomberg (2002–2013) sought to regulate soda consumption in the city by proposing a Portion Cap Rule to prohibit the sale of soda drinks above sixteen ounces. Under Bloomberg, the city government had been a pioneer of public health reform in the US with its ban on trans-fats, soda reduction campaigns and the calorie-posting requirement on food service establishments on the grounds that New Yorkers got

The Good Food movement

one-third or more of their calories eating outside the home and the mayor believed they needed help to make better-informed choices. Although this was the mayor's signature public health intervention, widely perceived as a global bellwether for a city's right to regulate the powerful fast food industry, the cap was overturned by the New York State Supreme Court on two grounds: (1) on *practical* grounds the cap was found to be arbitrary and capricious in its effects because it applied to some but not all food establishments and excluded other high sugar beverages; and (2) on *constitutional* grounds, as it would 'violate the separation of powers doctrine' according to Justice Tingling.[38]

The constitutional objection was firmly aimed at Bloomberg, who had introduced the cap in a high-handed fashion through the Board of Health, the executive branch which he controlled, rather than the city council (the legislative branch), and it was therefore deemed to be unconstitutional. But far more troubling for Bloomberg was the fact that the cap was unpopular with 60 per cent of New Yorkers, especially in the poorer boroughs of Queens and the Bronx.[39]

In *Soda Politics*, the most cogent analysis of the portion cap controversy, Marion Nestle dissects the complex politics of the battle and distils its implications for the Good Food movement. As regards the politics, she demonstrates how Bloomberg was totally outmanoeuvred by the American Beverage Association (ABA), which orchestrated an enormous public relations campaign to convince New Yorkers that the 'ban' on large soda sizes was an unwarranted intervention by the 'nanny state' as it infringed their freedom of choice. Framing the issue as a 'ban' was one of the most successful achievements of the ABA campaign because, while it was technically a cap and not a ban, the more evocative ban proved to be the dominant framing in the public mind. This framing was taken to extreme lengths by the ABA's 'attack dog', the Center for Consumer Freedom, which took out a full-page ad in the *New York Times* on 2 June 2012, portraying Bloomberg as 'The Nanny' (Exhibit 5.4).

The portion cap battle was an unequivocal defeat for Bloomberg's public health strategy, and Marion Nestle draws two important lessons from the experience. First, the Good Food movement needs to better appreciate the awesome lobbying power of the fast food industry, which targets far more people than we might imagine. Indeed, one of the most compelling aspects of her analysis revolves around what she calls 'the ABA's Strange Bedfellows'. These included not just the unions representing workers in soda bottling plants but, to the surprise of many public health advocates, the New York State chapter of the National Association for the Advancement of Colored People (NAACP) and the Hispanic Federation, the groups most at risk of obesity and type 2 diabetes. Although these organisations publicly opposed the cap on the grounds that it was paternalistic and damaging to minority-owned businesses, Marion Nestle shows that they also shared another important characteristic: 'for years, Coca-Cola and PepsiCo have generously supported their programs'. The same point applies to NYC Council members, a majority of whom opposed the cap, and Nestle argues that soda company donations to local politicians correlated with their voting behaviour.

The second lesson concerns the political tactics of the Good Food movement. As a billionaire who never took a salary from the city and who was allegedly impervious to public opinion, Bloomberg was a three-term mayor determined to deploy the city's public health mandate to counter obesity and other diet-related diseases. The ends may have been laudable, but the

The Good Food movement

Exhibit 5.4 The Nanny Bloomberg ad

means were lamentable because the city failed to engage with local residents and the lack of coalition building allowed Big Soda to win by default. So much was freely conceded by the president of the New York chapter of the NAACP when he said: 'This is about organizing ... The Mayor's got to come clean and actually humble himself to listen to his constituents and say let's solve this together. Our folks at the NAACP here in New York want to help him push through a comprehensive policy.'[40]

While the portion cap controversy might seem like a purely local affair, nothing could be further from the truth. As Nestle rightly says: 'What started out as a legal challenge to the portion cap had become a test of a much larger issue: whether city health departments had the authority to pass rules to protect and promote the health of citizens.'[41] Although the legal system ruled that they did not have the authority in this particular case, it was because the city council, not the health board, was deemed to be the responsible law-making body.

NYC is a significant part of the Good Food movement in the US because it highlights the scope for municipal activism as well as the limits to what a city can feasibly accomplish. Like all cities in the US, NYC is obliged to work within a multilevel polity that consists of state- and federal-level rules and regulations. Although it has built up more food policy capacity than other US cities, it still needs to draw on the support of national networks such as the Center for Good Food Purchasing to help it design and deliver a new, more sophisticated values-based procurement framework.

The Good Food movement

Alliances and networks: the social infrastructure for local movements

Local food movements need to be locally embedded and nationally engaged if they want to achieve two of their key goals – to be responsive to their local communities and effective in reforming federal food policy to ensure it fosters rather than frustrates the production and consumption of good food. The US food movement was much more successful than its UK counterpart in creating a national network that could serve as the social infrastructure for its local movements and this network was the Community Food Security Coalition (CFSC). Created in 1996 and dissolved in 2012, the rise and fall of the CFSC encapsulates the strengths and weaknesses of the Good Food movement in the US in its short sixteen-year life cycle. Significantly though, some of its work continued after its demise under the auspices of other organisations. For example, its work connecting FPCs was picked up and expanded by the Food Policy Networks project that is managed today by the Johns Hopkins Center for a Livable Future.[42]

According to Mark Winne, a founding member, the formation and growth of the CFSC can be attributed to three factors: (1) a growing recognition by food organisations that food insecurity could not be remedied by any single-interest approach or policy; (2) the urgent need to provide a common space, and a conceptual framework, for the activity that comprised the food movement; and (3) the federal funding that was released by reforms to the 1996 Farm Bill. The newly formed CFSC had successfully pressed for a new grant programme (the Community Food Projects Competitive Grant Program) to support the work of communities trying to become more food secure, a grant programme that was reauthorised in every subsequent Farm Bill. Although a minuscule part of the overall cost of a Farm Bill – the 2018 Farm Bill is projected to cost around $428 billion over its five-year life cycle – the community food projects grant is estimated to have provided some $100 million to hundreds of non-profit local food entities across the country since its inception.[43]

Recounting the rise and fall of the CFSC, Winne suggests that the Good Food movement has much to learn from the fate of this national network, especially from its demise. Although there were many reasons for its implosion, he highlights the fact that it failed to be inclusive. While it provided a common space that brought together very different perspectives – from those who had a large food system perspective to those who had a more conventional anti-hunger perspective – 'the unresolved issues of race and racism would eventually contribute to CFSC's demise'.[44]

For all its internal tensions, the CFSC hosted some of the most exciting national events in the history of the Good Food movement. From its first annual conference in Los Angeles in 1997 to the final conference in Oakland in 2011, the CFSC hosted cutting-edge debates about the systemic problems of the US food system and explored a variety of community-based solutions for a fairer, healthier and more sustainable system. The American Good Food movement had little or no idea what a unique achievement it was to have fashioned a national network such as the CFSC and to have held it together for sixteen years. There was certainly nothing remotely like it in the UK or Europe at the time. But the deep fissures of US society finally took their toll. The twin problems of race and class had bedevilled the US food movement from the beginning. Julie

The Good Food movement

Guthman had been outspoken about 'the unbearable whiteness of the alternative food movement', and Thomas Forster admitted that the American organic movement was not only 'a mostly white movement' but it was also 'largely blind to hunger, race, and class issues'.[45]

During its short life the CFSC achieved far more than it has been given credit for. For one thing, it played an important role in nurturing the Farm to School network, one of the fastest-growing parts of the Good Food movement in the US. The National Farm to School Network (NFSN) aims to increase access to local food and nutrition education to improve children's health, strengthen family farms and cultivate vibrant communities. Today the network covers 65 per cent of all US schools, in forty-six states, and has more than 20,000 members. Another unsung achievement was the way that the CFSC worked with the NFSN to change federal procurement law to allow school districts to express a geographical preference in their food purchases. As a result, new provisions in the 2008 Farm Bill signalled a major shift in the federal procurement policy landscape because school districts were empowered 'to give a bidding preference for minimally processed foods and fresh fruits and vegetables'.[46]

Procurement policy is also the core focus of another important national network, the GFP programme, which is inspiring and enabling public bodies to design and deliver a values-based procurement framework. Designed and developed by the Los Angeles FPC, the programme was first adopted in 2012 by the city of Los Angeles, closely followed by the second adopter, the Los Angeles United School District. In 2015 the programme was spun off into the Center for Good Food Purchasing, which was created to advance the national expansion of the programme. As a result of the national drive, the Center for Good Food Purchasing currently works with more than sixty-three public bodies in key cities and municipalities across the country. According to Paula Daniels and Alexa Delwiche, two of its key architects, the GFP programme 'is the first procurement model to support five food system values – local economies, environmental sustainability, valued workforce, animal welfare and nutrition – in equal measure and thereby encourages myriad organizations to come together to engage for shared goals'.[47]

The five food system values are designed to counteract the dominance of price in the weighting of public food contracts, though price still commands the highest single weight in the GFP system. One of the most distinctive features of the GFP framework is the inclusion of *labour* standards, which applies to both the purchasing institution as well as its supply chain, a social innovation that reflects the fact that the Food Chain Workers' Alliance played a key role in designing the programme. Another distinctive feature is that the Center for Good Food Purchasing works with a combination of national and local partners: 'local coalitions help to recruit institutions, secure formal programme adoption through policy, and influence public procurement processes to ensure that institutions and their vendors are held accountable to their policy commitments and that public contracts reflect community priorities'.[48]

The five values of the GFP system are designed to unite the Good Food movement and prevent it fragmenting by fixating on single-issue approaches to food reform. For the same reason, the GFP framework uses a capacious and inclusive definition of good food as food that is healthy, affordable, fair and sustainable. Looking ahead, the Center for Good Food Purchasing

The Good Food movement

plans to disseminate its values-based procurement system at two levels: *locally*, through a focus on key cities as hubs for regionalised food systems, and *nationally*, through its Anchors in Action (AiA) alliance.

The AiA alliance is one of the most significant developments in the history of the Good Food movement in the US. It describes itself as a national partnership that was established in 2015 by the Center for Good Food Purchasing, Health Care Without Harm and Real Food Generation. These three organisations support values-based food procurement at over sixty-five public institutions in twenty-five major cities, 2,000 hospitals, 7,800 elementary and secondary schools, and 100 colleges and universities across the country. These 'anchor institutions' are pioneers in a nationwide movement to use public food purchasing to invest in community values and well-being. The three organisations are equally committed to the following principles:

- *Leverage the collective purchasing power* across institutional sectors to increase the amount of ethically produced foods being purchased and served.
- *Increase tracking capacity throughout the supply chain* so that institutions can easily make choices for ethically produced foods.
- *Embed racial equity, climate justice, and food sovereignty* as core principles in values-based food procurement.
- *Transform the marketplace* to make ethically produced foods available and affordable to eaters served by institutions as well as the community it is situated in by supporting regional, sustainable production.[49]

Members of the AiA have orchestrated an even larger coalition, the Federal Good Food Purchasing Coalition, to advocate for changes to federal food policies such as the United States Department of Agriculture's commodity food programmes and the Food Service Guidelines for Federal Facilities, two of the most important policy targets for the American Good Food movement. These new national coalitions are now focusing on public institutions throughout the country because they collectively spend some $120 billion a year procuring food, $8.8 billion of which is spent by the federal government alone. While some federal agencies have implemented nutrition standards which align with the Dietary Guidelines for Americans – including more climate-friendly, plant-forward menus – these are still the exceptions to the norm because 'federal food procurement largely supports the status quo industrial food system, which has been denounced for its role in exacerbating climate change and biodiversity loss, preventable diet-related disease and health care costs, and exploitation of frontline workers and animals'.[50]

Retrospect and prospects

Being the first country to spawn a Good Food movement, the US was also the first to confront what Mark Winne called the twin challenges of 'unity and chaos' in its ranks. In a compelling history of the US food movement, Winne raises the question that tends to haunt food movements in every country: is the food movement *really* a movement given the plethora of single-issue groups? Lasting progress will not be made, he says referring to the US, 'until the numerous sub-movements that make up the larger food movement learn how to collaborate far better than they do now'.[51]

Although this question may never be fully resolved, most reformers seem to think of the Good Food movement as a

The Good Food movement

'movement of movements' or a 'network of networks'. This pluralistic perspective is more conducive to coalition building, a way of thinking that eschews the supposed iron discipline of the Leninist party and embraces instead an idea that is common to many contemporary social movements – the idea of *unity in diversity*. As imprecise as it is, the very ambiguity of the idea is a source of strength if it allows diverse groups to campaign for a common cause (e.g. good food) while retaining their core interest in a particular issue (e.g. workers' rights, organic food or UFSM).

But some of the issues that divide the American movement cannot be conjured away by invoking the mantra of unity in diversity. Perhaps the biggest and most intractable issue of all is the radically different perspectives between food system reformers, who are committed to the cause of a fairer, healthier and more sustainable food system, and the anti-hunger lobby that is charged with being indifferent to the quality of emergency food relief because it has aligned itself with what critics have called its 'unholy alliance with corporate America'.

In *Big Hunger*, Andy Fisher argues that the unholy alliance is epitomised by the 'anti-hunger industrial complex' that lies at the heart of federal food programmes, which manifests itself in two ways. First, anti-hunger groups have an umbilical relationship with multinational firms and the latter donate to their budgets and sit on their boards, ensuring that the agenda remains narrowly focused on hunger rather than the causes of hunger, such as wages, taxation and universal healthcare. Second, anti-hunger groups have tacitly accepted a market-based approach to federal food policies, with the result that much of the £100 billion spent annually on nutrition programmes such as SNAP ends up in the accounts of multinationals such as Tyson, Conagra, Walmart and Pepsi. 'The anti-hunger community', in Fisher's view, 'needs to become more aligned with the goals of the progressive community, with clearer and more direct alliances with labor, food system, public health, and other progressive organizations.'[52]

Bridging these differences will help to strengthen the internal coherence of the US movement. But on the external front, one of the key challenges is how to spread and scale the Good Food movement beyond its current strongholds. In the case of the Center for Good Food Purchasing, for example, it aims to promote its values-based procurement programme nationally by targeting the major cities, a strategy that makes sense given the progressive character of metropolitan America. But this strategy could be derailed by the fact that right-wing policy activists (orchestrated by ultra-conservative organisations such as the American Legislative Exchange Council and the State Policy Network) are using their legislative control of *state* governments to stymie the progressive agenda of liberal cities by blocking policies to raise the minimum wage, boost health insurance and promote good food. Progressives in the US have been preoccupied by the politics of Congress and the White House, ignoring the state level to their detriment because 'in their enthusiastic urban turn, liberal activists have overlooked a major barrier: most state legislatures can simply overrule (or "pre-empt") city action with which they disagree ... Given the distribution of political power across America's states and cities, then, progressives cannot retreat to their city strongholds and neglect the states.'[53]

Extending the Good Food movement to more cities, regions and municipalities is also the key challenge in the UK. Although local food movements are growing in number, as the membership of the SFP network attests, it is hard to avoid the conclusion that the gulf between aspiration and capacity remains

The Good Food movement

the biggest problem. Being far more centralised than the US, the UK political system concedes very little fiscal autonomy to local government, one of the main institutional pillars of the Good Food movement. Yet it remains little short of remarkable that the movement has developed as it has in recent years given the limited autonomy of local government and the austerity budgets that have denuded municipal capacity since 2010. Being fiscally constrained, municipalities have been forced to work more closely with their public sector partners, especially the NHS, and with civil society organisations to combine their efforts and pool resources in the common cause of food system reform.

Civil society organisations have been the most proactive part of the Good Food movement in the UK. As we saw in Part II, national alliances between civil society organisations – such as Sustain, the Soil Association and the Food Foundation – have managed to form highly effective advocacy coalitions, and these clearly helped to change the cognitive landscape about the quality of food in public institutions, particularly through their UFSM campaign.

Despite the inhospitable fiscal climate, cities have been energised by the advent of the Milan Urban Food Policy Pact (MUFPP), an international urban network launched by the mayor of Milan to mark the 2015 expo Feeding the Planet, Energy for Life. More than 100 cities signed up at the launch event and by 2023 there were 270 cities across the globe representing 450 million inhabitants. The MUFPP framework offers members a peer-to-peer support network to enable cities to pursue the common goal of sustainable food systems, and such international networks have succoured the good food policy agenda given the indifference of central government in the UK.

The federal funding for community food security projects in the US, a potential source of startup funds for local food schemes, simply has no equivalent in the UK.

Although devolution to the Celtic nations has created a somewhat more devolved state system, generating more scope for civic engagement and policy experimentation, the UK political system remains inordinately centralised by OECD standards; so much so that British local authorities are rapidly being transformed into fiscal serfs. No matter how socially innovative they are, local food groups will never get sufficient traction unless their municipal government partners are afforded more autonomy and resources to design and deliver good food reforms that are attuned to their local circumstances. Local food system reform, in other words, is inextricably bound up with and dependent upon wider political reforms to render the UK a more pluralistic and polycentric country, a question I explore further in the following chapter.

6
Prospects for change

Introduction

One of the common challenges facing food policy reformers in the Anglo-American world has been how to persuade their political elites to take food more seriously. 'It might sound odd to say this about something people deal with at least three times a day,' writes Michael Pollan, 'but food in America has been more or less invisible, politically speaking, until very recently.'[1] The fact that the food system has been rendered more visible in political circles in recent years is a tribute to the influence of the American food movement.

One of the turning points in the US was the NYC Mayoral Candidate Food Forum on 17 July 2013, at the New School Tishman Auditorium. The forum, moderated by the highly respected author Marion Nestle, was the first time that NYC mayoral candidates had ever agreed to appear on the same public platform to share their thoughts on food policy issues such as hunger, health, food access and school food reform. Nestle captured the significance of the occasion when she declared that 'the most important feature of the event was the event itself, because it was less about the candidates than the political coming of age of the food movement in the city.[2]

Although the UK has yet to grill its politicians in a similar vein, campaigners have succeeded in raising the political visibility of food system reform through innovative local campaigns. As we'll see in a moment, the Good Food for London campaign had the inspired idea of publishing an annual map highlighting what each borough was doing to promote good food in its area. The simple act of putting hitherto unknown information in the public domain had a ripple effect: raising awareness, galvanising action and catalysing change in what reformers believe is a race to the top among the boroughs. But the little victories of progressive localism can never be a substitute for more consistent and systemic support from *national* governments in the UK and the US, highlighting the need for more synchronised multilevel food policy interventions in which national and subnational policies are calibrated for greater effect.

Persuading political elites to take food system reform seriously is only the beginning of transformative change, which is a long and arduous process. As we have seen in previous chapters, the food industry deploys formidable lobbying power to protect its interests and forestall regulatory reform. In the following section I explore the prospects for change by assessing the clash between the power of ideas and the power of vested interests represented by Big Food, a corporate lobby that draws on the political playbook designed by Big Tobacco.

Navigating change: ideas and interests

At the very end of his magnum opus, John Maynard Keynes speculated as to how the ideas in his *General Theory* would be

Prospects for change

received in political society. 'Are the interests which they will thwart', he asked, 'stronger and more obvious than those which they will serve?' Although he resolutely refused to give a direct answer, he did address it obliquely with an observation that has fascinated scholars and policymakers ever since: 'I am sure that the power of vested interests is vastly exaggerated compared with the gradual encroachment of ideas.'[3]

If 'the gradual encroachment of ideas' is taken to mean the generally accepted scientific evidence, then we must acknowledge that, in certain cases, it can take an inordinate amount of time before new ideas trump vested interests. Think, for example, of one of the most protracted battles between new ideas and vested interests in the twentieth century: the controversy around the causes of lung cancer.

As early as 1912, Dr Isaac Adler established a link between cigarette smoking and lung cancer. But the definitive scientific breakthrough eventually came in the early 1950s, when Doll and Hill's research forced the discipline of epidemiology to officially recognise cigarette smoking as the primary cause of lung cancer.[4] Even so, it was still more than a decade later that the 1964 Surgeon General's report in the US recognised smoking as a cause of lung cancer in men, and this is often regarded as the official tipping point in the recognition of health harms from smoking.

The smoking example confirms that new ideas, even when they are strong and obvious, to use Keynes' words, are not sufficient to thwart vested interests. In this case the key ideas had been established in the 1950s. In 1956, for example, the scientific director of the American Cancer Society noted that 'if the same level of evidence had been arrayed against, say, spinach, no one would have objected to the banning of that plant from the national diet'.[5]

Serving the public

But it was not until 1971 that the US introduced the National Cancer Act and even later, in 1998, that the American tobacco industry was finally forced to pay $206 billion as part of the Tobacco Master Settlement Agreement, the largest lawsuit settlement in history, to cover the medical costs of tobacco-related illnesses. So how had vested interests trumped ideas for so long?

The answer is clearly pertinent to today's debates about climate change and diet-related diseases: the tobacco industry invented the playbook that taught industrial lobbyists how to embrace the rhetoric of science while denying its results.

Confronting an existential crisis in the 1950s, the tobacco industry adopted an audacious strategy to create scientific uncertainty about the harms of smoking by sponsoring research that was controlled by the industry but presented as independent. From 1953 onwards, the US tobacco industry sought to engineer the science around the harms associated with smoking: 'It moved aggressively into a new domain, the production of scientific knowledge, not for purposes of research and development but, rather, to undo what was now known: that cigarette smoking caused lethal disease. If science had historically been dedicated to the making of new facts, the industry campaign now sought to develop specific strategies to "unmake" a scientific fact.'[6]

For almost half a century vested interests trumped scientific ideas as Big Tobacco managed to forestall punitive regulation and litigation. But this sectoral success carried two long-term societal problems in and beyond the US. First, by enrolling scientists in its public relations campaigns, Big Tobacco had brought science into disrepute and set a dangerous precedent that would affect future debates on controversial subjects such as climate change and diet-related diseases. Second, the rhetoric of scientific uncertainty enabled the industry to promote the

Prospects for change

notion that smoking was an 'individual' risk freely chosen by the smoker: in other words, 'scientific uncertainty permitted the companies to attribute the very risks imposed by their product to individuals rather than to the companies themselves'.[7]

The public health communities in Europe and North America have established the parallels between the past tactics of Big Tobacco and the present tactics of Big Food. Although there are of course major differences between food and tobacco as substances, not least that the former is a necessity while the latter is an option, there are also many similarities in the playbook they use to promote their products and deflect criticism. The key tropes of the food industry playbook – tropes that are deployed by companies, their trade associations and their political allies – include the following:

- Focus on personal responsibility as the cause of the nation's unhealthy diet.
- Raise fears that government action usurps personal freedom.
- Vilify critics with totalitarian language, characterising them as the food police, leaders of a nanny state and even 'food fascists', and accuse them of desiring to strip people of their civil liberties.
- Criticise studies that hurt industry as 'junk science'.
- Emphasise physical activity over diet.
- State there are no good or bad foods; hence no food or food type (soft drinks, fast foods, etc.) should be targeted for change.
- Plant doubt when concerns are raised about the industry.[8]

Public health scholars rightly argue that the food industry is at a crossroads: one path involves fighting change (by targeting

Serving the public

children, forestalling regulation and selling as much product as possible no matter the consequences), while the other path involves a radically different strategy, such as working with the public health community, selling less harmful products and promoting healthier options. The question for the food industry is stark: 'Adopting the first option while laying claim to the second was the path taken by the tobacco industry. Is the food industry different, or is history repeating itself, this time with another substance?'[9]

The notion of a crossroads offering divergent paths serves to remind us that ideas and interests are not set in aspic. On the contrary, ideas and interests evolve and mutate through dialogue, conflict and crisis. The above discussion assumes that 'the food industry' is a static and homogenous entity with all its interests vested in the status quo. But in truth it is a hugely dynamic and highly diverse entity, and some parts of it are more receptive to positive change than others. For example, when Henry Dimbleby engaged the food industry to prepare an NFS for England, he found that many firms felt trapped in what he called the junk food cycle. 'Behind the scenes', he said, 'several company bosses have told me they would welcome government legislation designed to reduce junk food sales. They know the food they are selling is terrible for their consumers, and they want to do the right thing. But they need a level playing field. They can't act alone.'[10] Vested interests are clearly not static. However, some firms are so dependent on the junk food cycle that it would be naïve to think that they will 'do the right thing' and diversify into healthier and more sustainable products unless they are pressured to do so by the combined actions of consumers, shareholders and regulators.

On the consumer front, youth activist groups such as Bite Back are among the most articulate critics of the junk food cycle and its corporate perpetrators. In an alliance of change with researchers from Oxford University and NESTA (originally the National Endowment for Science, Technology and the Arts), they have shown the extent to which Big Food is peddling products that are high in fat, sugar or salt (HFSS), the products that fuel the noxious junk food cycle. Bite Back investigated the ten biggest global food and drink businesses operating in the UK and the findings, shown in Exhibit 6.1, reveal that more than two-thirds of their packaged food and drink sales came from HFSS products. It also found that the top-five categories of food and drink products by sales value are chocolate, savoury snacks, reduced sugar soft drinks, regular soft drinks and ice cream – none of which is reflected in the *Eatwell Guide*.[11]

The youth activists concluded their analysis by saying:

[T]he fact that so many businesses are still locked in a business model of production, promotion and sales of overwhelmingly unhealthy products, despite numerous government health strategies and failed voluntary programmes shows that comprehensive action from inside businesses, along with government regulation, is needed to shift the food system onto one that is not fuelled by driving food related illness. Business and governments hold the levers of change. We now need action.[12]

Some shareholders are also concerned that their investments could be in jeopardy if junk food assets morphed into stranded assets because of their association with diet-related diseases such as obesity. A group of Nestlé shareholders filed a resolution at the company's AGM in 2024 demanding that the company reduce the proportion of sales it makes from unhealthy goods, 'citing regulatory and reputational risks as well as growing public health concerns.'[13]

Serving the public

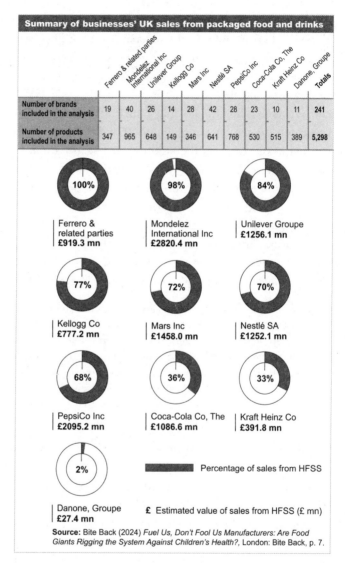

Exhibit 6.1 The vested interests in the junk food cycle

Prospects for change

In the food service sector, the evidence suggests that global companies behave in very different ways, even *within* the same company, when they are faced with different pressures and demands. A case in point is Compass Group, the world's largest food services company, which supplies school meals through Chartwells, its education-catering subsidiary. In the same year that the company was enjoying positive publicity for winning an FFLSH Gold Award for its school meals service in Bristol, it was excoriated by the headteacher of a school in Southampton for serving totally unacceptable food. In a letter to parents, the head apologised and explained that he was powerless to act as he had no control over the Chartwells contract because 'the school's services are restricted by a PFI contract, with a management company outsourcing the school's catering'.[14]

The difference in food quality is easily explained: to secure the contract in Bristol the company knew it had to meet exacting FFL standards, but there were no equivalent standards in Southampton.

Corporate behaviour is clearly malleable, and companies can and will redefine their interests when they are obliged to do so. For this to happen, however, regulators need to have the competence and confidence to design catering contracts that prioritise health and sustainability. Here the Good Food movement needs to reflect on how it responds to key trends in food service, a sector dominated by Compass Group, Sodexo and Aramark, the world's three biggest catering companies. The Big Three increased their share of the global food service market from 19 per cent in 2019 to 21 per cent in 2023, while regional players lost ground and the decline of self-operators accelerated. Although contract catering has boomed since the pandemic, small caterers have struggled with wage hikes and food inflation, two push factors that have 'turbocharged demand at the big-listed groups'.[15] While food policy campaigners often prefer local suppliers to the Big Three, the latter are not going away any time soon and the lesson of Chartwells in Bristol is that corporate players can be part of the good food revolution if they meet robust sustainability standards such as the FFL standards.

Mainstream economists have exaggerated the role of vested interests and underestimated the power of ideas, according to Dani Rodrik, which is why many political economy models do such a poor job at explaining policy change. But 'reform often happens not when vested interests are defeated, but when different strategies are used to pursue those interests, or when interests themselves are redefined ... What the economist typically treats as immutable self-interest is too often an artefact of ideas about who we are, how the world works, and what actions are available.'[16] In this view, there are different routes through which new ideas gain traction in the policymaking world – for example, through crises, through experimentation and through the emulation of practices that prevail elsewhere, which is perhaps 'the single most important source of new ideas and policy innovation'.[17] But emulation is a notoriously slippery route because *context* matters: the policy can be transferred but not the context in which it's applied.

If we apply the above ideas to the UK context, we can safely say that there is no shortage of crises to justify radical policy changes: looming climate change, burgeoning diet-related diseases and escalating inequalities would surely fit the bill. But what is missing is the political will in central government to experiment with policy solutions that are equal to the scale of these crises. As we'll see in the following section, local

Prospects for change

experimentation is underway, and so is the appetite to learn from practices that prevail elsewhere. But these routes to change need more than localised actions if we want to mainstream the good food revolution.

Tapping the potential of the public plate

The public plate is finally being recognised for what it is – a potentially powerful instrument to deliver multiple dividends. Among other things, it is being used to promote social justice, public health and ecological integrity, the quintessential values of sustainable development. Given the social and ecological significance of public sector food provisioning, one might have thought it would merit a mention in the official agrifood statistics. But public food and catering is conspicuous by its absence in DEFRA's statistical guide to the agrifood sector.[18] One of the rare occasions when the government estimated the economic scale of public food and catering in the UK was over a decade ago, when it was put at £2.4 billion, equivalent to 5.5 per cent of the food service sector.[19] Any plan to tap the potential of the public plate in the UK will clearly need to be informed by better data, not least because the power of purchase is expected to address more public policy agendas than ever before.

Indeed, one of the key trends in public food provisioning in recent years has been a decisive shift from a narrow neoliberal conception of value for money to a more capacious conception of *values-based* procurement. In schools, hospitals and prisons, there is now a rapidly growing recognition that the power of purchase can help cities, regions and countries to address societal challenges when it is deployed with professional skill and political purpose and when it is synchronised with food production and food consumption systems. Conceived in this way, the public plate can become a catalyst for wider food system reform by championing the values of health and sustainability, values that should be embraced by every other segment of the grocery market. To illustrate the possibilities, let's return to the school meals service to highlight developments that are underway in and beyond the UK.

School meals: the litmus test of sustainability

Originally framed as a means to redress hunger and malnutrition in the early twentieth century, the school meals service is today being radically redesigned to meet the well-being of people and planet in the twenty-first century. As we saw in Chapter 2, the school meals service in the UK is currently in the throes of the most significant changes since the founding of the welfare state in the 1940s. Two important shifts are underway: the shift to *universality* and the shift to *plant-based diets*.

The shift from means-tested to universal provision of nutritious FSMs is arguably the most important child-centred social policy innovation in the UK today, especially when we consider the high levels of poverty among British children and the punishing effects of a cost-of-living crisis in which food price inflation is such a prominent feature. But laudable as it is, the provision of UFSM remains a *partial* social innovation because it applies to primary schools but not secondary schools in Scotland, Wales and certain London boroughs and it remains a means-tested service in England beyond the infant years. Where it has occurred, the shift to universality is already delivering tangible health benefits. For example, Essex University researchers evaluated the effect of cumulative exposure to Universal

Prospects for change

Infant Free School Meals (UIFSM) over the course of the first year of school of children in England on bodyweight outcomes. By the end of the school year, they found that those exposed to UIFSM had significantly better bodyweight outcomes than they otherwise would, in terms of being more likely to be a healthy weight, being less likely to be obese and having a lower body mass index. Regarding take-up of school meals before and after the policy was introduced, the results showed that children from families not previously eligible for free meals increased their take-up considerably, though children previously eligible for free lunches increased their take-up by little.[20]

But partial universality is not enough. Further progress will be determined by politics and not academic research. Extending universality to all primary and secondary schools along the lines of the Finnish and Swedish models is the real goal of school food reformers, which is endorsed by all seven public health associations in the UK.[21] The Labour government elected in July 2024 will come under enormous pressure to embrace the principle of universality for all children to demonstrate its commitment to health, social justice and sustainability.

The shift to more plant-based school meals is widely expected to deliver a triple dividend because meals are designed to be healthier, cheaper and more climate friendly. That is certainly the message from ProVeg, a not-for-profit organisation that supports school caterers free of charge because it is funded from philanthropic sources. It aims to make school food healthier and more sustainable through the reduction of animal products (including 'blending' plant protein and vegetables in meat-based dishes) and increasing wholefood plant-based lunch options. Although its School Plates programme is barely five years old, it has expanded rapidly to cover over 6,500 schools

Serving the public

in the UK, with 14.4 million meals swapped from meat-based to plant-based since the programme was launched in 2018. In that time ProVeg has supported or is supporting over 25 per cent of all local authorities in the UK with responsibility for school food. In recognition of its contribution to more sustainable diets, ProVeg was nominated for the Earthshot Prize in 2024, which scours the globe for game-changing innovations that aim to repair the planet, awarding the best five solutions each year with £1 million to scale their work.[22]

The public plate now plays a prominent role in sustainable food strategies in all parts of the UK. Scotland has led the way by embedding its school meals policy in the Good Food Nation Act that was passed in 2022. The Act places a duty on Scottish ministers, local authorities and health boards to produce Good Food Nation Plans to address social and economic well-being, educational needs, child poverty and the environment. A statutory Scottish Food Commission is also being established to scrutinise the Good Food Nation Plans. While civil society partners welcome these developments, they are concerned that the new food strategy has still not been fully integrated into the official mindset because, in the programme for government, which sets out government priorities for the year ahead, nutrition wasn't one of them and nor was the Good Food Nation Plan.[23] Even so, the first Good Food Nation Plan was eventually launched in 2024 and its six outcomes will set a new direction of travel for Scotland and a new benchmark for food system planning in the UK that will hopefully inspire other nations and regions to follow suit.

In Wales, as we saw in Chapter 2, the provision of UFSM for all primary school children was the top item in the Cooperation Agreement between the Welsh Labour government and Plaid Cymru, the Welsh national party. Both parties perceive school

Prospects for change

meals as a litmus test of the WFG Act, the innovative legislation that introduced seven well-being goals to guide public policy in Wales. But the UFSM commitment is more challenging than it might seem because the policy is expected to combat child hunger, reduce child poverty, support educational attainment, promote nutritional health and foster local economic development by boosting the production and distribution of local food from local suppliers to encourage shorter supply chains.

While the public plate can indeed be a catalyst for reform, there is clearly a danger of policy overload, where too many political targets are attached to a single policy. This danger was highlighted in a study commissioned by the Welsh government which found that, on its own, the public procurement budget was too small to transform the fortunes of SMEs in the food sector in Wales. To be effective, public procurement had to be synchronised with other enterprise support policies to provide hard and soft infrastructure in the form of food parks that offered rented units to reduce the capital costs of expansion and food innovation centres that supported new product and process development.[24]

This is the prosaic world of policy coordination: the commitment to UFSM might be classified as a *social* policy innovation, but it needs to be calibrated with *economic* development policy if the local supply chain is to have sufficient capacity to meet the higher levels of demand associated with universality.

Along with Scotland and Wales, London has been a pioneer of UFSM for its state-funded primary schools. As we saw in Chapter 2, a minority of boroughs led the way before Sadiq Khan, the London mayor, extended the policy to all boroughs on a temporary basis for the 2023–2024 and 2024–2025 academic years to help alleviate the cost-of-living crisis.[25]

Serving the public

Newham was the first London borough to launch a UFSM service in its primary schools, a policy that was endorsed in a public consultation exercise when the service was threatened by financial pressures. The Eat for Free scheme is delivering multiple benefits according to the council, some of which are shown in Exhibit 6.2. The multiple benefits also include environmental benefits because the school food tender requires all menus to be accredited to meet the FFL standards or to an equivalent independent inspected standard.[26]

Globally, too, the school meals service is moving up the political agenda, which is why the School Meals Coalition (SMC) was launched at the UN Food Systems Summit in 2021. The coalition has attracted 98 countries and 116 partners, all supported by a secretariat hosted by the UN World Food Programme. The SMC is a new and powerful champion for a school meals service that can catalyse food system reform:

> When properly designed and accompanied by adequate policy and regulatory frameworks, as well as support measures, sustainable school food procurement can promote the adoption of planet-friendly production practices, broaden the local food basket and stimulate crop diversity, along with other social and economic development outcomes. This is particularly true when school food demand is linked to local and smallholder agriculture production, such as in the home-grown school feeding (HGSF) approach.[27]

For the poorest countries, where the need for a sustainable school meals service is most pressing, domestic action urgently needs more imaginative international support. In 2021, just 0.1 per cent of global official development assistance was devoted to school meal programmes, the equivalent to less than half a day's worth of spending on farm subsidies in OECD member

Eat for Free: Benefits and Impact

Newham London

In Newham, over 90% of KS2 pupils have a school meal, significantly higher than in boroughs without universal meal schemes. Before the scheme was launched in 2009 only 49% of children were eating a school meal each day. Despite 52% of Newham children living in poverty, only 33% qualify for benefits related free school meals (FSM). Eat for Free (EFF) helps more children to access nutritious meals each day, with grant conditions and principles in place to ensure that we also target the wider range of impacts and benefits.

What are the benefits of EFF to our community?

1. HEALTH AND WELLBEING

On the curriculum
Universal meals normalise healthy eating as a core part of the school day.

Less packed lunches
Only 16% of packed lunches meet the government's school meals nutritional standards.

Higher quality meals
All caterers who serve food as part of EFF, should also hold the Food For Life Served Here award.

Whole school approach
EFF grant principles have all schools working to develop a whole school approach to food.

2. EDUCATION

Disadvantaged pupils
EFF captures pupils who are living in low income households, who would otherwise miss out on a FSM. Universal has been shown to raise take up both as a whole and amongst those with FSM eligibility.

Concentration
Teachers have reported that a universal offer improves classroom behaviour and concentration, allowing for more teaching and less classroom management. Studies show that disruptive behaviour negatively affects teachers' well-being. Eating together benefits everyone in the classroom, whether they would have eaten a meal or not.

Performance & attainment
Hungry children can't learn. Recent data shows that the primary attainment score for disadvantaged pupils in boroughs with universal meals is higher compared to boroughs without a scheme.

More time
Time spent preparing packed lunches can be better spent with children (e.g. supporting activities such as homework and reading).

3. COMMUNITY WEALTH BUILDING

Local jobs
86% of employees working to deliver school meals are Newham residents. More meals eaten means more meals that need to be prepared creating rewarding skilled local jobs. Primary school kitchens employ around 500 workers in Newham.

Benefits to Newham workers
Eat for Free schools are required to pay London Living Wage and local government pensions. Certified meal standards as a grant condition means more cooking in each school which increases the volume and skill of work required locally.

Benefits to the Newham economy
Since the 1980s the school meals landscape has seen a significant decrease both in the number and size of local authority run education catering services. Large private sector caterers have grown with their remote national supply chains replacing more localised partnerships.

LA run school kitchens recognise unions and pay better than minimum Ts & Cs. EFF grant conditions seek to create a level playing field on labour costs when a school goes out to tender meaning caterers are competing on the quality of their meals and understanding of schools needs.

In Newham the Council owned caterer, Juniper Ventures, feeds the pupils in around two-thirds of all Eat for Free schools. The service uses local suppliers creating jobs accessible to residents.

4. SUSTAINABILITY

Climate Now
One of the six key futures outlined in Newham's Just Transition Plan is 'We Eat Well and Sustainably.' Grant conditions and principles have all 66 schools signed up as partners on this journey.

Food for Life Served Here
The scheme ensures all menus are inspected and accredited not just for health but against a standard that also prioritises the use of fresh, ethical and sustainable produce whilst championing local producers.

London Circular Purchasing Commitment
Newham Council was a founding signatory on this commitment that sets a measured pathway to reduce per plate CO2e on food waste and increase local buying. Grant conditions require all caterers to baseline and then commit to this journey by 2030.

Anchored spend
The Council invest around £6m every year in funding the KS2 element of the Eat for Free programme, by continuing to evolve the conditions of grant and support but this enables all money spent on primary school meals in the borough to be anchored by EFF conditions and principles.

What's next?
There are 66 schools who participate in the Eat for Free programme, by continuing to evolve the conditions of grant and support on offer we are able to increase outputs that advance our position on children's health, education, climate and community wealth building.

newham.gov.uk

WE ARE NEWHAM.

Exhibit 6.2 The benefits of the Eat for Free scheme

countries. Debt relief is part of the solution here. Under the Heavily Indebted Poor Countries framework, debtor governments promised to convert debt service savings into priority areas, generating new resources for health, education and other priorities. 'Debt-for-school-meal swaps' – along the lines of existing 'debt-for-nature' swaps – are now being proposed to provide direct financing for school meal programmes linked to wider food system reform initiatives. Smarter finance and better links between school food policy and climate policy would go a long way to plug the gaps in the global school meals agenda and help to get the Sustainable Development Goal for Zero Hunger back on track.[28]

Whatever the country context, policymakers need to recognise that school food reform is a far more complex challenge than their preconceptions might lead them to believe, not least because the goal of sustainability demands an unprecedented degree of coordination between policy departments and professional functions if synergies are to be maximised and trade-offs minimised. A five-country study of the school meals service highlighted the need for such integration when it sought to identify which actions have the greatest impacts on sustainability. It found that two types of action stood out. The first was a *sustainable menu* focus, which allowed the public catering service to address two sustainability measures (nutrition and carbon emissions) through a single policy instrument. But an exclusive focus on menu composition neglects the effect of food waste, so sustainable menu measures need to be integrated with those promoting infrastructure development and the installation of low-carbon waste disposal methods. The second type of action centred on the *valorisation of catering service staff*. The study found that, as well as contributing to local economies

Prospects for change

through the multiplier effect of their spending, catering staff were instrumental in implementing menu innovations and reducing plate waste, which have positive environmental and nutritional impacts.

These findings carry important implications for the design and delivery of the school meals service everywhere because they underline the need for coordination between policies and professions. All too often, the authors conclude, 'public institutions separate out the management and decision-making for catering service delivery from the management of procurement contracts. This means that the addressing of sustainability issues is often siloed in the realm of procurement, overlooking the very real potential of integrating the catering service delivery to address sustainability outcomes.'[29]

Healthcare and prisons

Tapping the potential of the public plate is no less urgent in healthcare and prisons, but these sectors have always struggled to compete with schools in the public mind. As we saw in Part II, the costs of the status quo in hospitals and prisons are becoming unsustainable. Although the quest for good food is not (yet) a top priority in political debates on healthcare reform in the UK, where it is sidelined by the more immediate crises of long waiting lists for hospital treatment and staff shortages, it is nevertheless part of the long-term solution to the paradox of the hospital. The paradox, as we have seen, consists of the impossible mission to which the NHS is condemned: the Sisyphean mission of offering *clinical* solutions to the *societal* problems of diet-related diseases. Sustainable diets are part of a societal solution because nutritious food will deliver a double dividend

Serving the public

by improving recovery rates within hospital and by reducing the demand for hospital treatment by placing more emphasis on prevention in the community.

We have seen how such programmes can work at the local level when we noted the sustainable food strategies in the Cornwall and Bristol health trusts in the UK, local initiatives that could have gone mainstream had they received more national support from the NHS hierarchy and from central government. Scaling sustainable diets within the healthcare sector is one of the goals of Health Care Without Harm, an NGO that seeks to transform healthcare worldwide so that it reduces its environmental footprint and becomes a community anchor for sustainability and a leader in the global movement for environmental health and justice. For the past decade it has sought to transform hospital food through programmes that harness values-based purchasing power to build a sustainable, equitable and health-promoting food system that benefits people and planet.[30]

Prisons are probably the most difficult environments in which to promote a good food revolution, not least because of the tenacious legacy of *less eligibility*, the proposition that prison conditions should be worse than, or certainly no better than, average conditions in free society, otherwise detention would cease to be a deterrent. But in the UK and the US, where mass incarceration is most pronounced, the human and financial costs of the carceral state are truly enormous. More nutritious diets have been shown to improve behaviour and access to more purposeful activity would enhance rehabilitation, the welfare support function that remains woefully inadequate in both countries.

The modest reforms that are underway suggest that so much more could be done to improve the human lot of prisoners *and* alleviate the burden on the public purse at the same time, because the cost of reoffending – which is partly due to the lack of training in prison and the lack of support after prison – has reached some £18 billion a year in the UK. Although the Clink's food training programme is currently confined to a tiny fraction of the prison population in the UK, it could easily be expanded if central government had the wit and the wherewithal to recognise that investing in rehabilitation makes fiscal as well as ethical sense.

Beyond the fragments: alliances for change

The good food revolution is a cause that attracts such a bewildering array of interest groups that they straddle every aspect of the food system from farm to fork. But as we saw in Chapter 5, diversity is both a strength and a weakness. It is a strength if diverse interests can act in concert and forge an alliance for change, but it is a weakness if they allow their differences to trump what they have in common. I have witnessed the pros and cons of diversity up close as a food system researcher and as a food policy campaigner and I'm inclined to agree with Raymond Tallis when he says: 'It seems to me likely that the deepest differences between human beings are not between man and woman, black and white, between intellectuals who aspire to the examined life and the thoughtless who do not, between those who do and those who do not believe in God, but between the hungry and the well-fed.'[31]

At a time of polarising politics and splintering identities in many countries, it becomes ever more important to reaffirm common bonds of citizenship and humanity because these bonds have been obscured by 'the postmodern nightmare of a world in which there is nothing but diversity'.[32] Common bonds can be reaffirmed in many different ways but none is surely more urgent or indeed more consequential than the need to address burgeoning levels of hunger. Of all the priorities that compete for our attention and resources, addressing hunger is second to none because it is the foundation on which all other goals are predicated. But while the relief of hunger has the greatest claim on our moral compass, we must also recognise that the good food agenda cannot be reduced to a narrow nutritional issue because food has such a multifunctional character.

Managing these different, and sometimes competing, food policy priorities can become an existential issue for any food movement. We need only recall the fate of the CFSC in the US, an organisation that sought to overcome the fragmentation of single-issue food politics, which eventually imploded because it failed to resolve the racialised tensions between the anti-hunger and sustainability wings of the movement.

If unity in diversity is the goal, then the Good Food movement needs to think of itself as a network of networks or a movement of movements, as was suggested earlier. Such a loose, pluralistic arrangement will be anathema to those of a Leninist disposition, who hanker after a tighter form of organisation that can function as the political vanguard of the movement. But the unequivocal lesson of history is that the single agent theory of change – be it the party, the proletariat or the populist leader – is the kiss of death for any movement that aspires to build alliances that are inclusive and transformative. Drawing on the UK experience, two agents have played prominent roles in building alliances for change in the food system: (1) civil society organisations that transcend single-issue demands and help to change the way we view and value food, and (2) public

Prospects for change

sector institutions that are able and willing to use their powers to promote the good food cause.

Sustain and the Soil Association are the best examples of civil society organisations that have managed to transcend single-issue food politics in the UK. They were often the prime movers in building alliances to launch experimental food projects in collaboration with public sector partners in local government or the health service. While these organisations continue their traditional advocacy work, they are increasingly committed to embedding sustainable food priorities in the regulatory rules and institutional practices of their public sector partners.

A case in point is the Good Food for All Londoners campaign. For more than a decade, Sustain has mapped and reported on Greater London's borough-level commitments to healthy and sustainable food through an annual survey and report. A highly effective tool for improving good food practice and policy among London councils, the survey and report act as an incentive for self-improvement, while providing guidance and a supportive network to help them along the way. Although Sustain refrains from saying so, the exercise has been effective because it includes a de facto 'naming and shaming' component in which a map of all thirty-three boroughs is put into the public domain to highlight high and low performers. Launching its 2024 report, for example, Sustain showcased the high performers, saying: 'Camden, Greenwich, Islington, Lambeth, Newham, Southwark and Tower Hamlets have been recognised for scoring highly across a broad range of measures, showing cross-cutting leadership. Wandsworth has been recognised as the most improved council, with special mention of its work on food poverty, school food, and developing a food strategy.'[33]

Serving the public

This food policy exercise is now being extended to the whole country under a new programme called Good Food Local, which is being piloted in north-east England, one of the poorest regions in the UK, where Sustain is partnering with the Association of Directors of Public Health and food partnerships from the region to tailor the survey to their local context and begin benchmarking local authority action on good food. Sustain is ideally placed to build alliances that straddle multiple spatial scales because it is a self-styled alliance of organisations and communities working together for a better system of food, farming and fishing by cultivating the movement for change.

But Good Food Local will confront the same challenges that faced the Soil Association's FFL programme: (1) how to build durable partnerships with local health trusts and local authorities, the key public sector anchor institutions that exist in all parts of the country; and (2) how to replicate or mainstream these arrangements nationally. Food campaigners would do well to learn from the field of social innovation, where these challenges are all too familiar. In a panoramic overview of the field, Geoff Mulgan asks how social innovation can become more than a series of interesting pilots and projects. 'The general lesson from most of these exercises', he says, 'is that structures help but are less important than processes, and that these in turn are less important than cultures.' The kind of culture he has in mind involves the strengthening of *horizontal* links and confidence between public sector staff, professionals, NGOs and others as 'a vital complement to top-down authorization from leaders and the use of formal metrics'.[34]

Another reflexive practitioner is Hilary Cottam. In *Radical Help* she resolutely eschews the idea of 'scaling' because it

Prospects for change

smacks of an industrial rollout process from the centre to the margins. She argues that the questions we need to ask are these:

> Can we seed the models in new places so that they can take root and be grown locally? Can we connect more and more people to the networks and platforms? And can we do this in a way that remains true to the principles, while enabling local adaptation? I know we can ... We learned that success was dependent on three factors: a shared vision, local leadership and a commitment to core values.[35]

Fostering collaboration through culture change, shared vision and core values sounds fine in principle, but what does it mean in practice? Translating these goals into a practical strategy for placed-based change is one of the great merits of the Foundational Liveability school of action research, which proposes three pragmatic ways of working to foster a discovery process of distributed social innovation: (1) engage with system and place specifics, (2) generate a robust evidence base to guide action and (3) mobilise alliances for change. 'Alliances for change', in this perspective, 'are the necessary but difficult precondition for initiating social innovation and for replication with variation for local circumstance'.[36]

Foundational Liveability is an intellectually compelling but politically challenging strategy for social innovation because, while it recognises that progressive localism is critically important, it also acknowledges that the central state cannot be bypassed since so much local delivery of 'essentials' is centrally formatted and funded. The 'essentials' in this conception rest on three foundational pillars of liveability – disposable and residual income, essential services and social infrastructure – each of which depends on central state funding in centralised financial systems such as the UK.

Serving the public

This brings us to the second type of agent referred to above: public sector institutions that are able and willing to use their powers to promote the good food cause. Even if civil society organisations such as Sustain are successful in changing the way we view and value food by shifting the cognitive landscape, their ideas about 'good food' and 'sustainable diets' will count for little unless they are translated into the policies of public sector bodies such as health boards and local authorities. But as earlier chapters have shown, public sector capacity in the UK has been eviscerated by the austerity policies of successive Conservative governments, which have been in thrall to a pre-Keynesian neoliberal creed.

Reforming this hostile macro environment is perhaps the single most important political priority if the UK is to create the conditions in which the Good Food movement can flourish rather than merely survive. The macro environment is invariably taken to mean the *economic* environment in conventional public discourse, where the UK's problems consist of low productivity, low investment and low growth, all of which contribute to the current crisis of foundational liveability. But the macro environment that I have in mind here is the *governance* environment, where political power is located and where public policies are designed and delivered. If political governance seems far removed from the nitty-gritty of public food provisioning, we should remember that this is where the rules of the game are established to determine how public sector bodies are to be managed, regulated and resourced.

In governance terms the UK is an international outlier. Food policy campaigners need to recognise the peculiarities of this governance system because a reform agenda that fails to address it is likely to end in tears. Two aspects of the UK

Prospects for change

system need to be addressed as a matter of urgency: the hyper-centralised nature of political power and the fiscal crisis of the local state.

The advent of devolution since 1999 may have obscured the hyper-centralised nature of the political system in the UK. While there has been a modest amount of devolution to the Celtic nations, to London and more recently to city-regions throughout the country, the primary powers over economic policy remain firmly in the hands of central government in Whitehall, specifically in the UK Treasury. At the core of the conservative fiscal mindset in the UK Treasury is the Green Book, which contains the cost–benefit analysis (CBA) methodology for deciding whether public investment projects pass the value-for-money test. The CBA methodology uses market prices and critics have shown that this 'gives rise to a "Matthew Effect" whereby further infrastructure investment occurs in places that are already productive'. To them that hath, in other words.[37]

Since this CBA methodology runs counter to the new political rhetoric of 'inclusive growth' and 'levelling up', the Green Book needs to be revised to remove the algorithmic bias against public investment in poorer regions. This is merely one of many problems associated with the peculiar UK governance system. In fact, there is now growing awareness that the hyper-centralised structure of the UK governance system has contributed to high inter-regional inequalities on the one hand and very low trust in central government on the other. But the key institutional feature that distinguishes the UK from other OECD countries is the lack of empowered middle-tier institutions between local and central government.[38]

Hyper-centralisation is closely linked to the fiscal crisis of the local state. Putting the local state on a sustainable financial footing will not be achieved without a major devolution of powers and resources to regional and local levels in the UK because the current central–local fiscal system is manifestly dysfunctional by the standards of comparable countries in the OECD, where local councils have more fiscal autonomy. Taxation in the UK is exceptionally centralised for a country of its size and level of development. Only 5 per cent of the UK's tax revenues in 2019 were collected by local government, compared to 14 per cent in France, 23 per cent in Japan, and 35 per cent in Sweden. Accordingly, local government relies on central government grant funding, with only 19 per cent of all local spending in the UK funded locally, compared to 37 per cent in the average OECD unitary state.[39]

Although the fiscal crisis of the local state has been in the making for many years, exacerbated by the systematic reductions in central government grants since 2010, the current fiscal position is unprecedented. The local government sector is now in a semi-permanent financial crisis, according to a 2024 survey, because over half the respondents said they were likely to declare effective bankruptcy in the next five years and 9 per cent said they were likely to do so in the next financial year.[40]

Fashioning a more devolved and effective governance system in the UK is essential if we want to promote a distributed capacity for social innovation in which local states and civil society organisations are empowered to act on their local knowledge. New models of experimental governance are emerging in which central government becomes more of an enabler of change and less of an ineffectual micro-manager. For their part, local and regional states and their partners need to assume responsibility for essential services, social infrastructure and place-based alliances for change because they have the democratic mandate to

Prospects for change

be place leaders in their localities. Significantly, the Good Food movement has now recognised that 'devolution is the key to unlocking UK food system reform'.[41]

Although the US has a more decentralised political system on account of its federal constitution, American federalism presents national and subnational governance challenges to the Good Food movement. At the national level the US party system has never been more polarised, with the result that transformative change becomes exceedingly difficult in the face of such political gridlock. At the subnational level, as we have seen, progressive urban food policies face the threat of being overruled or pre-empted by hyper-conservative state governments that are in denial about climate change and the rest of the good food policy agenda. Despite these problems, Joe Biden won plaudits in 2022 when he convened the first White House Conference on Hunger, Nutrition and Health in over fifty years. 'We are mobilizing the will to meet a bold goal', he said, 'to end hunger in America and increase healthy eating and physical activity by 2030 so fewer Americans experience diet-related diseases.'[42] Mobilising a broad-based coalition – consisting of federal, state and local governments along with civil society and business – is one of the preconditions to effect transformational change in the food system. But only time will tell if the White House, having willed the ends, has the capacity or the opportunity to will the means in a country where partisan politics are so corrosive to collective action.

Governance challenges are not confined to the UK and the US. The Good Food movement faces a common dilemma wherever it is active. While it is at the forefront of campaigns for a fairer, healthier and more sustainable food system, the localities, cities and regions in which it operates are neglected by both national governments and international bodies, especially in food and climate negotiations.[43] The principle of *subsidiarity* needs to be invoked here to resolve the political paradox at the heart of conventional models of multilevel governance: the sub-national level has the least power, yet it is the most important level for policy delivery and implementation.[44] Far from being a nice-to-have principle, in other words, subsidiarity can deliver a double dividend: as well as being the key to more impactful food policy, it also enables local citizens to be actively involved in the social innovations that are necessary to reform climate and food policies.

The upshot of this analysis is that the Good Food movement everywhere needs to be more fully engaged in campaigns for devolved and polycentric governance systems because this is the political environment in which multiple centres of power and decision-making can emerge and where good food systems are more likely to flourish.

Acknowledgements

All books incur debts, emotional as well as intellectual, and this book is no exception. Some of the following people have commented on drafts, while others have discussed the issues at the heart of the book, and I am eternally grateful to them for sharing their time and knowledge in such a generous spirit. In alphabetical order, a big thank you to: Gunilla Andersson, Tom Andrews, Leon Ballin, David Barling, Alison Blay-Palmer, Jonathan Bone, Myles Bremner, Mary Brennan, Helen Browning, Martin Caraher, Joy Carey, Hannah Caswell, Aditya Chakrabortty, Nevin Cohen, Karen Coombs, Barbara Crowther, Kath Dalmeny, Andy Davies, Rhys Davies, Robbie Davison, Peter Defranceschi, Alexa Delwiche, Naomi Duncan, Callum Etches, Andy Fisher, Thomas Forster, David Foad, Colette Fox, Peter Fox, Sinead Fury, Ruth Galpine, Bernard Gesch, Andy Gold, Bob Gottlieb, Anna Graham, Dan Gregory, Judith Gregory, Kirsty Hudson, Becca Jablonski, Rhys James, Ian Rees Jones, Jayne Jones, Mat Jones, Robert Jones, Tim Lang, Jo Lewis, Charlotte Long, Caron Longden, Jane Lynch, Kate MacKenzie, Terry Marsden, Mara Miele, Paul Milbourne, Raksha Mistry, Adrian Morley, Helen

Acknowledgements

Nilsson, Rich Osborn, Katie Palmer, Rob Percival, Cressida Pidgeon, Jenny Rathbone, Simon Reeves, Alex Richardson, Raychel Santo, Andrew Sayer, Emma Sirois, Lori Stahlbrand, Heather Stevens, Jonathan Tench, Yvonne Thomas, Angela Tregear, Matt Waskiewicz, Lee Waters, Gary Wilkins, Victoria Williams, Craig Willingham, Mark Winne, Simon Wood, Simon Wright, Samara Zuckerbrod.

Special thanks are due to Julie Froud and Karel Williams, the series editors, who painstakingly read every word and offered constructive challenges on style and substance from start to finish. At Manchester University Press, I must thank Kim Walker and Alun Richards for being firm but fair with respect to deadlines. I'm also grateful to Don Shewan for help with the illustrations.

Finally, I must thank my family – Sue, Louis, Robin, Jenny, Ioan and Maisie – for their steadfast support and encouragement. Diolch i chi gyd!

Exhibits

0.1	Health and environmental impacts of different diets	15
2.1	Food for Life meals by sector and award level (2021)	87
2.2	Amount of certified organic food served in Malmö	93
2.3	Greenhouse gas emissions from food procured by Malmö	94
3.1	Tackling obesities: building a sustainable response	110–111
4.1	Prison population of England and Wales since 1900	144
4.2	Mass production for mass incarceration	159
4.3	The punishing effects of the mainstream carceral diet	163
4.4	The Clink Integrated Rehabilitation Programme	169
5.1	What is a Food Policy Council?	197
5.2	A movement of movements	200
5.3	Goals for NYC's food future	203
5.4	The Nanny Bloomberg ad	209
6.1	The vested interests in the junk food cycle	228
6.2	The benefits of the Eat for Free scheme	237

Notes

Introduction

1 *Oldham Evening Chronicle* (2019) 'Oldham's school dinners are top of the class', 22 November.
2 A. Chakrabortty (2018) 'The school that shows good food is not just for posh kids', *The Guardian*, 25 April.
3 M. Bynke (2023) *Malmo's Policy for Sustainable Development and Food*, Malmö: Malmö Stad.
4 C. Peckham and J. Petts (eds) (2003) *Good Food on the Public Plate*, London: Sustain; K. Morgan (2006) 'School food and the public domain: the politics of the public plate', *The Political Quarterly*, 77(3), pp. 379–387.
5 The adage is usually attributed to William Gibson, the science fiction writer.
6 H. Pennington (2009) *The Public Inquiry into the September 2005 Outbreak of E.coli O157 in South Wales*, London: HMSO, p. 11.
7 *Ibid.*, p. 317. A phrase coined by Diane Vaughan to characterise the deviant culture in NASA that led to the *Challenger* space shuttle disaster in 1986.
8 Private communication from Mark Powell KC, the barrister for Mason's parents.
9 L. Swensson et al. (2020) 'Public food procurement as a game changer for food system transformation', in L. Swensson et al. (eds) *Public Food Procurement for Sustainable Food Systems and Healthy Diets*, Rome: FAO, p. 3.

Notes

10 T. Spector (2015) *The Diet Myth: The Real Science Behind What We Eat*, London: Weidenfeld & Nicolson, p. 276.
11 D. Cohen and M. McCartney (2023) 'We need to talk about ZOE: how scientific is the must-have health app?', *UnHerd*, 12 October.
12 United Nations (2023) *The Sustainable Development Goals Report 2023*, New York: UN.
13 F. Branca et al. (2020) 'A new nutrition manifesto for a new nutrition reality', *The Lancet*, 395, 4 January.
14 C. Hawkes et al. (2020) 'Double-duty actions: seizing programme and policy opportunities to address malnutrition in all its forms', *The Lancet*, 395, 30 January, pp. 142–155.
15 Joseph Rowntree Foundation (2024) *UK Poverty 2024*, York: JRF.
16 A. Hill (2023) 'Children raised under austerity shorter than European peers, study finds', *The Guardian*, 21 June.
17 Academy of Medical Sciences (2024) *Prioritising Early Childhood to Promote the Nation's Health, Wellbeing and Prosperity*, London: AMS.
18 Food and Agriculture Organisation (2012) *Sustainable Diets and Biodiversity*, Rome: FAO. See also P. Mason and T. Lang (2017) *Sustainable Diets: How Ecological Nutrition Can Transform Consumption and the Food System*, Abingdon: Routledge.
19 T. Garnett (2016) 'Plating up solutions: can eating patterns be both healthier and more sustainable?', *Science*, 353(6305), pp. 1202–1204.
20 *Ibid.*, p. 1204.
21 M. Nussbaum (2013) *Political Emotions*, Cambridge, MA: The Belknap Press, p. 383.

Chapter 1

1 C. Peckham and J. Petts (eds) (2003) *Good Food on the Public Plate*, London: Sustain.
2 A. Tooze (2022) 'Welcome to the world of the polycrisis', *Financial Times*, 28 October.
3 World Economic Forum (2023) *The Global Risks Report 2023*, Geneva: World Economic Forum, p. 6.
4 World Health Organization (2017) *The Double Burden of Malnutrition: Policy Brief*, Geneva: WHO.

Notes

5 A. Afshin et al. (2019) 'Health effects of dietary risks in 195 countries, 1990–2017: a systematic analysis for the Global Burden of Disease Study 2017', *The Lancet*, 393, pp. 1958–1972.

6 FAO (2023) *Climate Action and Nutrition: Pathways to Impact*, Rome: FAO.

7 P. Dasgupta (2021), *The Economics of Biodiversity: The Dasgupta Review*, London: HM Treasury, p. 221.

8 The Economics of Ecosystems and Biodiversity (TEEB) (2018) *Measuring What Matters in Agriculture and Food Systems*, Geneva: UN Environment.

9 FAO (2006) *Livestock's Long Shadow: Environmental Issues and Options*, Rome: FAO, p. 222.

10 A. Neslen (2023) '"The anti-livestock people are a pest": how UN food body played down role of farming in climate change', *The Guardian*, 20 October.

11 FAO (2023) *Achieving SDG 2 Without Breaching the 1.5C Threshold: A Global Roadmap*, Rome: FAO.

12 FAO (2023) *Climate Action and Nutrition: Pathways to Impact*, Rome: FAO, p. 6.

13 IPES Food *(2023) From Plate to Planet: How Local Governments Are Driving Action on Climate Change through Food*, https://ipes-food.org/report/from-plate-to-planet/.

14 F. Hayek (1945) 'The use of knowledge in society', *American Economic Review*, 35, p. 521.

15 P. Cooke and K. Morgan (1998) *The Associational Economy*, Oxford: Oxford University Press.

16 J. Buchanan (2003) 'Public choice: politics without romance', *Policy*, 19(3), pp. 13–18.

17 J. Buchanan and G. Tullock (1962) *The Calculus of Consent*, Ann Arbor: University of Michigan Press.

18 J. Buchanan (1975) *The Limits of Liberty: Between Anarchy and Leviathan*, Chicago: University of Chicago Press, p. 205.

19 N. MacLean (2017) *Democracy in Chains*, London: Scribe Publications, p. 161.

20 W. Brown (2015) *Undoing the Demos: Neoliberalism's Stealth Revolution*, Princeton: Princeton University Press. See also D. Harvey (2007) *A Brief History of Neoliberalism*, Oxford: Oxford University Press; and J. Peck (2013) *Constructions of Neoliberal Reason*, Oxford: Oxford University Press.

Notes

21 D. Marquand (2004) *Decline of the Public: The Hollowing Out of Citizenship*, Cambridge: Polity, p. 104.
22 *Ibid.*, p. 122.
23 Local Government Management Board (1997) *Service Delivery and Competition Information Service*, Survey Report No. 15, London: LGMB.
24 Department of Environment (1997) *CCT and Local Authority Blue-collar Services*, London: DoE.
25 D. Parker (1990) 'The 1988 Local Government Act and compulsory competitive tendering', *Urban Studies*, 27(5), pp. 653–668.
26 Marquand, *Decline of the Public*, p. 125.
27 A. Sen (2015) 'The economic consequences of austerity', *New Statesman*, 4 June.
28 A. Pratt (2023) *Food Banks in the UK*, London: House of Commons Library.
29 T. Helm (2013) 'Charities condemn Iain Duncan Smith for food bank snub', *The Observer*, 21 December.
30 The Trussell Trust (2019) *Universal Credit and Food Banks*, Salisbury: The Trussell Trust.
31 BBC (2024) *Fixing Britain: Hunger*, BBC Radio 4, 2 January.
32 G. Atkins and S. Hoddinott (2020) *Local Government Funding in England*, London: Institute for Government.
33 D. Walsh et al. (2022) 'Bearing the burden of austerity: how do changing mortality rates in the UK compare between men and women?', *Journal of Epidemiology and Community Health*, 76, pp. 1027–1033.
34 P. Butler (2022) 'Over 330,000 excess deaths in Great Britain linked to austerity, finds study', *The Guardian* 5 October.
35 See D. Rodrik (2014) 'Green industrial policy', *Oxford Review of Economic Policy*, 30(3), pp. 469–491; M. Mazzucato (2013) *The Entrepreneurial State: Debunking Public vs. Private Sector Myths*, London: Anthem Press; and A. Cumbers (2012) *Reclaiming Public Ownership*, London: Zed Books.
36 A. Bowman et al. (2014) *The End of the Experiment?* Manchester: Manchester University Press.
37 J. Stiglitz (2019) 'After neoliberalism', *Project Syndicate*, 30 May.
38 W. Brown (2019) *In the Ruins of Neoliberalism*, New York: Columbia University Press.
39 National Audit Office (2006) *Ministry of Defence: Major Projects Report 200*, London: NAO.
40 P. Gershon (1999) *Review of Civil Procurement in Central Government*, London: HM Treasury.

Notes

41 K. Morgan et al. (2006) *Worlds of Food: Place, Power and Provenance in the Food Chain*, Oxford: Oxford University Press.

42 World Trade Organization (2014) *Agreement on Government Procurement 2012*, Geneva: WTO, p. 86.

43 O. De Schutter et al. (2021) 'Public food procurement as a development tool: the role of the regulatory framework', in FAO, *Public Food Procurement for Sustainable Food Systems and Healthy Diets*, Rome: FAO, p. 51.

44 ClientEarth (2012) *Procuring Best Value for Money: Why Eliminating the 'Lowest Price' Approach to Awarding Public Contracts Would Serve Both Sustainability Objectives and Efficient Public Spending*, London: ClientEarth.

45 De Shutter et al., 'Public food procurement as a development tool', p. 54.

46 Sustainable Procurement Task Force (2006) *Procuring the Future*, London: DEFRA, p. 52.

47 DEFRA (2003) *Unlocking Opportunities: Lifting the Lid on Public Sector Food Procurement*, London: DEFRA.

48 Deloitte (2009) *Public Sector Food Procurement Initiative: An Evaluation*, London: DEFRA, p. 27.

49 National Audit Office (2005) *Sustainable Procurement in Central Government*, London: NAO.

50 Cabinet Office (2021) *Transforming Public Procurement: Government Response to Consultation*, London: UK Government, para. 127.

51 K. Morgan and R. Sonnino (2008) *The School Food Revolution*, London: Earthscan, p. 41.

52 H. Pearce (2003) *Food for Life: Healthy, Local, Organic School Meals*, Bristol: Soil Association.

53 House of Commons (2021) *Public Sector Procurement of Food*, London: House of Commons, Environment, Food and Rural Affairs Committee, HC 469, para. 40.

54 The reference to national government requires clarification here because, being a multinational state, the 'national' government could refer to the Scottish and Welsh governments as well as to the UK government in London. To avoid confusion, I refer to the London-based UK government as the central government and to either local authorities or city-regional governments as subnational governments.

55 K. Morgan and R. Wyn Jones (2023) 'Brexit and the death of devolution', *The Political Quarterly*, 94(4), pp. 625–633.

Notes

56 H. Dimbleby (2023) *Ravenous: How to Get Ourselves and the Planet into Shape*, London: Profile Books, p. 17.
57 J. Pickard and A. Gross (2024) 'Tory MP Chris Skidmore quits with attack on UK climate policy', *Financial Times*, 6 January.
58 Fruit and Vegetable Alliance (2023) *Cultivating Success: Priorities for Increasing Sustainable Production to Meet Growing Demand*, London: FVA, p. 5.
59 I. Hughes (2023) *Happy 5th Birthday to the Soft Drinks Industry Levy!*, The Food Foundation, 6 April, https://foodfoundation.org.uk/news/happy-5th-birthday-soft-drinks-industry-levy.
60 A. Gregory (2023) 'England heads for obesity disaster as minister frets about nanny state', *The Guardian*, 25 December.
61 Food, Farming and Countryside Commission (2023) *So, What Do We Really Want from Food?*, Bristol: FFCC.
62 P. Foster et al. (2024) 'New Brexit border rules will hit UK supply chains, food industry warns', *Financial Times*, 29 January.
63 T. Lang (2020) *Feeding Britain: Our Food Problems and How to Fix Them*, London: Pelican, p. 412.

Chapter 2

1 K. Morgan and R. Sonnino (2008) *The School Food Revolution: Public Food and the Challenge of Sustainable Development*, London: Earthscan.
2 *Ibid.*, p. xv.
3 This section on the three models draws on and develops the schema in K. Morgan (2006) 'School food and the public domain: the politics of the public plate', *The Political Quarterly*, 77(3), pp. 379–387.
4 J. Vernon (2007) *Hunger: A Modern History*, Cambridge, MA: The Belknap Press, p. 162.
5 *Ibid.*, pp. 87–88.
6 M. Cross and B. MacDonald (2009) *Nutrition in Institutions*, Chichester: Wiley-Blackwell, p. 9.
7 U. Gustafsson (2002) 'School meals policy: the problem of governing children', *Social Policy & Administration*, 36(6), pp. 685–697.
8 P. Fisher (1987) 'History of school meals in Great Britain', *Nutrition and Health*, 4, pp. 189–194.
9 *Ibid.*, p. 190.
10 Cross and MacDonald, *Nutrition in Institutions*, p. 10.

Notes

11 S. Passmore and G. Harris (2004) 'Education, health and school meals: a review of policy changes in England and Wales over the last century', *Nutrition Bulletin*, 29, pp. 221–227.
12 Morgan and Sonnino, *The School Food Revolution*, p. 92.
13 J. Orrey (2003) *The Dinner Lady*, London: Transworld.
14 Passmore and Harris, 'Education, health and school meals', pp. 223–224.
15 Scottish Executive (2002) *Hungry for Success: A Whole School Approach to School Meals in Scotland*, Edinburgh: TSO.
16 School Meals Review Panel (2005) *Turning the Tables: Transforming School Food*, London: DfES.
17 *Ibid.*, p. 9.
18 *Ibid.*, p. 35.
19 *Ibid.*, p. 9.
20 H. Dimbleby and J. Vincent (2013) *The School Food Plan*, www.gov.uk/government/publications/the-school-food-plan, p. 8.
21 C. van Tulleken (2023) *Ultra-processed People*, London: Cornerstone Press; K. Wilson (2023) *Unprocessed: How the Food We Eat Is Fuelling Our Mental Health Crisis*, London: W. H. Allen.
22 J. Dani et al. (2006) 'The remarkable role of nutrition in learning and behaviour', *Nutrition & Food Science*, 35(4), pp. 258–263; A. Richardson (2006) *They Are What You Feed Them*, London: HarperThorsons.
23 M. Belot and J. James (2011) 'Healthy school meals and educational outcomes', *Journal of Health Economics*, 30, pp. 489–504. For more evidence of the positive effects of diet on health, education and behaviour see Dimbleby and Vincent, *The School Food Plan*.
24 J. Orme et al. (2010) *Food for Life Partnership Evaluation*, Bristol: University of the West of England (UWE). This section draws on the UWE-led evaluation, the first comprehensive assessment of the FFL programme. Full disclosure: I was a member of the evaluation team.
25 *Ibid.*, p. 162.
26 M. Jones et al. (2016) *Evaluation of Food for Life 2013–2015: Summary and Synthesis Report*, Bristol: UWE, p. 43.
27 Soil Association (2021) *Food for Life Served Here 2020–2021: Our Impact*, Bristol: Soil Association.
28 K. Morgan (2021) 'Foodscapes of hope: the foundational economy of food', in F. Barbera and I. R. Jones (eds) *The Foundational Economy and Citizenship*, Bristol: Policy Press.

Notes

29 E. Gullberg (2006) 'Food for future citizens: school meal culture in Sweden', *Food, Culture & Society*, 9(3), pp. 337–343.

30 For this social engineering debate see J. Vernon (2007) *Hunger: A Modern History*, London: The Belknap Press.

31 C. Persson Osowski (2012) *The Swedish School Meal as a Public Meal*, PhD thesis, Uppsala University.

32 Gullberg, 'Food for future citizens', p. 341.

33 Malmö Stad (2010) *Policy for Sustainable Development and Food*, Malmö: Malmö Stad.

34 A. Moragues-Faus and K. Morgan (2015) 'Reframing the foodscape: the emergent world of urban food policy', *Environment and Planning A: Economy and Space*, 47(7), pp. 1558–1573.

35 M. Bynke (2023) *Malmo's Policy for Sustainable Development and Food: The Journey That Has Brought Us to Where We Are Today*, internal report, Malmö: Malmö Stad.

36 *Ibid.*, p. 7.

37 *Ibid.*, p. 17.

38 H. Nilsson (2022) *Malmo's Policy for Sustainable Development and Food*, presentation to Cynnal Cymru Roundtable, 28 July 2022.

39 K. Morgan (2007) 'The polycentric state: new spaces of empowerment and engagement?', *Regional Studies*, 41(9), pp. 1237–1251; T. Lang et al. (2009) *Food Policy: Integrating Health, Environment and Society*, Oxford: Oxford University Press.

40 P. Henderson (2022) 'Free school meals: story behind one of Holyrood's greatest achievements', *The National*, 5 January.

41 Scottish Food Coalition (2022) *A Good Food Nation for Scotland: Why and How*, Edinburgh: SFC.

42 G. Ryder (2022) 'Nicola Sturgeon under pressure to fund free school meals for secondary pupils amid cost of living', *Daily Record*, 29 May; Nourish Scotland (2016) *Listening to What Children Think about Food Insecurity*, Edinburgh: Nourish Scotland.

43 Welsh Government (2021) *The Cooperation Agreement*, Cardiff: Welsh Government, p. 3.

44 Audit Wales (2020) *So What's Different? Findings from the Auditor General's Sustainable Development Principle Examinations*, Cardiff: Auditor General for Wales.

45 K. Morgan (2023) *Values for Money: Public Food Procurement in Wales*, Cardiff: Welsh Government.

Notes

46 Welsh Government (2021) *Universal Primary Free School Meals: Terms and Conditions of Grant*, Cardiff: Welsh Government.
47 Food Policy Alliance Cymru (2020) *Priorities for a Food System Fit for Future Generations*, Cardiff: FPAC.
48 H. Dimbleby (2021) *National Food Strategy: The Plan*, www.nationalfoodstrategy.org. Dimbleby had earlier produced a government review of school meals which championed the whole school approach to school meals. See Dimbleby and Vincent, *The School Food Plan*.
49 H. Dimbleby (2023) *Ravenous: How to Get Ourselves and Our Planet into Shape*, London: Profile Books, p. 17.
50 S. Kitchen et al. (2010) *Evaluation of the Free School Meals Pilot*, London: Department for Education; D. Colquhoun et al. (2008) *Evaluation of Eat Well Do Well*, Hull: Centre for Educational Studies, University of Hull.
51 P. Butler (2021) 'Newham to keep Eat for Free school meal scheme after outcry', *The Guardian*, 21 January.
52 Tower Hamlets Council (2023) 'Council first in country to roll out universal free school meals in secondary schools from September 2023', www.towerhamlets.gov.uk/News_events/2023/September/Tower-Hamlets-Council-first-in-country-to-rollout-universal-free-school-meals-in-primary-and-secondary-schools.aspx.
53 Child Poverty Action Group (2023) *Free School Meals: Third of Kids in Poverty Miss Out*, London: CPAG.

Chapter 3

1 K. Wormersley and K. Ripullone (2017) 'Medical school should be prioritising nutrition and lifestyle education', *British Medical Journal*, 359, p. j4861.
2 R. Tudor et al. (2017) *Making Hospital Food Healthier and More Sustainable: A Toolkit for Bringing about Change*, London: Medact, p. 3.
3 M. Rayner and P. Scarborough (2005) 'The burden of food related ill health in the UK', *Journal of Epidemiology and Community* Health, 59, pp. 1054–1057.
4 H. Dimbleby (2021) *National Food Strategy: The Plan*, www.nationalfoodstrategy.org, p. 115.
5 Government Office for Science (2007) *Foresight: Tackling Obesities: Future Choices*, London: Government Office for Science; Frontier

Notes

Economics (2022) *Estimating the Full Costs of Obesity*, London: Frontier Economics.
6 Government Office for Science, *Foresight*, p. 5.
7 *Ibid.*, p. 47.
8 J. Adams et al. (2016) 'Why are some population interventions for diet and obesity more equitable and effective than others? The role of individual agency', *PLOS Medicine*, 13(4), p. e1001990.
9 H. Cottam (2018) *Radical Help: How We Can Remake the Relationships Between Us and Revolutionise the Welfare State*, London: Virago Press, p. 33.
10 T. Garnett et al. (2014) *Policies and Actions to Shift Eating Patterns: What Works?* London: Chatham House.
11 W. Willett et al. (2019) 'Food in the Anthropocene: the EAT–Lancet Commission on healthy diets from sustainable food systems', *Lancet*, 393, pp. 447–492.
12 *Ibid.*, p. 484.
13 S. Anandaciva (2023) *How Does the NHS Compare to the Health Systems of Other Countries?* London: The King's Fund, p. 86.
14 C. Ham (2023) *The Rise and Decline of the NHS in England 2000–2020*, London: The King's Fund, p. 25.
15 Age Concern (2006) *Hungry to Be Heard: The Scandal of Malnourished Older People in Hospital*, London: Age Concern, p. 4.
16 Department of Health and Social Care (2020) *Report of the Independent Review of NHS Hospital Food*, Leeds: DHSC.
17 NHS England (2015) 'Simon Stevens announces major drive to improve health in NHS workplace', press release, 2 September.
18 K. Dalmeny and A. Jackson (2009) *A Decade of Hospital Food Failure*, London: Sustain, p. 2.
19 Age Concern, *Hungry to be Heard*, p. 7.
20 BBC (2019) '"Pigswill. Slop. Not fit for dogs". Is hospital food that bad?', BBC News, 20 June.
21 N. Johns et al. (2013) 'Hungry in hospital, well-fed in prison? A comparative analysis of food service systems', *Appetite*, 68, pp. 45–50.
22 P. Shelley (2020) *Report of the Independent Review of NHS Hospital Food*, Leeds: Department of Health and Social Care. The review was officially focused on NHS England because health policy in the UK is a devolved matter.
23 *Ibid.*, p. 9.
24 *Ibid.*, p. 64.

Notes

25 K. Jochelson et al. (2005) *Sustainable Food and the NHS*, London: The King's Fund, p. 5.

26 K. Morgan and A. Morley (2002) *Relocalising the Food Chain: The Role of Creative Public Procurement*, Cardiff: The Regeneration Institute, Cardiff University.

27 Jochelson et al., *Sustainable Food and the NHS*, p. 13.

28 Shelley (2020), op.cit, p. 25.

29 T. Baum (2006) Food or Facilities? The changing role of catering managers in the healthcare environment, *Nutrition & Food Science* 36(3), pp. 138–152.

30 Shelley, *Report of the Independent Review of NHS Hospital Food*, p. 31.

31 *Ibid.*, p. 37.

32 *Ibid.*, p. 41.

33 *Ibid.*, p. 66.

34 R. Sonnino and S. McWilliam (2011) 'Food waste, catering practices and public procurement: a case study of hospital food systems in Wales', *Food Policy*, 36, pp. 823–829.

35 Cottam, *Radical Help*, p. 248.

36 K. Morgan and R. Sonnino (2010) *The School Food Revolution*, London: Earthscan.

37 D. Green (2016) *How Change Happens*, Oxford: Oxford University Press.

38 Dalmeny and Jackson, *A Decade of Hospital Food Failure*, p. 2.

39 Sustain (2016) *Taking the Pulse of Hospital Food*, London: Sustain.

40 P. Leith (2016) 'Foreword', in *ibid*.

41 Soil Association (2021) *Food for Life Served Here 2020–2021: Our Impact*, Bristol: Soil Association.

42 A. Neustatter (2008) 'Recipe for recovery', *The Guardian*, 11 December.

43 C. Foster et al. (2005) *The Cornwall Food Programme: Sustainable Food Procurement in the NHS*, Cheltenham: Countryside and Community Research Unit, University of Gloucestershire. This section draws on the analysis of this case study.

44 *Ibid.*, p. 46.

45 Soil Association (2007) *A Fresh Approach to Hospital Food*, Bristol: Soil Association.

46 Gary Wilkins, personal communication.

47 Simon Wood, personal communication.

48 *Public Sector Catering* (2014) 'Nottingham becomes first NHS hospital to achieve Food for Life Gold', 26 March.

Notes

49 P. Ram (2020) 'Hospital catering staff in Nottingham hold strike ballot over pay', *Nottingham Post*, 17 February.

Chapter 4

1 Prison Reform Trust (1991) *The Woolf Report: A Summary of the Main Findings and Recommendations of the Inquiry into Prison Disturbances*, London: PRT, p. 32.
2 National Audit Office (2006) *Serving Time: Prisoner Diet and Exercise*, London: The Stationary Office, HC 939, p. 1.
3 R. Godderis (2006) 'Dining in: the symbolic power of food in prison', *The Howard Journal*, 45(3), pp. 255–267; G. M. Sykes (2007) *The Society of Captives*, Princeton: Princeton University Press.
4 G. Sturge (2023) *UK Prison Population Statistics*, London: House of Commons Library.
5 *Ibid.*, p. 15.
6 HMIP (2022) *Prison Education: A Review of Reading Education in Prison*, London: HMIP and Ofsted.
7 HM Chief Inspector of Prisons for England and Wales (2022) *Annual Report 2021–22*, London: HMSO, p. 5.
8 F. Crook (2021) 'The reform of prisons has been my life's work, but they are still utterly broken', *The Guardian*, 10 August.
9 In the US system, prisons are facilities under federal or state control where convicted people serve their sentences; jails are county or local facilities where most people are awaiting trial (so still legally innocent), many because they can't afford to post bail. The US data in this section are largely drawn from W. Sawyer and P. Wagner (2023) *Mass Incarceration: The Whole Pie 2023*, Easthampton, MA: Prison Policy Initiative.
10 L. Wang et al. (2022) *Beyond the Count: A Deep Dive into State Prison Populations*, Easthampton, MA: Prison Policy Initiative.
11 H. A. Thompson (2016) *Blood in the Water: The Attica Prison Uprising of 1971 and Its Legacy*, New York: Pantheon.
12 McKay Commission (1972) *Attica: The Official Report of the New York State Special Commission on Attica*, New York: Bantam Books, p. xi.
13 *Ibid.*, p. xii.
14 M. Cavadino and J. Dignan (2005) *Penal Systems: A Comparative Approach*, London: Sage.

Notes

15 R. Wilkinson and K. Picket (2007) 'The problems of relative deprivation: why some societies do better than others', *Social Science and Medicine*, 65(9), pp. 1965–1978.

16 M. Mauer (2006) 'The causes and consequences of prison growth in the United States', *Punishment & Society*, 3(1), pp. 9–20.

17 J. Howard (1929 [1777]) *The State of the Prisons*, London: J. M. Dent & Sons.

18 J. Pratt (1999) 'Norbert Elias and the civilised prison', *British Journal of Sociology*, 50(2), pp. 271–296.

19 Prison Commission (1925) *Report of Departmental Committee on Diets*, quoted in M. Cross and B. MacDonald (2009) *Nutrition in Institutions*, Chichester: Wiley-Blackwell, p. 289.

20 National Audit Office (2006) *Serving Time: Prisoner Diet and Exercise*, HC 939, London: The Stationery Office.

21 UK Parliament (2019) 'Prisons: food', written answer, 30 October.

22 HMIP (2016) *Life in Prison: Food*, London: HMIP.

23 *Ibid.*, p. 13.

24 M. Vernewick (2021) 'Mailbag: poor diet', *Inside Time*, 5 August.

25 B. Gesch et al. (2002) 'Influence of supplementary vitamins, minerals and essential fatty acids on the anti-social behaviour of young adult prisoners', *British Journal of Psychiatry*, 181, pp. 22–28

26 *Ibid.*, p. 27.

27 B. Gesch (2011) *The Influence of Micronutrient Intake on Antisocial Behaviours*, PhD thesis, University College Cork, p. 289.

28 F. Lawrence (2006) 'Omega 3, junk food and the link between violence and what we eat', *The Guardian*, 17 October.

29 D. Ramsbotham and B. Gesch (2009) 'Crime and nourishment: cause for a rethink?', *Prison Service Journal*, 182, pp. 3–9.

30 *Ibid.*, p. 8.

31 B. Gesch, private communication, 3 May 2023.

32 A. Richardson (2006) *They Are What You Feed Them*, London: HarperThorsons,; K. Wilson (2023) *Unprocessed: How the Food We Eat Is Fuelling Our Mental Health Crisis*, London: W. H. Allen.

33 *Ibid.*, p 11.

34 M. Cross and B. MacDonald (2009) *Nutrition in Institutions*, Chichester: Wiley-Blackwell, p. 353.

35 L. Soble et al. (2020) *Eating behind Bars: Ending the Hidden Punishment of Food in Prison*, Impact Justice, https://impactjustice.org/innovation/food-in-prison/#report.

Notes

36 Prison Voice Washington (2016) *Correcting Food Policy in Washington Prisons*, Seattle: PVW, p. 2.
37 W. Sawyer (2017) 'Food for thought: prison food is a public health problem', Prison Policy Initiative Briefing.
38 S. Simon (2016) 'Prisoners organise countrywide strike to demand better working, living conditions', National Public Radio, 1 October.
39 Unless otherwise stated, the details of the nutraloaf controversy are drawn from J. Cuellar (2023) 'Gruel and unusual: prison punishment diets and the eighth amendment', *Minnesota Law Review*, 107, pp. 475–527.
40 *Ibid.*, p. 509.
41 W. McKeithen (2022) 'Carceral nutrition: prison food and the biopolitics of dietary knowledge in the neoliberal prison', *Food and Foodways*, 30(1–2), 58–81.
42 E. Nonko (2021) 'Abolitionist organisation takes on Maryland's prison food system', *Next City*, 22 September.
43 K. Kathuria (2021) *'I Refuse To Let Them Kill Me': Food, Violence and the Maryland Correctional Food System*, Baltimore: Maryland Food & Prison Abolition Project, p. 19.
44 House of Lords (2017) *Rehabilitation in Prisons*, Library Briefing, London: House of Lords.
45 Ministry of Justice (2019) *Economic and Social Costs of Reoffending*, London: Ministry of Justice.
46 Soble et al., *Eating behind Bars* is the main source of information on Maine unless otherwise stated.
47 *Ibid.*, p. 117.
48 M. Angst (2023) 'How Gavin Newsom plans to transform California's infamous San Quentin State Prison', *The Sacramento Bee*, 19 March.
49 R. W. Gilmore (2007) *Golden Gulag*, London: University of California Press.
50 The Clink Charity (2023) *Annual Review: 2022*, Banstead: The Clink Charity, HMP High Down.
51 Pro Bono Economics (2020) *The Clink Charity: An Economic Impact Analysis*, www.probonoeconomics.com/Handlers/Download.ashx?IDMF=2f257459-4a78-4d16-8534-710fd4ae5397.
52 C. Rutter (2023) 'Food for thought', *Public Finance*, 1 March, pp. 28–32.
53 The Clink Charity (2023) *The Clink Kitchens*, London: The Clink Charity, p. 6.

Notes

54 A. Graham (2020) *Serving Time: An Ethnographic Study of the Clink Restaurant*, D.Phil. thesis, Cardiff University, p. 104.
55 Food Matters (2024) *Food Matters in Prisons*, Brighton: Food Matters.
56 *Ibid.*, p. 11.

Chapter 5

1 C. Steel (2008) *Hungry City: How Food Shapes Our Lives*, London Chatto and Windus, p. 307.
2 K. Morgan and R. Santo (2018) 'The rise of municipal food movements', in S. Skordili and S. Kalfagianna (eds) *Localizing Global Food*, London: Routledge.
3 K. Pothukuchi and J. Kaufman, J (2000) 'The food system: a stranger to the planning field', *Journal of the American Planning Association*, 66(2), pp. 112–124.
4 K. Morgan and R. Sonnino (2010) 'The urban foodscape: world cities and the new food equation', *Cambridge Journal of Regions, Economy and Society*, 3(2), pp. 209–224.
5 A. Moragues-Faus and K. Morgan (2015) 'Reframing the foodscape: the emergent world of urban food policy', *Environment and Planning A: Economy and Space*, 47(7), pp. 1558–1573.
6 W. Roberts (2001) *The Way to a City's Heart Is through Its Stomach*, Toronto: Toronto Food Policy Council.
7 Brighton and Hove Food Partnership (2006) *Spade to Spoon: Making the Connections*, Brighton: BHFP.
8 T. Andrews (2020) 'Celebrating Brighton and Hove: UK's first Gold SFP Award', www.sustainablefoodplaces.org/news/brighton_and_hove_gold_award_nov20-/.
9 BHFP (2020) *Good Food Is Good for Business: Good Food Procurement Group*, Brighton: BHFP.
10 R. Murray (2012) *The New Wave of Mutuality: Social Innovation and Public Service Reform*, London: Policy Network.
11 J. Carey (2011) *Who Feeds Bristol? Towards a Resilient Food Plan*, Bristol: Bristol City Council.
12 I have to declare an interest at this point because Barbara Jenke, the leader of Bristol City Council in 2011, invited me to chair the Food Policy Council and I served in that capacity for the first three years of its existence.

Notes

13 Bristol Food Network (2023) *Bristol Good Food 2030: A One City Framework for Action*, Bristol: Bristol Food Network.
14 J. Carey, personal communication, 28 April 2023.
15 Esmée Fairbairn Foundation, https://esmeefairbairn.org.uk/about-esmee/.
16 S. Davies (2017) *Food Partnership Structures*, Bristol: Sustainable Food Places.
17 *Ibid.*, p. 30.
18 S. Davies (2018) *Engaging with Local Authorities*, Bristol: Sustainable Food Places, p. 5.
19 A. Marceau (2021) *Good Policy for Good Food: A Toolbox of Local Authority Food Policy Levers*, Bristol: SFP.
20 M. Jones and S. Hills (2021) 'Scaling Up Action on urban sustainable food systems in the United Kingdom: agenda setting, networking, and influence', *Sustainability*, 13(2156), p. 11.
21 *Ibid.*, p. 6.
22 *Ibid.*, p. 9.
23 A. Fisher (2017) *Big Hunger: The Unholy Alliance between Corporate America and Anti-Hunger Groups*, Cambridge, MA: The MIT Press, p. 6.
24 M. Desmond (2023) *Poverty, by America*, London: Penguin; and A. Case and A. Deaton (2020) *Deaths of Despair and the Future of Capitalism*, Princeton: Princeton University Press.
25 A. Harper et al. (2009) *Food Policy Councils: Lessons Learned*, Oakland, CA: Food First.
26 R. Santo et al. (2021) *Pivoting Policy, Programs and Partnerships: Food Policy Councils' Responses to the Crises of 2020*, Baltimore: Center for a Livable Future, Johns Hopkins University.
27 *Ibid.*, p. 13.
28 Harper et al., *Food Policy Councils*, p. 6.
29 N. Freudenberg et al. (2018) 'Ten years of food policy governance in New York City: lessons for the next decade', *Fordham Urban Law Journal*, 45(4), pp. 951–994.
30 R. Gottlieb and A. Joshi (2013) *Food Justice*, Cambridge, MA: The MIT Press.
31 A. Velez (2010) 'FoodWorks unveiled: a new vision for NYC's food system', *Civil Eats*, 26 November; S. Stringer (2010) *FoodNYC: A Blueprint for a Sustainable Food System*, New York: Borough of Manhattan.
32 C. Quinn (2010) *FoodWorks: A Vision to Improve NYC's Food System*, New York: The NYC Council, p. 17.

Notes

33 Freudenberg et al., 'Ten years of food policy governance in New York City', p. 989.
34 NYC (2021) *Food Forward NYC: A 10-Year Food Policy Plan*, New York: City of New York, p. 32.
35 Public Plate Working Group (2014) *The Public Plate in NYC: A Guide to Institutional Meals*, New York: NYC Food Policy Center, Hunter College.
36 NYC Council (2017) 'Chancellor Farina announces free school lunch for all', press release, 6 September.
37 Mayor's Office of Food Policy (2021) *Citywide Goals and Strategy for the Implementation of Good Food Purchasing*, New York: Mayor's Office of Food Policy.
38 M. Tingling (2013) *American Beverage Association v NYC Department of Health*, 11 March 2013, New York: New York State Supreme Court, p. 13.
39 M. Grynbaum (2013) 'Judge blocks NYC's limits on big sugary drinks', *New York Times*, 11 March.
40 Quoted in M. Nestle (2015) *Soda Politics: Taking On Big Soda (and Winning)*, Oxford: Oxford University Press, p. 359.
41 *Ibid.*, p. 354.
42 Thanks to Raychel Santo for highlighting the continuity of this FPC support work.
43 M. Winne (2018) *Stand Together or Starve Alone: Unity and Chaos in the US Food Movement*, Colorado: Praeger, p. 99.
44 *Ibid.*, p. 104.
45 Quoted in K. Morgan (2015) 'Nourishing the city: the rise of the urban food question in the Global North', *Urban Studies*, 52(8), 1379–1394.
46 Fisher, *Big Hunger*, p. 164.
47 P. Daniels and A. Delwiche (2022) 'Future Policy Award 2018: the Good Food Purchasing Program, USA', *Frontiers in Sustainable Food Systems*, 5, p. 576776.
48 *Ibid.*, p. 5.
49 Anchors in Action Alliance (2023) *Anchors in Action Aligned Framework*, AiA Alliance, www.anchorsinaction.org/the-framework.
50 R. Santo and J. Silverman (2023) *Values-Aligned Food Purchasing and Service: Promising Examples from US Federal Agencies and Programs*, Federal Good Food Purchasing Coalition, www.fedgoodfoodpurchasing.org.
51 Winne, *Stand Together or Starve Alone*, p. 5.
52 Fisher, *Big Hunger*, p. 270.

Notes

53 A. Hertel-Fernandez (2021) *State Capture: How Conservative Activists, Big Businesses and Wealthy Donors Reshaped the American States – and the Nation*, New York: Oxford University Press, p. 239.

Chapter 6

1 M. Pollan (2010) 'The food movement, rising', *New York Review of Books*, 20 May.
2 S. Kamin (2013) 'The NYC mayoral candidate food forum: big ideas or real policy change?', *HuffPost*, 26 July.
3 J. M. Keynes (1936) *The General Theory of Employment, Interest and Money*, London: Macmillan, p. 383.
4 R. Doll and R. B. Hill (1950) 'Smoking and carcinoma of the lung: preliminary report', *British Medical Journal*, 30 September, pp. 739–748.
5 R. Proctor (2012) 'The history of the discovery of the cigarette–lung cancer link: evidentiary traditions, corporate denial, global toll', *Tobacco Control*, 21, pp. 87–89.
6 A. M. Brandt (2012) 'Inventing conflicts of interest: a history of tobacco industry tactics', *American Journal of Public Health*, 102(1), pp. 63–71.
7 *Ibid.*, p. 70.
8 K. D. Brownell and K. E. Warner (2009) 'The perils of ignoring history: big tobacco played dirty and millions died – how similar is big food?', *The Milbank Quarterly*, 87(1), pp. 259–294.
9 *Ibid.*, p. 264.
10 H. Dimbleby (2023) *Ravenous: How to Get Ourselves and Our Planet into Shape*, London: Profile Books, p. 47. Some social enterprises are not waiting for a level playing field. Can Cook, for example, claims to be 'the only food provider in the UK to be Ultra Processed Food Free'. See www.cancook.co.uk/about-can-cook/.
11 NHS (2022) *The Eatwell Guide*, www.nhs.uk/live-well/eat-well/food-guidelines-and-food-labels/the-eatwell-guide/.
12 Bite Back (2024) *Fuel Us, Don't Fool Us Manufacturers: Are Food Giants Rigging the System Against Children's Health?*, p. 32, https://biteback.contentfiles.net/media/documents/WEBSITE__Bite_Back_Manufacturers___high_res.pdf.
13 M. Speed (2024) 'Nestlé shareholders call on food giant to reduce reliance on unhealthy products', *Financial Times*, 14 March.

Notes

14 R. Adams (2024) '"How difficult is it to bake a potato?": fed-up head hits out at school's caterers', *The Guardian*, 13 March.
15 J. Slingo (2024) 'Three catering stocks that are cooking up a storm', *Investors' Chronicle*, 12 February.
16 D. Rodrik (2014) 'When ideas trump interests: preferences, worldviews, and policy innovations', *Journal of Economic Perspectives*, 28(1), pp. 189–208.
17 *Ibid.*, p. 204.
18 DEFRA (2024) *Food Statistics in Your Pocket*, London: DEFRA.
19 DEFRA (2014) *A Plan for Public Procurement: Food and Catering*, London: DEFRA.
20 A. Holford and B. Rabe (2022) 'Going universal: the impact of free school lunches on child body weight outcomes', *Journal of Public Economics Plus*, 3, pp. 1–19.
21 Faculty of Public Health (2024) *Health of the Next Generation: Good Food for Children*, London: FPH.
22 E. Wadell (2024) 'Plant-based school food programme receives nomination for £1m Earthshot Prize', *Public Sector Catering*, 4 March.
23 P. Richie (2023) *Sleeping on the Job*, Edinburgh: Nourish Scotland.
24 A. Bowman et al. (2021) *What Can Welsh Government Do to Increase the Number of Grounded SME Firms in Food Processing and Distribution?* Cardiff: Welsh Government.
25 Mayor of London (2024) *Free School Meals: No Child Should Go to School Hungry*, London: Mayor of London.
26 A. Gold (2023) *Scaling up Universal Free School Meals*, London: Newham Council.
27 School Meals Coalition (2023) *School Meals and Food Systems*, Rome: World Food Programme, p. 13.
28 K. Watkins (2023) *School Meal Programmes: A Missing Link in Food System Reform*, Geneva: Sustainable Financing Initiative, United Nations.
29 A. Tregear et al. (2022) 'Routes to sustainability in public food procurement: an investigation of different models in primary school catering', *Journal of Cleaner Production*, 338, pp. 1–10.
30 Health Care Without Harm (2024) 'HCWH launches national Food is Medicine strategy', https://noharm-uscanada.org/articles/news/us-canada/health-care-without-harm-launches-national-food-medicine-strategy.
31 R. Tallis (2008) *Hunger: The Art of Living*, Stocksfield: Acumen, p. 5.

Notes

32 D. Smith (2000) *Moral Geographies: Ethics in a World of Difference*, Edinburgh: Edinburgh University Press, p. 137.
33 Sustain (2024) 'London councils support good food work in spite of funding cuts', 29 February.
34 G. Mulgan (2019) *Social Innovation: How Societies Find the Power to Change*, Bristol: Policy Press, p. 103.
35 H. Cottam (2018) *Radical Help: How We Can Remake the Relationships Between Us and Revolutionise the Welfare State*, London: Virago, p. 242.
36 L. Calafata et al. (2023) *When Nothing Works: From Cost of Living to Foundational Liveability*, Manchester: Manchester University Press, p. 254.
37 D. Coyle and M. Sensier (2019) 'The imperial treasury: appraisal methodology and regional economic performance in the UK', Bennett Institute for Public Policy working paper no. 02/2018, University of Cambridge, p. 2.
38 P. McCann (2023) *Levelling-up economics*, London: Institute for Fiscal Studies.
39 A. Breach et al. (2023) *In Place of Centralisation*, London: The Resolution Foundation.
40 Local Government Information Unit (2024) *The State of Local Government Finance in England 2024*, London: LGIU.
41 Eating Better (2024) *Eating Better in the Nations: A Policy Review*, www.eating-better.org/news-and-reports/reports/eating-better-in-the-nations-a-political-review/.
42 (2022) *White House National Strategy on Hunger, Nutrition, and Health*, Washington, DC: The White House.
43 IPES-Food (2023) *From Plate to Planet: How Local Governments Are Driving Action on Climate Change through Food*, https://ipes-food.org/wp-content/uploads/2024/03/PlatetoPlanetEN.pdf.
44 A key part of democratic governance, the principle of subsidiarity aims to ensure that decisions are taken at the closest possible level to citizens.

Index

Page numbers in **bold** refer to exhibits.

A Decade of Hospital Food Failure (Sustain) 129
Academy of Medical Sciences 12–13
Age Concern 115, 117
Agenda 21 action programme 91
Agreement on Government Procurement (GPA) 47–48
agrifood system 4, 26, 28–33
American Beverage Association (ABA) 207–208
American Planning Association (APA), Community and Regional Food Planning policy guide 180
Anchors in Action (AiA) alliance 215–216
Andrews, Tom 185
animal products, reduction of 233–234
animal welfare 14
anti-hunger industrial complex 217–218
antisocial behaviour, diet and 20, 154–158
Argentina 31
Army Medical Service 71
austerity programmes, 2010–2023 41–44
Aylesbury mystery, the 20, 154–158

behavioural change, demand for 28
Best Value regime 40–41
Better Hospital Food initiative 116–117, 120, 129, 131
Biden, Joe 249
Big Food 199, 222, 225–227
Big Lottery 82, 85–86, 187
biodiversity loss 29–30
Bite Back 226–227
Bloomberg, Michael 206–208, **209**, 210
Boer War 71
Brazil 31

Index

Brexit 53, 59, 61
Brighton & Hove Food Partnership 183–187
Bristol Food Network 187–190
Bristol Good Food 2030 Partnership 189–190
British Medical Journal 105–106
Brown, Wendy 37, 46
Buchanan, James M. 34, 35–37, 40
budget deficits 36
Burns, Anne 2, 88

carceral diet *see* prisons
Cardiff and Vale University Health Board 125
Carey, Joy 190
Carillion 139–140
Carlisle, Mark 74
Caroline Walker Trust 55
catering service staff valorisation 238–239
Center for Good Food Purchasing 205–206, 210, 213–215, 218
central planning, neoliberal critique of 34–35
change
  agents of 22
  alliances for 241–250
  dimensions of 22
  prospects for 222, 222–227, 229–231
Charles, Prince 136
Chartwells 229, 230
child health and wellbeing, early years 12–13
child poverty 12, 12–13
children, health and diet 80
Chile, Pinochet regime 37

China 27
citizen engagement 33
civil society groups 5, 22, 27, 183, 184–185, 188, 201, 219, 242–245
climate change 4, 29, 32–33, 45, 94–95, 125, 181, 224, 230
clinical dietitians 123
Clink Integrated Rehabilitation Programme (CIRP) 20, 168, **169**, 170–174, 241
Community and Regional Food Planning policy guide (APA) 180
Community Food Security Coalition (CFSC) 211–213, 242
Compass Group 229
compulsory competitive tendering (CCT) 26, 39–40, 75
Concordia Bus case 49
Conservative governments 18, 26–27, 58–59, 114, 246
contract catering 229–230
COP28 summit, Dubai, 2023 32–33
Cornwall Food Programme (CFP) 133–135
corporate behaviour 229–230
cost–benefit analysis (CBA) 170, 171, 247
cost-of-living crisis 44, 103, 235
Cottam, Hilary 112, 127, 244–245
COVID-19 pandemic 44–45, 59, 61, 113, 115–116, 126, 170, 186–187, 197, 201–202
Crisci, Albert 168
Crook, Frances 145–146

Index

Cuellar, Jackie 162–163
cultural economy 16

Daniels, Paula 214
Dasgupta Review 29–30
Davis, Angela 164
deaths 29
deforestation 29–30
Delwiche, Alexa 214
Department of Food and Rural Affairs (DEFRA) 26–27, 50, 134, 231
departmental silos, and policymaking 28
deviance, normalization of 7
diet, antisocial behaviour and 154–158
diet-related diseases 4, 9, 11, 19, 106–108, 108, 181, 183, 208, 224, 230
Dimbleby, Henry 26–27, 59–60, 101–102, 226
direct service organisations 39–40
double-duty strategy 11
Duncan Smith, Iain 42
Dundas, Ruth 44
Durham 103
duty of care 5, 9, 16, 174

early childhood 12–13
Earth Summit, Rio, 1992 25
EAT–Lancet Commission 113
Eatwell Guide 226–227
ecological model, school food provisioning 18, 76–78, 79–80
economization 37
Education (Provision of Meals) Act, 1906 70–71

Education Act, 1944 70, 71–72
Education Act, 1980 74
efficiency/sustainability tension 50–52
environmental impacts 4, 14, **15**, 27
Esmée Fairbairn Foundation 186, 187, 191
Europe 2020 agenda 50
European Commission 54
European Court of Justice 49
European Union 45–46, 48–50, 54, 121, 134–135

fast food industry, lobbying power 208
Federal Good Food Purchasing Coalition 215–216
Feed the Future coalition 104
Finland 148
Fisher, Andy 217–218
Food, Farming and Countryside Commission (FFCC) 62–63
food, social significance 8–10
food audits 188
food banks 42
Food Behind Bars 173
food choice 61
food consumption 61
food culture reform 106–113
food education 56, 79, 95
Food for Life (FFL) programme 18, 19, 54–57, 69, 81–86, **87**, 88, 244
Food for Life Partnership (FFLP) 56
Food for Life Served Here (FFLSH) Awards 1–3, 82, 86, **87**, 88, 135–140

Index

Food for Life Sustainable Catering Standards 132
Food Forward NYC programme 202, **203**
Food Foundation 104, 219
food governance 58, 63
food industry, lobbying power 13
food insecurity 9, 11
food justice movement 160–161
Food Matters Inside and Out Programme 172–173, 190
food miles 54, 55–56
food policy 20–21, 182
food policy councils 21, 183, 196–199, **197**, **200**
food policy forums 8
food poverty 181, 185
food price inflation 94, 99, 180
food procurement 18, 189–190, 194
   efficiency/sustainability tension 50–52
   Good Food Purchasing (GFP) programme 205
   low-cost purchasing culture 46
   NHS 120–121
   prisons 151, 166–167
   sustainable 26–27, 53–58
   values-driven 53–58, 231–232
food provenance 67–68
food security 180
food sourcing 84
food system 17–18
   context 25
   fragmentation of 179
   holistic approach 29–30, 201
   infrastructure 194
   reform 22, 221–222
   urban planning agenda 180
   visibility 179–180
food system strategy 58, 59–63
food systems planning 188
food training programme 20
food waste 3, 124–126, 194
FoodNYC report 201
food-related ill-health costs 107–108
foodscapes, sustainable 20–21
foodscapes of hope 69, 89–104
FoodWorks policy 201–202
Foresight: Tackling Obesities (GOS) 109, 110–111, 111
Forster, Thomas 213
Foucault, Michel 20
Foundational Liveability 245
France 148
Freud, David 43

Garnett, Tara 14, 16
geopolitical crises 27
Germany 148
Gershon Review 47
Gesch, Bernard 156
Gilmore, Ruth Wilson 164
Glasgow Centre for Population Health 44
Global South 10–11
globalisation 26, 28
good food agenda 16
good food cause, the 5
good food, conceptualisation 1
Good Food for All Londoners campaign 243–244
Good Food for London campaign 222
Good Food Local programme 244

Index

Good Food movement 20–21, 54, 177–183, 229, 242, 246, 249–250
  agents of 178–179
  Brighton & Hove Food Partnership 183–187
  Bristol Food Network 187–190
  civil society groups 183, 184–185, 188, 201, 219
  food policy councils 196–199, **197**, **200**
  legal challenges 206–208, **209**, 210
  local infrastructure 182, 211–216
  New York City 199–202, **203**, 204–208, **209**, 210
  political tactics 208, 210
  Sustainable Food Places network 190–195
  UK 177–178, 183–195, 218–220
  US 177–178, 195–202, **200**, **203**, 204–208, **209**, 210–218, 249
Good Food Nation (Scotland) Bill, 2022 99
Good Food Purchasing (GFP) programme 54–55, 205–206
good food revolution 5, 17, 241
Gothenburg European Council, 2001 50
governance environment 246–250
Great Food Transformation, the 113
Green, Duncan 127
greenhouse gas emmissions 14, 29–30, 59, 91, 92–93, 94–95, **94**

Greenwich 80
Grossman, Loyd 116–117
gut microbiome, biological significance of 9
Guthman, Julie 213

Hall, Chloe 106
Hancock, Matt 126
Harper, A. 199
Hayek, Friedrich 34–35, 37
Health Care Without Harm 215, 240
health crises 27
health inequalities 9
holistic food system approach 29–30, 201
Home-Grown School Feeding System 68
horticulture sector 60–61, 63
hospitals and hospital food provisioning
  agents of change 126–140
  catering 122–124
  cognitive landscape 128, 128–133
  concerns 115–118
  local food experiments 133–140
  malnutrition risk 115
  NGOs 128, 128–133
  procurement 120–121
  Shelley review 118–120, 122–123, 125–126, 132
  Sustain food standards report, 2016 129–131
  sustainability 239–240
  waste 124–126
  workplace tensions 122–123
How Change Happens (Green) 127
Howard, John 149–150

278

Index

hunger 10–11, 16, 21, 242
Hussey, Trevor 155
hygiene standards 6–7
hyper-centralisation 247–248

industrial disputes 38
Inside Time 153
institutional settings 1, 18, 64
integration, lack of 32–33
Inter-Departmental Committee on Physical Deterioration 71
interdependencies 28
International Monetary Fund 34

John Tudor and Son 6–7
Johnson, Boris 126
Jones, Mason, death of 6–7
Joseph Rowntree Foundation 12
junk food culture 109, 226–227, **228**

Kaufman, Jerry 180
Keynes, John Maynard 222–223
Khan, Sadiq 103, 235
King's Fund 120–121

labour standards 214
Leicestershire Traded Services 86
Leith, Prue 126, 130–131
Liberty, Randall 167
livestock farming 29–31
Livestock's Long Shadow (UN FAO) 30–33
lobbying power 31–32, 208
Local Agenda 21 183
local authorities 39–40, 43, 57, 193–194, 195, 244, 248
local education authorities 71, 74

local food partnerships *see* Good Food movement
local food policies 20–21
local food policy groups, fragility of 177–178
Local Government Act, 1988 39–40, 75
local sourcing 54
localisation 68
lose-lose diets 14
Loss and Damage Fund 33
low-cost catering culture 57, 75
low-cost culture 40
low-cost purchasing culture 46–47

McBrine, Mark 166
Macfarlane, Neil 74–75
MacKenzie, Kate 205–206
macro-economic environment 195, 246
Malmö 69
  Policy for Sustainable Development and Food 3–4, 91, 95
  school food provisioning 89, 90–97, **93**, **94**
malnutrition, double burden of 11, 28, 32–33
Marquand, David 41
meat consumption 30, 92–93
medical professionals, nutrition education 105–106
mental health 80
Milan Urban Food Policy Pact 219
Mills, Sonia 136
mortality rates 44
most economically advantageous tender (MEAT) 49

Index

Mulgan, Geoff 244
multilevel governance 33
municipal activism, New York City 199–202, **203**, 204–208, **209**, 210
Murray, Robin 187

nanny state trope 4, 61, 62
National Audit Office 51–52
National Farm to School Network (NFSN) 213
National Food Strategy (NFS) 26–27, 59–60, 101–102, 226
National Institute for Health and Care Excellence guidelines 106
Nationally Determined Contributions 33
nation-states 26
Neale, Chris 139
neoliberalism 13, 26, 34–46, 246
  critique of state 34–37
  school food provisioning policy 18, 40, 73–76
  UK 38–45
Nestle, Marion 207–208, 210
net zero target 59
Netherlands, the 148
new food equation, the 180–181
New Labour 40–41, 76, 79
New York City 21, 199–202, **203**, 204–208, **209**, 210, 221–222
Newham 102–103
Newsom, Gavin 167
NHS 104, 105–106, 239–240
  cognitive landscape 128, 128–133
  food costs 108
  food culture 106–113

food procurement 120–121
healthcare culture 107, 113
local food experiments 133–140
malnourished patients 19
medicalised culture 19
staff diet 115–116
see also hospitals
North Bristol NHS Trust (NBT) 135–139, 140
Northern Ireland 97, 101–102, 143–144
Norway 165
Nottingham University Hospitals (NUH) 139–140
Nursing and Midwifery Council 123
Nussbaum, Martha 17
nutraloaf controversy 20, 158, 160–165, **163**
nutrition, personalised 9
nutrition education, medical professionals 105–106
nutritional targets 55, 56

obesity 4, 11, 62, 80, 109, 110–111, 111, 181, 208, 233
Oldham 1–3, 86, 88
Oliver, Jamie 76
Organic South West (OSW) 134–135
outsourcing 140
Oxfam 127

Paris Agreement, 2015 25, 45
Pearson, Mike 133, 135
personalised nutrition 9
planning 193
plant-based diets 232, 233–234
policy coherence 58–59

Index

policy implementation 33
policymaking, and departmental silos 28
political context 8, 13, 16, 17–18, 21, 58, 113
Pollan, Michael 221
polycrisis 25–26, 27–33
poorest countries, school food provisioning 236, 238
Pothukuchi, Kami 180
poverty 2, 10–11
  child 12, 12–13
prison abolition movement 164–165
prisons 20, 117
  the Aylesbury mystery 20, 154–158
  carceral diet 20, 141–142, 149–158, **159**, 160–165, **163**
  Clink Integrated Rehabilitation Programme 20, 168, **169**, 170–174, 241
  conditions 145–149
  food procurement 151, 166–167
  food spending 152
  food training programme 20
  nutraloaf controversy 20, 158–165, **163**
  population 142–145, **144**
  reform 145–146, 240–241
  rehabilitation regimes 20, 165–168, **169**, 170–174, 241
  significance of food 142
  US 146–149, 158, **159**, 160–165, **163**, 166–168, 240
privatisation 38
Procurement Act, 2023 60
ProVeg 233–234
proxy markets 38

public choice theory 35–37
public expenditure 73
public food provisioning 238–241
public health 4, 111–112, 114
public plate, the 4
  as a catalyst for reform 235
  potential tapping 231–236, **237**, 238–241
  reclaiming 17–18, 58–63
public procurement 7–8, 39
  deployment 58–63
  efficiency/sustainability tension 50–52
  Gershon Review 47
  low-cost purchasing culture 40, 46–47
  most economically advantageous tender (MEAT) 49
  reform 52–53, 60
  regulatory landscape 47–53
  values-driven 53–58
  values-for-money approach 53
public sector 4, 5, 39–40, 64, 246–250
Public Sector Food Procurement Initiative (PSFPI) 50–51
Public Services (Social Value) Act, 2012 52–53
public spending cuts 114
purchase power 8, 18
Purchasing and Supplies Agency (PASA) 120–121, 134

Quinn, Christine 201

race and racism 149, 198, 212–213
Ramsbotham, Lord David 156
Real Food Generation 215

Index

reform
  focus 62
  food culture 106–113
  food system 221–222
  healthcare culture 113–115
  livestock sector 30
  opposition to 26
  prisons 145–146, 240–241
  public procurement 52–53, 60
  public sector 39–40
  regulatory 18
  school food provisioning 68, 238–239
  welfare 42–43
regulation 4, 5, 7, 18
Roberts, Wayne 182
Rodrik, Dani 230
Royal Cornwall Hospital Trust (RCHT) 133–134

School Food Plan, 2013 59–60, 79
school food provisioning 1–3, 67
  benefits 79–80, 81
  catering service staff valorisation 238–239
  complexity 68
  compulsory competitive tendering (CCT) 75
  cost 88, 94
  cultural stereotype 68
  Eat for Free scheme 236, **237**
  ecological model 18, 76–78, 79–80
  Food for Life (FFL) targets 55–56
  food education 56
  Food for Life (FFL) programme 55–56, 69, 81–86, **87**, 88
  food miles 55–56
  food sourcing 84
  foodscapes of hope 69, 89–104
  free school meals 74, 90–97, 101–102, 104
  instrumentalist rationale 83–84
  Jamie Oliver effect 76
  localisation 68
  low-cost catering culture 57, 75
  models 18–19
  national context 67
  neoliberal model 18, 40, 73–76
  nutritional targets 55, 56
  organic food 92, **93**
  pedagogical meals 95
  plant-based 232, 233–234
  poorest countries 236, 238
  provenance 67–68
  reform 68, 238–239
  SMRP report 77–78
  social context 96–97
  supply chains 55–56
  sustainability 232–236, **237**, 238–239
  Sweden 89, 90–97, **93**, **94**
  take-up 83
  universal free school meals campaign 19, 69, 97–104, 232–236
  universality 232–233
  welfare model 18, 70–73
  whole school approach 18–19, 76–78, 81–86, **87**, 88
School Meals Coalition (SMC) 236
School Meals Review Panel (SMRP) 77–78
Scotland 58, 76–77, 97–99, 101, 143–144, 234
Scottish Food Coalition 98–99

Index

Second World War 79–80
Shelley, Philip 118–120, 122–123, 125–126, 132
Skidmore, Chris 60
S.M.A.R.T model 91
Social Value agenda 51–52
Social Welfare 73
socio-economic crises 27
Soft Drinks Industry Levy (SDIL) 61–62
Soil Association 55, 56, 69, 81, 82, 104, 128, 129, 132–133, 133, 136, 190, 219, 243–244, 244
Spade to Spoon food strategy 184–185
Spector, Tim 9
spillover effects 84–85
Steel, Carolyn 179
Steinfeld, Henning 31
Stevens, Simon 116
Stiglitz, Joseph 46
Stringer, Scott 201
subnational actors 32–33, 181–182
subsidiarity 22, 250
Sugar Reduction Programme 61–62
supply chains 55–56
Sustain 116, 128, 128–132, 133, 190, 219, 243, 246
sustainability perspective 25
sustainable development 32, 50
Sustainable Development Goals (SDGs) 10–11, 45, 238
sustainable diets 13–14, **15**, 16, 113, 115
Sustainable Food Cities (SFC) network 190–191

sustainable food movement 54, 55
Sustainable Food Places (SFP) awards 185, 187
Sustainable Food Places (SFP) network 20–21, 183, 190–195
sustainable food system 17, 20–21, 58–59, 63, 133–140
see also Good Food movement
sustainable public food procurement system 26–27
Sweden 3–4, 89, 90–97, **93**, **94**, 148

Tallis, Raymond 241
Taylor, Charlie 145
TEEB study 29–30
Thatcher, Margaret and Thatcherism 18, 26, 37, 38–40, 67, 73, 73–76
Think Through Nutrition 173
Thomas, Yvonne 171
Tooze, Adam 27
Trussell Trust 42
Tudor, William 6–7
Turning the Tables (SMRP) 77–78
Tyree, Randy 196

Ukraine War 27, 59, 61
ultra-processed foods 4, 11, 19, 28, 157, 160, 165
UN Food Systems Summit, 2021 236
UN World Food Programme 236
undernutrition 11
UNICEF 12
United Nations 13–14, 30–33, 45, 68

Index

United States of America 27, 48
   Anchors in Action (AiA) alliance 215–216
   carceral diet 158, **159**, 160–165, **163**
   Center for Good Food Purchasing 213–215, 218
   Community Food Security Coalition (CFSC) 211–213, 242
   Farm Bill, 2018 211–212
   Federal Good Food Purchasing Coalition 215–216
   food justice movement 160–161
   food policy councils 21, 196–199, **197**, **200**
   food system reform 221–222
   Good Food movement 21, 177–178, 195–202, **200**, **203**, 204–208, **209**, 210–218, 246–250
   Good Food Purchasing Program 21, 54–55, 213–215
   hunger 21
   livestock lobby 31
   National Farm to School Network (NFSN) 213
   New York City 221–222
   nutraloaf controversy 20, 158, **159**, 160–165, **163**
   NYC Mayoral Candidate Food Forum 221–222
   portion cap controversy 206–208, **209**, 210
   prison abolition movement 164–165
   prisons 20, 146–149, 158, **159**, 160–165, **163**, 165–168, 240
Universal Credit 42–43, 104
universal free school meals campaign 19, 69, 97–104, 232–236
urban food policy, New York City 199–202, **203**, 204–208, **209**, 210
urbanisation 28, 181

value, non-economic forms 53
values-based procurement 231–232
values-for-money approach 53
vested interests 2, 223–226, 230

Wales 5–7, 58, 96, 97, 99–101, 125, 143–144, **144**, 234–235
Waste and Resources Action Programme 124
weaponised food 161–165, **163**
welfare model, school food provisioning 18, 70–73
welfare reform 42–43
Well-being of Future Generations (WFG) Act (Wales) 100–101
Who Feeds Bristol? (Carey) 188, 190
Wilkins, Gary 136–137
Wilson, Kimberley 157
Winne, Mark 211, 212, 216
Wood, Simon 136–137
World Bank 34
World Health Organization 13
World Trade Organization 34, 47–48, 60